THE ARCHITECT OF KOKODA

HACHETTE MILITARY COLLECTION

THE ARCHITECT OF KOKODA

BERT KIENZLE – THE MAN WHO MADE THE KOKODA TRAIL

ROBYN KIENZLE

hachette
AUSTRALIA

hachette
AUSTRALIA

First published in Australia and New Zealand in 2011
by Hachette Australia
(an imprint of Hachette Australia Pty Limited)
Level 17, 207 Kent Street, Sydney NSW 2000
www.hachette.com.au

Second edition published in 2013
This edition published in 2017

10 9 8 7 6 5 4 3 2 1

National Library of Australia
Cataloguing-in-Publication data:

Kienzle, Robyn, author.
The architect of Kokoda/Robyn Kienzle.

ISBN: 978 0 7336 3915 9 (paperback)

Kienzle, Herbert Thomson, 1905–1988.
Veterans – Australia – Biography.
Kokoda Trail (Papua New Guinea).

305.90697092

Cover design and illustration by Luke Causby/Blue Cork Design
Cover image: AdobeStock
Internal photos: Kienzle family collection, and a private collection
Text design by Bookhouse, Sydney
Typeset in Sabon LT Std
Printed and bound in Australia by McPherson's Printing Group

The paper this book is printed on is certified against the
Forest Stewardship Council® Standards. McPherson's Printing
Group holds FSC® chain of custody certification SA-COC-005379.
FSC® promotes environmentally responsible, socially beneficial
and economically viable management of the world's forests.

CONTENTS

FOREWORD

Exhausted troops climb an immense stairway cut into the jungle. A line of soldiers move uneasily along a bush track. Then a shot rings out, a man collapses. His mates peer into the dank green foliage trying to see an almost invisible enemy. Papuan carriers deftly manoeuvre a stretcher across a fast running stream and up the steep bank on the other side. At Isurava, lines of yelling Japanese erupt from the jungle in a desperate banzai charge. Then the deadly chatter of machine guns comes from the Australian positions and the 'Japs' are cut down. Warrant Officer Jim Cowey waits in the darkness outside the Kokoda Plantation for some of his men who have been left behind then coolly picks off one Japanese soldier after another as they try to man a mountain gun. Brigadier Arnold Potts walks down to the latrine with Private Gill. There is a shot, Gill falls and the battle for Brigade Hill begins. Pathetically depleted lines of men from the 39th Battalion are addressed by their colonel, Ralph Honner, while a black bearded photographer with a box-like camera to his eye unobtrusively captures the moment. A powerfully built man accompanied by some dangerous looking Papuans armed with shotguns moves easily past a carrier line, checking to see the loads are not too heavy. These are some random incidents from the battles on the Kokoda Trail in 1942.

The powerfully built man was Bert Kienzle, and he played a vital part in the Kokoda fighting; events that are unique in Australia's military history. They were not like Gallipoli, where defeat was redeemed by the bravery of the participants, nor were they like the siege of Tobruk, where the Australian troops were one of the very few forces in World War II to match the German army when they met on equal terms. The Kokoda battles were not decisive victories such as the Charge at Beersheba or when the Australians broke the Hindenburg line in the Great War. Nevertheless, the fighting on the Trail was an extraordinary tactical victory achieved in the face of overwhelming odds and ultimately the Kokoda battles brought about a series of decisive engagements on the beachhead that virtually wiped out the Japanese invaders.

In the last twenty years the experiences of the troops who fought on the Trail have captured the Australian imagination. There have been hikes, celebrations of the Battle of Isurava and numerous books about the campaign. To be sure, these have included a lot of sentimental nonsense about the spirit of Kokoda, but there have also been some fine narratives like Peter Fitzsimons's *Kokoda*, and above all, Peter Brune's classic treatments of the campaign *Those Ragged Bloody Heroes* and *A Bastard of a Place*. Those works establish that the 21st Brigade executed that most difficult of military manoeuvres – a fighting withdrawal. Outnumbered approximately six to one by the Japanese in any one engagement, the field commander Brigadier Arnold Potts switched tactics and pulled back his force making the enemy pay in blood for their every advance. It is a tactic that can only be employed by extremely good troops. You can't stay too long in one position otherwise your force will be wiped out, and if the pull-back is too early the rearguard will be overrun. By doing this the Australians succeeded in whittling down the Japanese forces, compelling them to go beyond their supply lines, all the while keeping a viable force between the enemy and its principal objective,

Port Moresby. Throughout, adequate supplies for our troops was essential. Bert Kienzle's task was to ensure those supplies reached our troops.

Kienzle had been a successful planter in New Guinea in the 1930s known to have excellent relations with his Papuan workers. With the outbreak of war he was taken into the army, first as warrant officer, then lieutenant and finally as captain. Kienzle comes into the Kokoda story at the very beginning when he guided B Company of the 39th Battalion across the Trail to secure the airfield at Kokoda. He was among the first to realise the extent of the ignorance of the Australian high command about conditions on the Kokoda Trail when he was given one of the more preposterous orders of the campaign:

> CO Angau to fulfill requirements up to a maximum of one thousand native labourers. Construction of road to Kokoda to commence not later than 29th June. Road to be completed 26th August 1942.

In some documents he sent to Peter Brune, Kienzle wrote, 'I have heard of Superman but have yet to see him in action.' Nevertheless, thanks to Kienzle and his Papuan carriers, B Company's journey up the Trail was less arduous than it was for the rest of the battalion. Kienzle must have seemed an imposing figure to the young men of the 39th Battalion. At the time he was a ruggedly handsome man, six foot two and eighteen stone with muscles hardened by years of hiking in the New Guinean jungle.

Understandably Kienzle, as Robyn Kienzle records, saw the battalion as untried and inexperienced and, indeed, they were officially graded F – their unit training not yet complete. But the battalion included a number of experienced soldiers and on 21 June, 36 AIF officers were posted to the unit. In the fighting that followed the Japanese landing near Buna there were some blunders but the battalion acquitted themselves well and managed to convince the Japanese they were opposed by a much larger force. The 39th were also fortunate that, after being forced back to Isurava, the newly promoted Lieutenant Colonel Ralph Honner took over command. He altered the dispositions and when the Japanese attacked, the Australians proceeded to tear them to pieces.

Kienzle quickly realised that the 21st Brigade, who were about to be sent up the Trail to relieve the hard pressed 39th Battalion, could not be supplied solely by Papuan carriers. There would have to be aerial dropping of supplies. This had also been realised at Australian Headquarters in Port Moresby but it was Kienzle who discovered Myola, the dried lake, that became one of the principal drop zones. It can be seen in war photographer Damien Parer's documentary *Kokoda Frontline* where supplies are being pushed out the doors of low flying transports – the famous biscuit bombers.

Viewing these events through Kienzle's eyes gives us a unique perspective on the campaign. For the 21st Brigade to advance and withdraw across the Kokoda Trail there had to be relays of Papuan carriers and staging camps, many of which were set up by Kienzle.

The carriers' contribution is also recorded in Parer's documentary. At times they look magnificent, but Parer was too good a reporter to be satisfied with a few heroic images. There are shots of exhausted Papuans at Eora Creek breathing heavily, their eyes bulging as they look into the camera. 'How tired the carriers are,' Parer wrote on his shot list. Kienzle knew that, even though they had been virtually conscripted into the army, many of his carriers would never have passed the medical for the AIF and they were often quite sick. Their health was a constant concern for Kienzle and his friend, the marvelously eccentric Doc Vernon, one of the main characters in Robyn Kienzle's narrative. Understandably many of the carriers deserted. However, soldiers I interviewed were adamant that the 'natives' never abandoned the wounded. As Damien Parer noted, 'If they [the casualties] need a drink, a shit, the natives will fix it.' One of Kienzle's major achievements was to persuade so many of the Papuans to remain loyal. Throughout the campaign he was accompanied by a group of workers from his plantation armed with shotguns. The Japanese usually treated the Papuans brutally; the very few who behaved decently were, of course, our most formidable adversaries.

Another of Bert Kienzle and his workers' tasks was to prepare the Trail as far as possible for the movement of first, a battalion, then a brigade and, finally, when the counter attack came, a division. Revealed here for the first time is the fact that the wily Brigadier Potts instructed Kienzle to cut extra tracks at Brigade Hill that later enabled Potts and the troops at Brigade headquarters to escape when the Japanese encircled their position and cut them off from the main body of the Australian forces.

One of the great ironies of the Kokoda battles is that Potts's tactical victory was not recognised at the time. This was more than understandable for Corps Commander Lieutenant General Rowell and the Divisional Commander Major General 'Tubby' Allen. Both were trying to keep track of a series of fast moving engagements on the Trail while Rowell was also responsible for repelling the Japanese landings at Milne Bay. (Wisely he backed his subordinate commander, Major General Clowes, who inflicted the first land defeat on the Japanese in the Pacific War.) Later it became expedient to rewrite history when Land Forces Commander General Sir Thomas Blamey relieved Rowell and Potts then pretended that the subsequent turnaround in the campaign had come about because he had re-energised the situation. He then proceeded at the now infamous parade at Koitaki to virtually accuse the 21st Brigade of cowardice. After the war all this became profoundly embarrassing. Many eminent men in public life owed their positions to Blamey and just before his death he had been made Australia's first Field Marshall. Inevitably, any adequate history of the Kokoda battles would expose Blamey's lies and incompetence so for nearly sixteen years nothing was written about the campaign.

Along with many of the other participants, Bert Kienzle strived to get the full story of Kokoda told to the Australian people. He collaborated with Raymond Paull who wrote the first account of the campaign, *Retreat from Kokoda*, in

1958 and, many years later, with Peter Brune who contacted Kienzle when he was researching *Those Ragged Bloody Heroes*. Impressed by the questionnaire Peter had sent him, Kienzle decided to send the young historian all his papers. The day after the package containing the papers arrived, Bert Kienzle died. They were, however, embodied in both *Heroes* and Brune's definitive *A Bastard of a Place*. These books vindicated Potts's tactics and the reputation of the 21st Brigade, as well as doing justice to Kienzle's own part in the campaign. As Brune is the first to admit, he owes much to Raymond Paull, who was able to interview both Arnold Potts and Bert Kienzle at length, and to Dudley McCarthy's official history *Kokoda to Wau*. But Peter uncovered much new material that not only enabled him to correct the mistakes of his predecessors but to lay the foundation for just about all the books about Kokoda that have been published since. He could not, of course, tell the story of Bert Kienzle's life. Now, thanks to Robyn Kienzle, we have the long overdue biography of this extraordinary Australian.

Neil McDonald

LIST OF ABBREVIATIONS

ADC	Assistant District Commissioner
AAMC	Australian Army Medical Corps
ADF	Australian Defence Force
ADH	Assistant Director Health
ADMS	Assistant Director Medical Services
ADS	Advanced Dressing Station
AIF	Australian Imperial Force
AMF	Australian Military Force
ANGAU	Australian New Guinea Administrative Unit
ANGPCB	Australian New Guinea Production Control Board
ARM	Assistant Resident Magistrate
ASOPA	Australian School of Pacific Administration
CBE	Commander of the Order of the British Empire
CIC	Commander in Chief
CO	Commanding Officer
COSC	Combined Operational Service Command
CRE	Commander Royal Engineers
DA and QMG	Deputy Adjutant and Quartermaster General
DC	District Commissioner
DCA	Department of Civil Aviation

DO   District Officer
DSC   Distinguished Service Cross
DSO   Distinguished Service Order
FRCM   Fellow of the Royal College of Music
GHQ   General Headquarters
GMD   Government Medical Officer
GOC   General Officer Commanding
HMAS   His Majesty's Australian Ship
HMAT   His Majesty's Australian Troopship
HMS   His Majesty's Ship
HQ   Headquarters
L of C   Line of Communication
MBE   Member of the Order of the British Empire
MC   Military Cross
MD   Military District
MDS   Main Dressing Station
MO   Medical Officer
MV   Motor Vessel
NGVR   New Guinea Volunteer Rifles
OIC   Officer in Charge
PCB   Production Control Board
PHD   Public Health Department
PIB   Papuan Infantry Battalion
PIR   Pacific Islands Regiment
PNG   Papua New Guinea
PRP   Papua Rubber Plantations
PO   Patrol Officer
PSP   perforated steel planking
RAAF   Royal Australian Air Force
RM   Resident Magistrate
RMO   Regimental Medical Officer
RPC   Royal Papuan Constabulary
STOL   Short take-off and landing
TAA   Trans-Australia Airlines
VC   Victoria Cross
WO   Warrant Officer

HERBERT THOMSON 'BERT' KIENZLE
FAMILY TREE

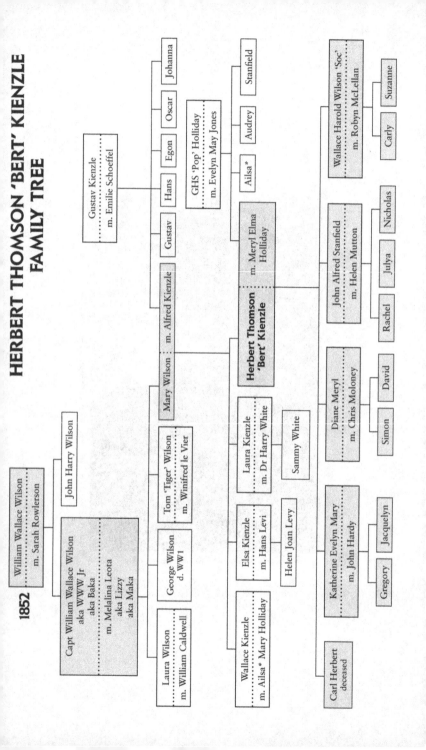

PROLOGUE

Herbert Kienzle was a man who commanded respect from the moment you met him.

I first met Mr Kienzle when I went to stay at Kokoda in 1974. While staying in Port Moresby on the way through with the parents of a university friend, they mentioned to me a little about what a great man Herbert Kienzle was and what a magnificent plantation he owned, the Mamba Estates. They also mentioned that he had one bachelor son called Soc.

By the end of my two-week stay at Kokoda, I had seen quite a lot of Soc and we had become quite interested in each other. In fact, not long after I returned home, he arrived on my doorstep. The following year and a half involved trips to and from Kokoda every holiday until we were married in December 1975, three months after PNG received its independence.

The evening routine at Mamba was dress for dinner and drinks at 6 p.m. sharp. It was during this ritual that I got to know my father-in-law and a little about his fascinating life. My mother-in-law Meryl and I also spent a lot of time together in those years, Bert encouraging me to take a break from office duties and talk to her over a cup of tea. Not being a student of history, I did not take the opportunity to ask the questions I so wish I could ask them now. Sometimes we would get Dad talking and he would 'hold forth' from his end of the big dining room table until Mum, who loved to imitate the way he remonstrated with his hands, and often teasingly called him a 'Teutonic old bugger', would embarrass him into quietening down.

Meryl, or Juju as she was affectionately called once her first grandchild arrived, never called her husband Bert – it was always Herbert or some other term of endearment. His brother Wallace called him Herbert and to his children and grandchildren he was Dad or Grandad.

In 1980, the family sold the estates at Kokoda to the PNG Development Bank for about one-tenth of their true worth. Soc and I were the only ones left and Bert's dreams of a dynasty were shattered. We stayed on to manage the plantation for three years but it was not the same, and in July we moved to a farm near Allora in Queensland, to be close to my parents in Warwick. Grandad and Juju (Bert and Meryl) soon bought the adjoining farm and so we saw a lot of them as they commuted between there and their unit at Tweed Heads. All those lost opportunities to learn so much from Bert! It was only after he passed away in January 1988, followed by Meryl in November of that year, that I sat down and read a short summary of his life that he had penned some years previously and realised that, in addition to all he had done on the Kokoda Trail during World War II, his life from day one to death was extraordinary and should be recorded and shared.

In 2006, Soc decided he wanted to take his two daughters back to Kokoda to see their roots and to walk the Kokoda Trail. So began a resurgence of family interest in Grandad's life, and a serious delving into the camphorwood box where all his papers and mementos were stored. How lucky I was that Bert was a 'hoarder and recorder' and that he had noted down the core of his life story. And how interesting the journey has been as I learnt about his life, his achievements, his loves and losses, and what was going on in the world around him at the various points in history.

This is not a military history and I do not claim to be a historian. Plenty of books have been written by others more qualified than I detailing the military aspects of the Kokoda Campaign. This book is about a man, how he became who he was, and what he achieved before, during and after the war.

My apologies to those who find my prose sometimes politically incorrect but I choose to use the vernacular of the time and place. For example, Papuan natives are often referred to as 'boys': this is not meant – nor was it ever used by members of the Kienzle family – in a condescending manner. It was the term for indigenous men passed down from the British colonialists and adopted by the expats in the Territory. In Bert's case, it was used with affection and a sense of these people being family – not the derogatory form 'boi' that was banned in the 1950s. Employees were identified according to occupation – houseboy, laundry boy, cowboy – surely even John Wayne did not object to this! It was that deep affection for his Papuan friends that played such a huge part in the success of the Kokoda Campaign and why those who know the true story of Kokoda know the enormous role Bert played in the lives of the 'fuzzy wuzzy angels'.

My apologies also to the diggers who insist it is Track not Trail, but this is a debate that will go on forever, and after finishing this book I am sure readers will get the picture that Bert Kienzle and his family call it the Trail and hopefully will understand why they do.

In summary, Bert called it the Trail from very early in the campaign. It was a mail trail before the war. As he said in his speech in 1972, a trail is 'a path through the wilderness'; and that is indeed what it was to him and his men. He also made the point that there are myriad tracks along and around the route over the Ranges, but there is only one Kokoda Trail over which the Campaign was fought and along which his boys carried ammunition, wounded and supplies to and from the various staging points.

In recent years, Soc and I have been honoured to meet some of the surviving diggers of the campaign. Great blokes like Bill

Bellairs, George Palmer and Stan Bisset to name but a few, who are adamant it is Track because Trail, they believe, is a name given it by the U.S. Command – but the Yanks were 'never bloody there'! No one can really pinpoint at what point it became Trail and who first called it that although various claims have been made. All I know is that amongst the many papers I have of Bert's and Doc Vernon's, they seemed to be calling it Trail almost from the 'get-go', and we certainly all grew up knowing it as Trail. The PNG Government has gazetted it as Trail and their decision and right to do so should be acknowledged.

Our respect for the diggers and what they did for us during the horrific time that was the Kokoda Campaign is such that if they want to call it Track, that is their prerogative and we do our best to remember to call it that in their presence. Trouble is if Bert was still alive, we'd be in trouble with him! One other real character, Cec Driscoll, who was with 'Sam' Templeton and B. Coy when Bert led them across the Ranges in July 1942, says he recalls being told they were going on the Kokoda Trail but once they were there and throughout the Campaign they called it 'the bloody track'.

Bert is best known for the huge part he played along this wartime path in 1942, but his whole 83 years were significant and memorable. His was indeed an extraordinary life, and he was truly an 'Architect' of Kokoda in all senses of the word.

Robyn J. Kienzle

1

CHILD OF THE PACIFIC

Mary Kienzle was heavily pregnant with her first child when the cyclone hit Levuka on the Fiji island of Ovalau in the year 1905. The devastating weather phenomenon had left a trail of destruction throughout the southern Pacific Islands, starting in the Marshall Islands down through Kiribati then Samoa, arriving in the Fiji Islands in the last week of April.

Mary had closed down all the shutters on her beautiful home in the hills that hovered close over the town of Levuka. The cyclone was approaching from the northern end of the island and so her house, which faced south-east, would be somewhat protected from the full wrath of the storm. Off Ovalau, several hundred metres out, stood the Lekaleka Reef, with a gap through which ships could safely pass in nearly all weathers, meaning that the township of Levuka was a welcome, safe harbour at most times.

Levuka – where Mary's English father, Captain William Wallace Wilson, was harbourmaster – is quite a significant place in the history of Fiji during the 19th century. It is situated at the centre of 'Lomaiviti', the heart of Fiji, which is a series of islands scattered about the horizon around Ovalau. Around 1806, sandalwood traders began stopping in its safe harbour for food and water and, under protection provided by the chief of Levuka, Tui Levuka, Europeans were settling there by the 1830s. By the middle of the 19th century, it had become an important trading post where American, French and British interests vied distrustfully with each other because of fears of imperialist intent. This seaside settlement had developed a reputation as a lawless shanty town, populated with pirates, escaped convicts and fortune hunters. Viewed from the harbour at the time, Levuka was not an attractive site. With its ramshackle huts and storage sheds built of weatherboard and corrugated iron, it presented a sorry picture to arriving vessels. The 'main street' ran along the beachfront, and at high tide only a narrow path, aptly named Beach Street, remained, washed and eroded by every storm. Horses, cattle, pigs and goats roamed freely among the buildings, the beach was permanently strewn with waste, and the lack of proper sanitation meant an incessant, unpleasant odour hung over the town. Every second shop sold liquor and it was joked that ships' captains just needed to follow the line of floating empty rum and gin bottles to enter the harbour; not surprising, because at one stage the little township boasted 52 pubs.

§

As the storm raged and the shutters rattled, Mary must have pondered the interesting ancestry this child she was carrying would inherit. Mary's mother Lizzy, whose real maiden name was Melalina Leota, was the daughter of a village leader from Eastern, now American, Samoa. Her husband Alfred was of ancient German stock, and her father, Captain Wilson, was British through and through, with a long seafaring history tied to the South Pacific.

William Wallace Wilson Jnr arrived in Fiji while still in his teens. William was the son of William Wallace Wilson, born in England in 1825, and his wife Sarah Rowlerson, daughter of farmer William Rowlerson. They married in London on 18 May 1851 and produced two sons – John Harry, born 2 March 1852, and William Wallace Jnr, born 7 December

1853. When the boys were still infants, the call to the South Pacific saw the Wilsons emigrate to New Zealand, where Wilson senior worked as a customs officer. Young W.W.W. Jnr apparently was not very cooperative at his school in Auckland, and at not quite 17 years of age, ran away to sea with a mate, sailing to Fiji in a small ketch. His arrival in the islands was at a time when there was a veritable rush of adventurers and enterprising young men looking to fulfil dreams borne of rumours of instant wealth.

Levuka at the time was crowded with offices of arbiters, advocates, auctioneers, brokers and commission agents, with not enough business or work to go around. For a young W.W.W. to take up his first job being a tax collector must have been no easy task. Collecting tax from the many renegades occupying all parts of Fiji, with very little established law and order to back him, would have been a huge challenge. After a short time in this difficult occupation, he opted to become a master mariner and was soon captaining various ships as they traded among the South Pacific Islands, east to San Francisco and south to Chile, even spending some time as ship's pilot for Fiji's King Cakobau (pronounced Thakombau).

On one of his journeys in his ship the *Elizabeth* in 1881, Captain Wilson befriended – or more accurately had a short dalliance with – a young Samoan, Melalina Leota. Melalina was the daughter of one of the ruling chiefs of her *aiga* or family, her father being part of the *maita*, who are traditionally selected for their leadership abilities as well as their birthright. This young Polynesian girl was obviously besotted with the handsome, blue-eyed European with his own ship, dressed in his dashing captain's uniform. She expressed a desire to run away with him but by then it was illegal to remove young maidens from their villages, so the captain, perhaps somewhat jokingly, told Melalina if she wanted to come with him she would have to swim out to his schooner at night. She did just that; and so he took her back to his home at Levuka.

It was doubtful that Wilson intended this to be a permanent relationship, but Melalina quickly became pregnant, and on

3 April 1882, Mary was born. Life for Melalina as a captain's woman was not the idyllic existence she had envisaged. Wilson was away a lot at sea and when he was at home, preferred his own company, burying himself in his study with his books. He was a highly intelligent man but rather selfish, and a loner. Reading and acquiring knowledge were his great loves and over the years he had taught himself smatterings of French, Spanish and Latin. He did not allow Melalina to have any male Samoan relatives to stay in the house, although over the years a variety of female friends and relatives visited. In these early days, travel back and forth to Pago Pago was not easy. Melalina quickly learnt Fijian and got on well with the local people. She also learnt a lot more English than she ever let on. The Captain insisted she anglicise her name to Elizabeth (perhaps naming her after his boat!), which he shortened to Lizzy. Thus, when Mary was born, her 15-year-old mother was lonely and a little confused and frightened and maybe this is why she never really bonded with her firstborn child.

Once Mary was born, life developed a pattern for Lizzy and the captain. Regularly, Lizzie would get fed up with her lonely existence and take off back to Pago Pago, hauling whatever children she had at the time with her. Reports would reach the captain from his fellow seafarers that his offspring were running wild with the village urchins in Pago Pago and so he would call in and collect her on his next voyage, or make a special trip to Samoa and bring her home. She would fall pregnant again, eventually producing five more children – Thomas in 1886, then George in 1894 followed by three daughters, Laura in 1897, then Matilda and Ginny. Tragically, the last two girls died during infancy.

Luckily for Wilson and his fast-expanding family, Levuka was the first town in Fiji to establish a school. As soon as the colonial government gazetted its Public School Ordinance, a group of education-conscious citizens set about forming a school board, which first met on 23 April 1879. They applied for a headmaster and his wife to come from New South Wales and on 25 August 1879 opened the school for teaching.

Mary first appears on the roll at Levuka Public School in 1886, five years after a permanent building for the school had been constructed on a site on the banks of the Totogo Creek. Her siblings followed as they each reached four years of age. Mary, however, continued to have a strained relationship with her mother, no doubt being affected by Lizzy's unreliable and wandering ways. At the age of eight she was sent off to stay with Wilson relatives in Auckland and attend school there, where her younger sister Laura would later join her. Mary did not return to Fiji until she was 18 years old, virtually a stranger to her parents.

Captain Wilson had little patience with any of his children until they reached an age where he could communicate with them as adults. Laura and Tom were almost afraid of him but George held him in no real awe and would gabble away at him incessantly, occasionally holding long conversations with Lizzy in Samoan, which Wilson did not speak, just to annoy him. In fact, all the children spoke to her in Samoan, which infuriated the captain, who was still not really comfortable with these little half-castes he had produced. He once told them they were like little animals, howling and yowling around his house, damaging his precious books and disturbing the peace he craved when he came home from sea or his job at the harbour. On one occasion, he became most upset when young Tom emerged from his bath wearing one of Lizzy's *lavalava*s, the traditional knee-length skirt of the Samoans, and told him to go and get dressed properly immediately. Tom is purported to have said, 'I am what you made me, Father. You cannot say to do what you say, not what you have done.' The captain just turned and walked away in a stunned and seething silence.

Despite his apparently remote and unaffectionate relationship with his children, others who knew him said the captain was a well-respected identity throughout the South Pacific, known for his honesty, integrity and strong independence. They believed he loved his family deeply and he always spoke fondly of them in their absence. He was admired for his sobriety in a hard-drinking world and his skill as a mariner was legendary.

When Mary did return in 1900, perhaps because now as an adult she had indicated that she was ashamed that her parents were unmarried, and the captain having adapted to life with Lizzy and his children, he decided to finally make an honest woman of her and they were married in the Anglican Church of the Holy Redeemer by the Vicar Rev. William Floyd. Mary then stayed in Levuka, and in 1903 she met Alfred Kienzle. On 23 March 1904, they too married in the same picturesque church, which lies at the northern end of Beach Rd, its fine stained-glass windows reflecting the morning sun with dazzling rainbows of colour that fell across the polished timber pews.

Alfred was originally from Stuttgart in southern Germany but had spent quite a lot of his youth in England. He was sent out to manage the Fiji office of the German-owned company Hedemann & Evers. He was joined in 1908 by his first cousin Alfred Schoeffel, who came out to work for another German company at Levuka at the age of only 16. Along the way this Alfred had become a naturalised British citizen and on a trip to New Zealand he met an Australian lass, Daisy Pearse, from a well-known Perth family, and, against furious opposition from her family, they married in 1913. The Hedemann family were investors in two companies in Levuka, one being called Hedemann & Co and the other Alfred's employer Hedemann & Evers. The latter was involved in import and export, particularly of plantation produce of copra and sugar. The fortunes of Levuka rode very much on the back of plantation productivity and marketing.

Captain Wilson had acquired interests in several plantations on the island of Vanua Levu and one on the island of Makogai – this was later sold to the government and set up as a leper colony. Around the time Makogai was sold, George was sent off to King's College in Auckland from where he went to Agricultural College and then to Australia to learn surveying. It was the captain's dream that George would one day come home and manage the family's plantation interests.

Alfred also invested some money in copra plantations on the island of Wakaya only a short hop from Levuka, and on other Ovalau Islands so that, like his father-in-law and the town where he lived, his financial situation was very much tied to the vagaries of the copra industry.

Despite the 1890s having seen an increase in German presence in Levuka, by the early 1900s the main influences were very much British, and Queen Victoria held pride of place in the hearts of most of the European citizens, even those of German origins – after all, Victoria came from a Teutonic background. The Victoria League flourished, Empire Day was celebrated with gusto and many Germans, including Alfred Kienzle, chose to become naturalised British citizens.

§

Mary's firstborn child, Herbert Thomson Kienzle, was brought safely into the world on 19 May 1905 – 19.05.1905, a special date that signified the beginning of a special life, and just one month after Mary rode out the horrendous cyclone alone. A little over two years later, Mary produced her first daughter, Laura, followed in 1910 by Elsa. All were born at their picturesque home on the hill.

Despite their rather strict father and grandfather, life for Bert and his younger sisters was pretty idyllic for some years. Their gentle mother Mary encouraged them to enjoy life on this tropical island, and their days were filled with fishing in the harbour for tasty lagoon and reef fish and exploring the dense jungle in the hillside behind their home, always alive with the sound of the abundant birdlife. Just below them on the hillside lived the Eastgate family, who would walk with them to school down the endless steps, past the breadfruit and mango trees laden with luscious fruits and over the bridge across the fast-flowing Totogo Creek, which roared over the rocks after the perpetual rains. One of Bert's mates was the young Daniel Whippy, grandson of the American sailor David Whippy, the founder of Levuka. Despite their Samoan ancestry, the young Kienzles were discouraged from mixing with the local Fijian children, very few of whom attended Levuka Public School in the early years. Only the children of village chiefs enrolled at the school, the most notable being the young Cakobaus, Edward in 1917 and George in 1920. This did not stop Bert learning to speak Fijian and sneaking time with the children of the local women who worked in the family home and helped care for him and his sisters.

As Bert grew old enough, he would go with his father and sometimes his grandfather to check on their copra plantation interests on the various surrounding islands. It was in these formative years that Bert developed a deep love and respect for the South Pacific, its way of life and its people. This passion stayed with him through years of forced separation from the tropics and his deep understanding of Pacific Islanders, particularly Melanesians, would stand him in good stead the way his life panned out; indeed, it helped direct the choices that he made.

Bert was very fond of his grandparents, whom he was the first to call Baka and Maka – probably mispronunciations of a combination of English and Fijian words for grandpa and grandma. He and his cousins recalled visits to the house they called 'Qima', pronounced Gima, which sat on an acre of land further up the hill from Alfred and Mary's home. One of Bert's cousins, Elima, related her memories of the house in a letter to Bert many years later:

> I loved it as a child with all the pumice paths between the gardens which I always remember as being full of euchrist [sic] lilies, tea roses, gerberas and gardenias with a big lagilagi tree with smelly yellow flowers that Maka would use to perfume the coconut oil that was rubbed all over us after baths.

On their visits to their grandparents, the children were always sent to bed straight after dinner. They would lie on their simple cots, the kerosene lamps flickering on the tallboy, large mosquito nets covering them like tents, the smell of camphorwood and sandalwood boxes all around them, and moths and cockroaches bombarding their protective nets. They would inhale the smoke of Maka's salukas (native tobacco wrapped in banana leaves), which wafted up from the 'big room' downstairs. This room had a vast wooden floor, with French doors at each end and big glass cases full of Baka's beloved books. The floor was covered in fine mats where Maka would sit with her daughters, telling tales of her old life in a Samoan village, and of her interest in the political intrigue and history of the South Pacific.

Maka (Lizzy) had been born in Pago Pago on the island of Tutuila, which is one of six islands that make up what is now the American Samoa group. Similar to Ovalau, these islands consist of low but sheer cliffs and rugged tropical forest-covered peaks with limited coastal plains. The coastline is ringed by an aquamarine sea with blue tide pools, lava beaches and cliffs and geyser-like blowholes. It has a tropical marine climate and, like Fiji, lies in the hurricane belt. Tutuila is the main, most populous island in the group and Pago Pago at its centre is its capital and site of one of the best deepwater harbours in the South Pacific.

Like Levuka in Fiji, Pago Pago in Samoa was occupied in the mid-1800s by the flotsam and jetsam of the Pacific, as well as fortune seekers from America, Germany and Britain, and by the 1880s a three-way tug-of-war had developed between these nations for the right to colonise Samoa. At one stage, ships from the three countries were involved in a 'Mexican stand-off' in the harbour, and legend has it that they were so busy watching each other, they forgot to watch their barometers! Suddenly a hurricane of mammoth proportions was upon them, and when the mayhem finally ended, only the British ship, the *Calliope*, was still afloat. The madness of this event moved them to make some sort of decision about the future of the island group and, eventually, what was Eastern Samoa entered willingly into a covenant with the United States while Western Samoa was claimed by Germany. By the end of the 19th century, all the Pacific Islands except Tonga, which somehow had remained a sovereignty under the arm of British protection, had been colonised by America or a European power.

Lizzy had left Pago Pago by the time the annexation to America became official in 1900 but being born in 1867 she witnessed the crazy events and intrigues of the 1870s and always remained interested in the political history of her home country. She shared her ongoing love for Samoa with her children and grandchildren and enthralled and terrified them with tales of the many dramas of village life on her home island.

§

Like his mother before him, Bert attended Levuka Public School, appearing on the roll in 1911, followed by Laura in 1912 and Elsa in 1915. Soon after the school was built in 1881, the board set out on a beautification program, planting *luaci* or candlenut trees for shade and creating garden beds of tropical shrubs. It was probably the most attractive building site in Levuka, although its position next to the temperamental Totogo Creek with the steep hillside behind meant the lack of room for expansion was always going to be a problem. In 1894, a gentleman called Captain D. Garner Jones arrived from New Zealand to take up the job as principal, a position he held until after Bert and his family left the school. He was a highly educated man, ahead of his time, who believed in a practical education relevant to the environment in which his pupils lived, adding wireless telegraphy, boatbuilding and sailmaking to the curriculum.

Bert and his sisters' teacher in their first few years was a Mrs Hathaway, who joined the staff in 1899 and did not retire until 1922. She was patient, kindly and an excellent teacher, instilling in all her students a love of knowledge, England and the English language. One idiosyncrasy of Principal Jones was that he encouraged his pupils to write and draw equally well with both their right and left hands. Both Jones and Hathaway put great value on discipline, so combining this with their strict paternal relatives, the Kienzle children had a reputation for exemplary behaviour. Bert was not looking forward to being sent off to boarding school in Melbourne but that was the plan.

Meanwhile, both their father and grandfather continued to lead prominent lives in the Levuka expatriate community, regularly joining fellow businessmen, planters and civil servicemen at the Ovalau Club for the traditional evening drink of the tropics, the gin and tonic affectionately called 'planters punch'.

In 1912, Alfred was appointed master of the masonic lodge and took on the title of The Right and Worshipful Master Brother A. Kienzle. It was at this time that he had a major difference of opinion with his father-in-law over the use of lodge funds. Captain Wilson was trustee of the estate left to the lodge by Peter Murray: in fact, with the resignation of Brother George Smith, he was sole administrator. There were moves afoot to use these funds to erect a permanent temple for the lodge and land had already been donated for this purpose. Members felt the lodge was prosperous and popular enough to have a building of its own and not have to move from rented premises to premises. To do this they would need to use a significant portion of Murray's estate. Wilson, however, took literally the terms of the will, which stated funds should be 'devoted to the relief of the poor and the suffering who shall be considered worthy of their bounty'. To use these funds to build an edifice for the exclusive use of the brethren he felt was an abuse of their responsibilities to administer the inheritance under the terms that it was given. Apparently he was in the minority in this opinion, and the lodge committee voted to go ahead and withdraw the necessary funds to complete the construction. Wilson resigned in protest, and fatefully, responsibility for administering the estate was handed over to his son-in-law, Alfred. The captain would feel justified in his decision when he later learnt that all the liquid funds were used for the project and permission had to be obtained to mortgage the assets of the estate to continue.

The building was completed and the foundation stone laid with all due celebration on 28 February 1913. The Right Reverend the Bishop of Polynesia Thomas Clayton Mitchell performed chaplain duties at the opening ceremony and Brother Kienzle gave an address to the gathering labelled 'The Nature and Objects of Freemasonry'.

It may be significant that only a year after this event, in early 1914, Captain Wilson retired from his post as harbourmaster. During his years in the civil service he had also taken on other positions of responsibility including Receiver of Native Taxes, Bondkeeper and Boarding Officer, Manager of Levuka Cemetery, Sub-Collector of Customs, and Deputy Commissioner of Water Supply. In a newspaper article at the time of his retirement, it was written: 'Our old and genial friend will be most missed by the seafaring community who have received many obligations and strenuous services at his hands.' A farewell was to be organised and it was noted that Wilson had purchased land on the east end of Vanua Levu where he intended to establish his own copra plantation. He called this new estate of 554 acres 'Nabaka' and he was to spend a lot of his time there over the ensuing years. He later acquired several adjoining estates called 'Midri' (270 acres), 'Naso Sobu' (83 acres) and 'Navuo' (383 acres). In addition, he owned a 1,000-acre island, Vatu Vara. No doubt he was accumulating all this land with his ambitions for George in mind.

Nineteen-fourteen proved to be a watershed – indeed a devastating – year for the Kienzle family. On 18 June, the day began with great joy in the morning when Bert's new baby brother Wallace arrived safely and he and Laura rushed home from school, quickly scaling two at a time the 80 or so steps to their hillside home, to see mother, new baby and sister Elsa sitting up in bed and seemingly well. Then, tragedy in the afternoon when, unexpectedly, Mary passed away. As with her other children, this baby was born at home, so medical assistance was limited and delayed shock at the trauma of the birth apparently caused Mary's stressed heart to suddenly just stop beating. Some members of the family believe that Mary was very depressed during her fourth pregnancy and that her lack of a will to live contributed to her death. Her niece Elima would write years later that her family believed Mary was blessed, or more realistically, cursed, with 'the second sight' and she had foreseen some imminent disaster during her confinement.

Captain Wilson happened to be back at sea relieving as captain on the *Ranadi* when this tragedy occurred, and on board with him was ship's mate and good friend and roommate of Tom's, Hubert Sabben, who recalled many years later in a letter to Bert that Captain Wilson was devastated by this news. He had become very fond of Mary since her return to Levuka 14 years earlier and because of his already strained relationship with Alfred it would appear he partly blamed him for her death. Perhaps he felt she should not have had this fourth baby, or maybe he was just looking for someone on whom to vent his anger and sorrow and Alfred, for whom he had no time since the lodge dispute, was an easy target.

The Captain and Lizzie's other surviving children soon also married and went their separate ways. Laura married the postmaster at Levuka, a William Mill Caldwell, and had four children – Elima, Mabel, Barbara and Wallace. Tom married a Winifred le Vier and lived in Suva, where he was a junior merchant marine engineer, having served his apprenticeship with his mate Hubert Sabben at Rarawai Sugar Mill. They produced two daughters, Feleni and Rua.

Mary Kienzle is buried in the cemetery at Levuka where her grave can be seen to this day. The members of the Masonic Lodge formed a grand funeral procession along the winding seaside path to the cemetery, dressed uniformly in their 'aprons' and holding aloft the coffin of this beautiful young mother for the entire distance. Mary's grave lies in a prominent position in what was described in a delightfully written late 1800s document as 'a most charming Cemetery . . . offering one of the sweetest resting places to be desired in the Southern Hemisphere'. Her headstone, a pink marble scroll-shaped tablet, lies safely in a large rectangular concrete gravesite, sitting high on the main volcanic outcrop of the graveyard, with the majestic hills behind and the azure Pacific in front. It reads: 'In loving remembrance of Mary Kienzle, beloved wife of Alfred Kienzle, who died 18th June 1914. Auf Wiedersehen.'

2

ENEMY ALIENS

The absurdity and futility of war was exemplified by what happened to Bert Kienzle and his family from 1914 right through until 1945.

When World War I broke out in August 1914, baby Wallace was only two months old and Alfred's main concern was keeping his job with Hedemann & Evers and his plantation interests going while grieving for his lovely wife Mary and trying to raise four young children. The Schoeffels had been good and loyal friends to Alfred and Mary and helped as best they could. Alfred's relationship with his father-in-law was still strained and although Lizzy occasionally came back from Suva where she and the captain now spent most of their time – her calm presence around the children relieving him for short times – his situation was not easy.

Germany was now at war with Britain, and so the old rivalries and enmities that had existed between the various nations that had vied for sovereignty of Fiji in the 1800s resurfaced. The German nationals in the islands were on the whole men of peace, quite content to carry on in their agricultural pursuits. The Kienzles and the Schoeffels purposefully kept their heads down and, to quote Daisy Schoeffel in a letter she would later write to the Hon H. Gregory, the Member of Parliament for

Fremantle: 'We lived there quietly without ever having any trouble personally with anyone, we contributed to every fund and helped as much as possible in all patriotic functions.'

Altogether, the Colony of Fiji contributed over £600,000 to various patriotic funds and the people worked generously raising money through festivals and direct levies, and it is to this sort of activity that Daisy is obviously referring. In a preposterous demonstration of bigotry, the British refused all offers from Fijians, Indians and part-Europeans to enrol in military service and fight side by side with the English soldiers of the King. Mary's younger brother George's attempt to enlist was initially knocked back because he was not 'a pure white man' but when this happened the captain exploded with rage and is reputed to have verbally – some versions of the story even say physically – attacked the governor of Fiji to force him to make an exception. The response of 'pure' Europeans in Fiji was enthusiastic and so George along with around 50 other Fiji residents, joined the First Fiji Voluntary Expedition Force, which departed Suva on board the RMS *Majura* on 1 January 1915, bound for Europe.

These men, including 101 Fijians in the Transport Corps, would perform with distinction, winning more than 100 commissions and 34 decorations.

Mary's brother Tom Wilson also joined up and because of his qualifications as a marine engineer was gladly accepted by the Royal Australian Navy. His tour of duty was not without controversy, and experiences of discrimination and his determination to stand up for himself resulted in a few stoushes. First, as officer of the day he had to reprimand a sailor who returned from shore leave very drunk and obnoxious. The loudmouthed bigot threw a punch at Tom, who reciprocated with one hard fist, knocking his opponent to the ground. Unfortunately, the sailor hit the deck so hard he was knocked unconscious and subsequently died, but evidence given by witnesses to the event meant no charges were laid against Tom. His ship was involved in transport of Anzac troops and supplies, but on arrival in the European war zone, many of the 'colonial' officers, including

Tom, were replaced by very junior and inexperienced British officers. Tom was very outspoken about this move, saying the incompetence of these green sailors would be sure to sink the ships. He was arrested, removed from the ship and placed in the brig awaiting court-martial for insubordination. Somehow he got off on this charge too, probably because his engineering skills were badly needed for the war effort, and he was given a commission on another vessel. The story goes that as he predicted, his old ship was lost on the way to Gallipoli. It is not surprising that Tom earned the nickname 'Tiger' Wilson.

Through late 1914 and early 1915, in all the Pacific Islands, tensions continued to rise between German nationals or naturalised subjects of German descent and other Europeans in the population.

During the first half of 1915, Daisy Schoeffel invited her older unmarried sister, Mena Hallet Pearse, known to her family as Hally, to come to Levuka for a visit. Perhaps she wanted her company during these troubled times, or maybe she wanted help with her children as she was not always in good health but more than likely there were some matchmaking plans in mind.

On 8 May 1915, Mary Kienzle's brother George Wilson was killed at the Battle of Ypres in Belgium. The death of this boy, who had become his favourite son, devastated Captain Wilson and once again he turned on Alfred, directing his hatred at all Germans and refusing to ever speak to his son-in-law again. All attempts by Laura and other members of the family to exhort the captain to heal the rift proved futile. Either he had forgotten, or was looking to assuage his guilt for having begged the governor to let George enlist in the first place. Whatever his reasons, the inevitable outcome was that Alfred was indeed a lonely widower, and the arrival of an unattached Australian woman with the maturity to take on a ready-made family was quite fortuitous.

Thus it transpired that on 11 September 1915, Alfred Kienzle married Hally Pearse in the Anglican Church at Levuka and, as history was soon to attest, the union proved fortunate for

Alfred and the children, and for Daisy and Hally, who would need each other's mutual support during the ensuing years. Hally, however, was a different kettle of fish from Mary. Alfred's three older children had trouble accepting her as their mother. She found it easiest to bond with the baby Wallace and it was noticeable in correspondence and conversations with Bert over the years the different feelings he had towards his mother and stepmother. He always spoke of Mary with a deep sense of love and loss, whereas with Hally, it was more a tone of almost grudging respect.

A series of unusual events combined with the divisions caused by war in Europe were soon to bring a most unfortunate fate upon the Kienzle family.

As mentioned, Alfred Kienzle had been an active member of Lodge Polynesia No. 52. He had served as master of this lodge in 1912 and, as such, had his name engraved on the foundation stone listing all past masters. The story goes that sometime in 1916, Alfred joined in a session at a kava saloon one evening with other brothers of the lodge. Whether they adjourned to the lodge or it occurred in some other location, the story does not relate, but apparently, in a rather inebriated state, Alfred tried to straighten a picture of King George that was hanging crookedly on the wall, using his walking stick. The stick slipped, the picture fell to the ground and the glass smashed. In the paranoia of the times, as the story of the event spread, ulterior motives were read into the accident, and even the so-called Brotherhood of the Masonic Lodge were carried along in the heat of the moment, and expelled Alfred from the lodge, going so far as to chisel his name off the foundation stone.

One who latched onto the sinister implications of the exaggerated rumours was the local vicar, a widower whose son had just been killed on the Western Front. This vicar became an active proponent of the moves afoot to intern German nationals and German naturalised citizens of Fiji and to expropriate their estates. Many of these agitators were planters and businessman who no doubt saw an opportunity for cheap expansion of their own assets. Initially, the governor conceded to some of their demands by limiting the movement of these 'aliens' in Fiji, restricting their residence and curtailing some of their freedoms, including the right to carry arms. By April 1916, patriotic fervour and hysteria had risen to fever pitch, and the first batch of Germans was sent off to be interned in Australia.

Of course, these anti-German sentiments were not restricted to Fiji. Everywhere, including Australia, where Germans resided, no matter what their current allegiances, they were treated with suspicion. Within one week of war breaking out, all German subjects in Australia were required to report to the nearest post office and to notify immediately of any change of address. As the number of Australian casualties in Europe grew, so did the hostility to anyone of German descent back home. They found it harder to obtain employment and often ended up volunteering themselves for internment in order to survive and feel safe.

On 7 April 1916, Alfred was fined £75 for possessing a firearm, which of course was confiscated. No doubt this, along with the King George picture incident and perhaps even the influence of his own father-in-law, resulted in Alfred Kienzle also being on the first shipment from Levuka, leaving behind his wife of less than a year with her four new stepchildren. Alfred arrived in Sydney on 3 May 1916 and was handed a warrant for his arrest, made out to Alfred Thomas Karl Kienzle of Levuka in the State of Fiji, written on 5 May and signed by the defence minister. Alfred appears in prisoner of war records as Alfred T. Kienzle Barcode: 350360 1917/89/267 Series A1183.

Alfred was taken by sea to Trial Bay Gaol, on the north coast of New South Wales north of Kempsey and near the estuary of the Macleay River, some 500 kilometres from Sydney. Building of Trial Bay had commenced in 1884 and it opened in 1886 as part of a reform of the NSW prison system. It was intended that prisoners towards the end of their sentences would attend these 'Public Works Prisons' where they would learn skills as part of their preparation for rehabilitation into mainstream society. At Trial Bay it was planned that they would be involved in the construction of a breakwater that would turn the bay into a safe anchorage during storms. This concept soon proved to be unfeasible as the wall kept collapsing with the high seas and also caused silting of the harbour it was built to protect. Simultaneously, the enthusiasm for reform of the prison system waned, so the facility was closed in July 1903 and lay dormant until August 1916, when the Australian Government decided to use it for the internment of POWs and German detainees.

Fortunately for Alfred, Trial Bay was known as the camp for the elite of the detainees and among the 'upper 500', as they came to be known, were naval officers, merchants, physicians, priests, university lecturers and several German consuls. Many of the residents had been moved there from the Holsworthy camp near Liverpool, a separation based on a desire to reduce social tensions where divisions had developed based on rank, position and class. Conditions at Trial Bay were much better than Holsworthy, where between 5,000 and 6,000 detainees were accommodated in far less attractive surroundings and with far fewer facilities. The sturdy granite rock of Trial Bay meant that it was at least cool in summer even if the winters were unpleasantly cold.

Quite an active social life was organised by internees but this could still not detract from the fact that many of them were unjustly detained. They were a very patriotic lot who actively supported the efforts of their much-loved Emperor and, amazingly, they were allowed a lot of freedom to feed this nationalism. They were even permitted to print a weekly newspaper called *Welt am Montag* (The World on Monday), which gave reports on the war from the German perspective and espoused the superiority of their Teutonic race. For this reason, Alfred did not really fit in. He was married to an Australian and had many Australian and British friends, plus he had no desire to go back to Germany – his first love was now the South Pacific. From day one, Alfred spent much of his time alone in his 4 metre x 7 metre cell, which was sparsely furnished with a bed, table and desk, writing to his family and lodging his objections to his situation through every channel available. Initially he wrote to the governor-general, stating that he had been forcibly deported from Fiji and landed against his will. The letter read:

> As it is apparent that the Commonwealth authorities have detained me at first upon my involuntary landing in Australia without any warrant, which is contrary to Law, and furthermore it is apparent that the warrant issued by the minister for the State for Defence is 'ultra vires' as he has no jurisdiction or power of any kind over or in the Crown Colony of Fiji, I therefore herewith take the liberty to request your Excellency to have my case investigated and if the facts should be found as stated above, it would in my opinion be expedient if I were returned to the Fiji Govt. Upon investigation your Excellency will find that I am the only naturalised British subject that has been sent to Australia as a prisoner of war, no other British Crown Colony having dared to put the Australian government in the embarrassing position which it has created in my case by the detention of a British subject who is not under the jurisdiction of the government of Australia.

Unfortunately for Alfred, despite the legal advice he had obviously received, he was not cognisant of the facts with regard to the many naturalised British ex-Germans already interned elsewhere, and of the complicity of the Australian Government with many other Pacific nations to intern their so-called 'enemy aliens'. The internment of both German and Austrian naturalised citizens, even those with Australian wives, was justified by the acting prime minister, Senator Pearce, when he stated in the *Sydney Mail*: '. . . naturalization to a German or Austrian was a very different thing from naturalization to an American or Frenchman. Any German or Austrian naturalized in the Commonwealth could, by merely signing his name in the book at the office of the consul-general, divest himself of that naturalization'.

In other words, he implied that these naturalisation certificates were not worth the paper they were written on and were no guarantee of loyalty to the Commonwealth, and so internment of these persons, along with German nationals and even visitors to our shores, began from early 1915. Why Australia volunteered so willingly to carry out this onerous task on behalf of the whole Commonwealth, at a time when it was otherwise trying to firmly establish independence and sever its apron strings from Britain, is a mystery. Britain's enthusiasm for the project can be partly put down to seeing an opportunity to dilute, hopefully even destroy, German interests in the Pacific, Asia and Africa where they had continually competed with the British Empire for sovereignty over many years. Those who have studied this whole situation can only conclude that, for Australia, it was still a case of politicians continuing the sycophantic attitude to their sovereign power and an almost childlike acceptance that Australia was historically a dumping ground for Commonwealth prisoners. This is what they did well and how they could continue to contribute to the greater good of the Empire. The reality is that it damaged Australia's reputation in Europe, Asia and the South Pacific and confirmed the German belief in the moral superiority of their German imperial traditions.

Alfred's case was routinely referred to the prime minister, who passed it on to the defence minister, who then sent it on to Fiji. Four months later, the governor-general responded, stating that the governor of Fiji was 'unable to vary the terms of the order under which Mr Kienzle was interned'.

Immediately, Alfred made a second request for exemption on medical grounds. Release on the basis of medical conditions was dependent on the report of one examining doctor who had to establish if the applicant was medically 'fit for garrison duty i.e. office work, if he had been resident in Germany at the present time'. Alfred was accordingly advised 'the medical report does not entitle you to repatriation as medically unfit', and so once again his request was refused by the Defence Department. Naturally, he was furious, and he wrote to both the official visitor to the camps and to the governor-general, protesting:

> If I would be in Germany at the present time or have stayed
> there at the outbreak of war, I would be interned in Ruhleben,
> if the German authorities would think me medically fit for
> internment ... I beg to point out that I am a British subject
> naturalized in the Crown Colony of Fiji and that volunteers are
> only accepted up to the age of 35 years, and that therefore I
> am over age according to the ordinance in force in my country.

This time, the governor-general did not refer the matter to his ministers for consideration but sent the curt reply that he was 'unable to see that any good purpose would be served by reopening this matter'. Alfred was a typical victim of the bureaucratic ball game that had resulted because, even though Australia was more than happy to accept the internees, it neither wanted nor accepted any jurisdiction over them. It insisted on an intermediary role only, not wanting to be involved in decisions with regard to prisoner status, requests for release or even access to monies in bank accounts. All such matters were referred back to the government of the colonies from which internees came, and of course from there they bounced straight back again.

Alfred was left no alternative but to grin and bear it; at least at Trial Bay he was in esteemed company with the many prominent gentlemen interned there at the time. Most notable were two German scientists, the physicist Pringsheim and the anthropologist Grabner, both of whom had been invited by the Australian Government to attend the Congress of the British Association for the Advancement of Science – bad luck for them that war broke out while they were 'down under'. Also present, somewhat controversially, was the naturalised Australian medical practitioner and first orthopaedic surgeon in Australia, Dr Max Herz. Herz was a respected member of the British Medical Association but the power of xenophobia and professional jealousy was enough to see him blacklisted by that association and interned as an enemy alien on 19 May 1915, only a few weeks after the birth of his first child.

Inmates of Trial Bay were afforded quite a lot of freedom, with the doors being open during daylight hours. The men were free to walk around the peninsula and onto the beach, where they revelled in the opportunity to swim, sunbathe and fish.

Food was good, with official rations being supplemented by produce from a vegetable garden. There was even a beachside cafe called the Artist's Den and a restaurant called The Duck Coop operated by enterprising inmates. The camp was run by a series of committees that organised many cultural and educational activities, all of this enhanced by the cosmopolitan character of the interned population. Detainees came from such diverse countries as Singapore, Ceylon, Hong Kong, New Guinea and Samoa. Gerhard Fischer, in his book *Enemy Aliens*, went so far as to state: 'The atmosphere of the fashionable sea resort and the relative freedom enjoyed by the internees thus created a kind of holiday spirit.'

As already suggested, however, this did not negate the fact that these men were suffering quite significant psychological distress. They had been uprooted from their homes and businesses, lost their old social contacts and been separated from their families. In their absence, their businesses were being wound up or sold at auction by the public trustee. To top it all off, they had in most cases been treated despicably during their transport to Australia. The feeling of helplessness and impotence must have been overpowering, and one can understand their attempts to cope with all this by immersing themselves in German culture and traditions as much as possible in this forced environment, even if it made a few like Alfred feel very uncomfortable. Despite the relative comfort in which they were interned, and perhaps because they were allowed the freedom to do so and had the time and intellect, a lot of the men at Trial Bay wrote to whoever they could think of complaining of their lot. More letters came out of Trial Bay than any other camp, one fellow actually confessing in a poem: 'We protested every bit, Had simply got used to it!'

§

Back in Fiji, life continued reasonably peacefully for Hally and the children and the Schoeffels in Levuka until another bizarre incident

In September 1917, the infamous commander of the German raider, the *Seeadler*, Count Felix von Luckner, ironically himself a brother of the lodge, paid an unexpected visit to the Fijian Islands.

The *Seeadler*, meaning 'sea eagle' in German, had managed to run the British blockade in the North Sea in December 1916 by posing as a Norwegian vessel. It was actually an American cotton ship, the *Pass of Balmaha*, which had fallen into the hands of the Germans, but by going to extreme lengths of preparation, von Luckner even tricked the British when they boarded her at sea. All the crew spoke Norwegian, chewed Norwegian tobacco and in their cabins displayed photos of their 'sweethearts' taken by Norwegian photographers. Von Luckner went so far as to have 'Knudsen', a good Norwegian name, embroidered on his underwear.

Once through the British blockade, he proceeded to leave a trail of destruction of Allied ships from the Atlantic all the way to Cape Horn. Included among his many victims were the *Antonin*, *Buenos Aires* and *Charles Gounoud*. To give von Luckner his due, during his attacks, no enemy sailors were left to drown and all were treated fairly and by the rules of war.

By the time the *Seeadler* reached the Pacific, however, her 64-man crew was riddled with beri-beri and scurvy and badly in need of fresh supplies. Von Luckner opted to try to land at the Mopelia Atoll, a dot in French Oceania about 360 kilometres west of Tahiti in the Society Islands. While attempting to navigate the narrow passage through the reef, a freak wave threw the *Seeadler* onto the rocks. No crew were lost but the ship was unsalvageable.

Having set his crew up in a tent-town on shore and burnt the wreck of the *Seeadler* so they would not be spotted, von Luckner set off in a 5.5-metre lifeboat, which he christened

Kronprinzessin Cecilie, with his lieutenant and four men. Their plan was to find a good-sized ship to steal and return to collect the rest of their crew. Their first stop was in the Cook Islands about three days sailing from their starting point, but here they received a hostile reception, so they turned about and set off for Fiji.

Von Luckner and his men had travelled more than 3,000 kilometres in extremely rough conditions when they finally struggled ashore at Katafaga in the northern Lau group of Fiji, and in the absence of the local plantation owner helped themselves to his supplies and had a good rest. They politely left him a note saying:

> We are very sorry we have not meet you here. I and my mates sleep in your house. We had a good meal and are now quite fit to proceed on our sporting trip. The wonderful stroll around your island we shall never forget – all things we took is paid for – turkey 10 shillings, bananas 2 shillings. Me and my men are thankful to you.

In a bold and facetious twist, von Luckner signed the letter 'Max Pemberton'.

From Katafaga, they sailed west to Wakaya Island. This island, where both the Kienzles and the Schoeffels had held some interests in a plantation, is not far from Levuka, and at the time was still privately owned, and occupied by only a few native labourers. Anchored in the bay was a handsome, new three-masted schooner, the *Eleanor D*, provisioned with large stores of fruit and vegetables for six months' cruising. Von Luckner could not believe his luck and had already christened her the *Seeadler II* in his mind. In Norwegian guise, he approached the skipper, who in his ignorance generously offered to take him and his men to Australia.

As von Luckner planned the takeover of the schooner with his men, an ugly little cattle boat called the *Amra* slid into the bay beside him. On board was Inspector Hills of the Fiji Constabulary along with five policemen, who von Luckner would later describe as 'Indians who wore puttees and those funny little pants'. With arms and the element of surprise at his advantage, Von Luckner could easily have overpowered this small group of law officers, but, as he then told his men, to make war in civilian clothes would see them hung from the yardarm as international bandits. Much to the consternation of his men, including surely those back at Mopelia if they had known, he ordered his troops to throw their weapons over the side, raised his arms and said to Inspector Hills, 'We are at your service.'

The prisoners were first taken to Levuka then Suva and from there, they were sent on to New Zealand. Not surprisingly, the story does not end there, as soon after arrival von Luckner stole a boat and a New Zealand army officer's uniform, and escaped. He was soon recaptured but apparently was planning a second escape when the armistice was signed, at which point he was returned to Germany on the transport *Willochra*.

Of course, this scenario is not the story that reached the Fijian populace. The tale grew to the extent that accusations abounded that hundreds of Germans had landed on Wakaya and were being aided and abetted by local naturalised German planters to escape. A *Fiji Times* editorial at the time suggested that, as the Germans had just carried out a moonlight raid on London, it was time for a moonlight raid on the 'enemies within our gates'. Fiji even requested permission to mount an attack on German Samoa but fortunately this was not granted.

Daisy Schoeffel wrote in her letter: 'I should not have believed it possible that a British community could behave as they did, had I not been there and stood the many insults: I can only forgive them when I know that they were temporarily mad.'

Letter after letter in the press began demanding the arrest and internment of all Germans, whether British citizens or not. In October, the governor of Fiji gave in to the pressure, stating that he had received orders from London, and that he was concerned about the threat to British rule if these persons whose homeland was at war with Britain were to join forces with the natives and start an uprising. He also expressed concerns that internment of these persons in Fiji would be difficult to control, even though there really was no evidence to support this. He set about arranging for all other persons of 'doubt' to be deported, their properties to be confiscated and their businesses seized and sold at auction. One of the first casualties of this decree was Hedermann & Evers, Alfred's old employer.

It was at this time that Hally and her stepchildren, along with Daisy Schoeffel with her husband and two young children, aged three years and 15 months, were forced to board the SS *Atua*, which departed Suva on 1 November 1917. They were not given any option to stay in Fiji. Bert was 12 years of age, his sisters Laura 10, Elsa seven and Wallace only three years old when they were bundled into steerage on a ship whose decks were covered in hundreds of bunches of bananas. On board with them were 18 men (three of whom were naturalised British subjects and five German nationals) 11 women and 11 children guarded by one officer, two non-commissioned officers and six soldiers. The men on board were merchants, planters, retailers, professionals including an accountant and a surveyor, and even a lay Marist Brothers missionary. Among these were Karl Krafft, a timber merchant and acting German consul in Fiji, plus Reichart the baker and Volk, a retired publican. The Fijian Governor did not see fit to record the details of the women's citizenship, but most were from Australia and the United Kingdom.

Despite being guarded by these soldiers with bayonets, Daisy and Hally still believed, as told to them by several officials in Levuka, that they were really being deported for their own protection from the bigotry and hysteria of the European populace of Fiji. They assumed that on arrival in Sydney they would be free to continue to a destination of their choice and that their main challenge would be to convince authorities in Australia that their two German-born but naturalised British husbands were no threat to the nation's security. Despite the relative comfort in which Alfred Kienzle was residing at Trial Bay, communications with Hally since his internment had been restricted and unreliable. She therefore was not fully aware of the brick wall he had met so far trying to argue his case to Australian Government officials.

The two women intended to contact their father George Pearse in Western Australia as soon as they docked in Sydney. The Pearses had been prominent residents of Western Australia and Pearse was a successful and well-respected owner of a boot-making company, Pearse and Bros in Fremantle. They hoped to use his influence to free both their husbands from the perceived need for internment. In addition, they would point out that Alfred Kienzle's brother-in-law George Wilson had died fighting in Belgium for the Allies with the first Fiji Voluntary Expeditionary Force and Daisy and Hally's two brothers, Ken and Sep Pearse, were currently fighting with the AIF in Gallipoli and France.

Imagine their outrage and despair when, on arrival at the Sydney wharf at daybreak on 9 November 1917, they were heavily guarded by military forces with fixed bayonets, refused all communications with Australian relatives or friends, and herded unceremoniously into the 'black maria' to be taken from the wharf to Central Railway Station. In future years, Bert would often state that this whole experience was etched painfully on his mind, and the indignity and unfairness of it all would stay with him forever. At the station, they heard for the first time that they were to be transported to Bourke in far west New South Wales and interned there. Young Wallace would later often bitterly bemoan that as a mere babe-in-arms he had been ripped from the comfort of his childhood home and thrown into 'a concentration camp'.

Conditions for children on the 'banana boat' had been most unsuitable, with no facilities for bathing and no proper food for infants, but at least they had not suffered from the weather. Coming from the tropics, none of the internees had warm clothing and the trip across the Blue Mountains proved unbearably cold. The journey from there took two long days and nights, and once down off the mountains, the scenery that greeted them as they gazed endlessly out their carriage windows grew more and more arid each hour. For Hally and Daisy, coming from Western Australia, it was no novelty, but for Alfred Schoeffel and both families of children it was like a journey into outer space. Bert had never before seen the likes of it – this harsh, brown landscape such a contrast to anything he had ever imagined during life in lush Fiji.

The train ploughed on through the endless sundried landscape past tiny settlements with one or two rickety wooden huts and the occasional more sturdy stone cottages, stopping at stations with names like Mungeribar, and Girilambone. Bert would never forget the stretch of track from Nyngan to Bourke – two metal lines that seemed to stretch to infinity, not a bend in the track or change in the scenery to break the monotony. The dry heat rising off the earth hit his face as Bert strained out the window and he found this far more stifling than the high humidity of his home. The willy-willies that swirled in across the flat landscape occasionally crossing paths with the train, combined with the fine ash disgorging from the locomotive's sooty funnel, added to the feeling of suffocation. He felt that surely he would drop off the end of the world at any minute!

Bourke was the end of the line and the railway station that had been built in 1885 was quite an attractive structure, but the view south that greeted them as they stood on the platform was no different from the miles and miles of scattered trees on a sandy, grassless plain they had chugged through for the last 24 hours. Bert felt a huge weight settle on his shoulders and was overcome by a feeling of claustrophobia despite the open spaces that surrounded him. He gasped for moisture in the hot dry air. The ubiquitous dust and blowflies stifled him at every turn and he could not understand why anyone would want to live in this environment. He certainly couldn't fathom what he and his family had done to deserve exile to such a place.

From the train they were bundled onto uncomfortable wooden drays pulled by draught horses and taken a few kilometres to their accommodation, which for the Kienzles and the Schoeffels was a delicensed, broken-down hotel with no electricity, that had been unoccupied for more than two years.

Daisy wrote: 'On the night of our arrival . . . once I was able to get some candles from a store nearby and we were able to see the state of the rooms we had to live in, we women just broke down – I wished to God I could die and my babies with me!'

The rooms were filthy, with broken bedsteads. They were offered sacks of straw for bedding but no pillows. For eating they were provided dirty rusty tin plates and mugs and an old tin wash bucket for cooking. When Daisy asked the sergeant major on duty for a clean plate to feed her children, he almost spat at her, 'These are the plates that the Australian Government gives German prisoners.' When Daisy responded, 'I am neither a German nor a prisoner, but an Australian woman,' he retorted, 'If you were not a German prisoner you would not be here.'

Both Daisy and Hally had to wash their children under a tap in the backyard and cook on a stove they created from four bricks and an iron bar. They had not been allowed to bring any money from Fiji, and if it had not been for the generosity of other German prisoners, who had been there for some time and had managed to get some of their possessions and funds brought to town, they believed they would have perished. For the first two months, rations consisted of bread and meat that was often flyblown so decent food had to be purchased from local stores.

It can only be assumed the military officials who selected a place such as Bourke did so with a sadistic pleasure in punishing these 'Huns', as they were called. Temperatures regularly reached 40 degrees in the shade, and arriving as they did in November in the midst of an extended drought, the internees were soon submitted to the extremes of outback New South Wales weather. What a shock it must have been to these Europeans, stepping off the train at the end of a railway line, 1,300 kilometres from Sydney in a hot, dusty broken-down old town at the end of the earth. Those not housed in the old Empire Hotel were interned in the gaol on the banks of the Darling River, alongside the common criminals serving their sentences for the usual array of crimes. Families with some accessible funds were scattered round the town in old cottages that they had to rent from local landowners. The whole set-up was overseen by a lieutenant, sergeant, guards and a matron.

Bourke was the only camp at the time that interned families as one unit, so at least in this early part of their stay Daisy had her husband to support her. Alfred Kienzle was not able to join his wife at Bourke for six weeks, making it just in time for a hot, depressing Christmas. He had to travel by ship from Jerseyville upstream from Trial Bay to Sydney, then that long train journey to Bourke. Alfred must have wondered what he had struck arriving in this hell hole, and a week after his arrival, not surprisingly under the conditions, the hotel inmates all contracted dysentery for which they received scant medical attention. Daisy's youngest child spent three weeks in hospital and Daisy herself by now was most unwell and had reached new depths of despair. Hally was relieved to have the extra support of Alfred, although his shock at the conditions at Bourke, the soul-destroying boredom and the lack of real freedom made him angrier than ever about the fate that had befallen him and his young family through no fault of their own.

The unpleasantness of life in this isolated outpost was only softened slightly by the concession that internees were given parole during daylight hours as long as they stayed within the boundaries of the village and did not enter the station, post office or any of the hotels. The boredom was also slightly relieved by the occasional supervised picnic on the banks of the nearby muddy, meandering Darling River, and the kindness and generosity of some of the local townsfolk who provided toys and pets for the camp children and helped in the throwing of a Christmas party. The people of Bourke were used to the arrival of foreigners – the town already had a multicultural feel, being populated by Chinese, Greeks, Norwegians and even a group of Afghans and their camels. They were therefore a fairly tolerant townspeople but this only slightly detracted from the woes of the internees. The constant heat and flies were unbearable and the unhygienic conditions meant that the children regularly suffered from eye conditions, meningitis and even typhoid, and what would have been most upsetting was the implication from authorities that this was caused by the internees not being conscientious enough about cleanliness.

Once again a series of incidents were about to change the course of life for the Kienzles.

On 17 September 1917, a cablegram had arrived from the secretary of state for the colonies at the office of the governor-general asking the government to receive 3,000 'enemy aliens' from China. A further request was then received to accept 3,290 Germans and Austrians from German East Africa. The government consented, no questions asked, and set about preparing accommodation for the prisoners. The building of a whole new camp at Pialligo, 6 kilometres west of Queanbeyan near the Molonglo River in the Federal Territory, commenced in February 1918 and was ready for occupation in April. On hearing of the project, the German foreign minister in China wrote to the Swiss minister in Berlin: 'The plan for this horrible step which shows equal contempt for the principles of international law and the dictates of humanity does not proceed from the Chinese Government but must be attributed to English influence.'

Via the Spanish ambassador in London, Germany sent clear warnings that if the deportation went ahead, they would be forced to carry out reprisals against Allied nationals interned in Germany, in particular not ratifying an agreement made with Great Britain for an exchange of POWs. Fortunately for the potential internees from both the colonies, their governments heeded these warnings and also began questioning the legality of such transportation, so that in the end they saw sense and it did not occur.

Meanwhile, back at Bourke, the Kienzles' fellow passenger on the *Atua* Karl George Krafft, aged 57, died from heat apoplexy on Tuesday 5 February. As a result of this death, word reached the German Foreign Office that German detainees in Australian internment camps were being mistreated, and a request was sent to the Swiss consul-general to send a representative to inspect the camps with a view to demanding an improvement in conditions.

Then, in April, at about 4.45 a.m. on Good Friday, a fire broke out in a weatherboard cottage in Short Street in Bourke occupied by one of the German internees named Wulff with his wife and child. The family were woken in time to be saved, but all their belongings and the cottage were destroyed, with no insurance to cover the loss.

These events, combined with numerous problems with costs of water supply and rent of the various hotel and housing accommodation for internees, plus perceived difficulties monitoring the movements of detainees around the township of Bourke, resulted in a decision to move all internees out of Bourke and into the new facilities at Molonglo, now no longer required for prisoners from China and Africa. The Kienzles, the Schoeffels and nearly 200 others from Bourke were transported to the new camp, arriving on 27 May 1918.

Another long, hot train journey ensued from Bourke all the way back to Sydney, then a change of trains for the winding trip to Canberra. No wonder Bert hated and tried to avoid train travel for the rest of his life, but what a relief it was to finally see some green foliage and tree-covered hills, some decent roads and prosperous-looking business houses. Their arrival was somewhat intimidating when they were made aware that there were almost as many soldiers stationed there to guard them as there were internees, this being because the camp authorities were expecting a much larger contingent of prisoners. However, the move was a real blessing, and Daisy was to write: '. . . oh the difference in the treatment here was very marked indeed and we all said if only we had been sent here in the first place!'

Molonglo Camp was far better run and much more comfortable than Bourke and Holsworthy, although not as pleasantly situated as Trial Bay. Also located at the end of a freight railway line, it was more than 300 kilometres from Sydney. It had been built over about 3.3 hectares of vacant undulating land that sloped away to the Molonglo River. As well as the weatherboard and corrugated iron huts for family accommodation, there were baggage stores, a baker and butcher shop, an assembly hall, hospital, fire station and post office. Water, electricity and sewerage services were installed, accommodation built on-site for military personnel and, as a none-too-subtle reminder to internees that they were still prisoners, a watch tower.

By now, Bert was a strapping teenage boy, having had his 13th birthday just before their removal to Molonglo. He was tall and thin but strong, with an adventurous spirit and a thirst for knowledge. Life in an internment camp therefore offered many frustrations for such a lad, and no doubt he caused his father and stepmother some grief. He was the oldest boy in the camp, with the other children, including his sisters, ranging in ages younger than him, down to toddlers. Because of this, Bert spent a lot of his time alone, or in the company of adults or his little sisters. As a result he was very mature for his age, and developed a rapport and respect for members of the opposite sex that he carried with him through life, and that set him apart from many of his peers.

He learnt to speak fluent German and became fascinated by his father's home country and its history. What was going on back there that had caused all this upheaval in his life and had resulted in him and his family being treated like common criminals?

At Molonglo, daily life took on a more interesting routine than at Bourke. The children attended school each week day and were even allowed out of camp grounds if accompanied by a teacher. On weekends they were able to swim and picnic by the river and play various sports including tennis on the courts the inmates constructed. The community hall had a piano, so regular concerts, sing-alongs and even dances helped to fill the evenings. There was a good library and a canteen and attractive gardens to break the monotony of the otherwise bare surroundings. Despite the ever present shadow of the watchtower, no guards were mounted near internees' quarters and once the internees were settled there was really no obvious police presence.

Daisy and Hally's only real complaint about Molonglo was the fact that even though there were plenty of huts available, and each family was allocated three rooms for their exclusive use, the occupied tenements were crowded in a group close together and the incessant noise of chatter in French, German, Chinese and English, all day and night, almost drove them insane. They asked to be moved to accommodation away from the noise but were refused. Daisy also noted that the huts were not very well built and were neither properly rainproof nor windproof. In winter, the wind straight from the Snowy Mountains whistled up the hill to the tenements shaking their very foundations and rattling through the gaps in the floorboards and doorways. She believed all this contributed to her deteriorating health but at least there was a well-equipped hospital at the camp and doctors carried out regular rounds. It was one of these doctors who encouraged Daisy to put in writing the story of her ordeal of deportation and internment to Hon. H. Gregory, a member of the federal parliament who had recently visited the camps and was from her home town. This letter remains on file in the archives of Prime Minister's Department correspondence files.

And so the Kienzles and Schoeffels gradually adjusted to their existence at Molonglo. Still, it must have come as a great relief to them when Armistice Day was declared on 11 November 1918, but then a further shock and frustration when they learnt they were not to be immediately released. Unbelievably, Hally and the children were not let out until 22 May 1919 and Alfred was moved to Holsworthy, where he was held until October. One can only assume that the authorities did not quite know what to do with them and there was some talk of them all even being deported to Germany, a policy proposed by both the British and Fijian governments. The Fiji Legislative Council had passed an ordinance in August 1919 prohibiting former 'enemy aliens' from returning to the island, thus thrusting the decision back on Australia as to what to do with these subjects, many of whom held British passports. Commencing in May 1919, other German and

Austrian internees auctioned their few possessions and with what little funds they had managed to liquidate, went back to their homelands on eight British transport ships including the *Willochra*, which had von Luckner on board. Alfred and Hally obviously wished to remain in Australia and it was only through continual pleading to the authorities by the Kienzles and Schoeffels and their Australian in-laws, and the intervention of MP Gregory, that the deportation order was finally rescinded.

When at last they were eventually all free again, they were almost destitute, with nowhere to go and very little accessible money. Bert recalls that they spent some time in a Salvation Army facility in Pitt Street, Sydney, while Alfred searched for employment. This was not an easy task, as returned soldiers who were having trouble getting jobs were adamant that these persons of German descent should not take any of the limited positions available. Fortunately, because of his pre-war history Alfred eventually found a job in an import–export company and was then able to lease a house in Cronulla. The school year was virtually over so there was no point in the children attending at this stage. Hally, still suffering from the nervous disorders that many internees had developed, was lumped with four idle children, with no friends of their own age, trying to start a new life after five very disrupted and unsettling years.

3

IN SEARCH OF ROOTS
AND REASONS

The confusion and inequity of what had happened to Alfred Kienzle and his family during World War I apparently led to what seemed a very strange decision on his behalf in 1920.

Hally was still unwell, having been affected both mentally and physically by her time in the internment camps. A combination of health problems had caused her skin to go blotchy and muddy coloured, most likely caused by scurvy, and she therefore dressed in long-sleeved and high-collared clothes at all times. This only added to her severe appearance that in later years her grandchildren would say made her rather an intimidating presence. Hally does deserve some sympathy for her plight: she had only been married to Alfred for just over a year when he was taken from her, leaving her to adjust alone to her instant family of four. The future would tell us that Bert, Laura and Elsa were all strong-willed youngsters who no doubt would have questioned her authority and made her life as a new mother a challenge to say the least. Thrown into this equation was the traumatic experience of being shipped to Australia and interned in concentration camps like prisoners of war, for no real reason and with no forthcoming explanation, apology or redress after the war.

This was surely the main reason that can be fathomed for Alfred's decision to make arrangements for young Herbert, now aged fourteen and a half years, to be shipped off to Germany to stay with his grandparents to complete his education. Bert had become quite fluent in German in the camps but although he had attended school at Molonglo, his education had been badly interrupted. Elsa and Laura were to follow Bert to the Continent soon after, leaving only the baby of the family, Wallace, in the care of Hally. It is not surprising that it was only Wallace in later years who continued to call Hally 'Mum', when the rest of the family would refer to her as 'Mother' or 'Nan'.

Alfred appears to have decided that despite all that had happened, his life and future were in Australia and he would do all in his power to make that future safe and secure for his family. He was busy, along with the Schoeffels, chasing up some sort of compensation for his lost properties in Fiji, and for his unjust internment and the hardships it had caused. He must have felt he could do this better from a sound position in Sydney, while caring for Hally and allowing her to regain her health without four children to handle.

After extended negotiations, the Schoeffels were allowed to return to Fiji in 1920; but neither they nor the Kienzles ever received compensation for their lost businesses and properties; nor was there any likelihood of successful legal action. Alfred Kienzle's name was eventually recarved on the Foundation Stone of the Masonic Lodge at Levuka and the vicar who contributed to his early exile expressed some regret at his behaviour – none of this any help to Alfred in his current state.

Maybe Alfred also believed Bert should learn about his German roots and try to gain some understanding of the conditions and conflicts in that country that had led to World War I. Whatever the reasons, in January 1920 Alfred put young Bert on the SS *Commonwealth*, a one-class ship bound for London via Melbourne, Adelaide and Fremantle, where he was able to briefly meet his stepmother's family, the Pearses. He then travelled on through Durban and Cape Town, eventually arriving in London in late February – quite a journey for a teenage boy on his own.

In London, he was met at the Tilbury Dock by a friend of his father's, Mr Butterworth, whose family took Bert under their wing and accommodated him for five weeks. While in London, being a British citizen born in the Colony of Fiji, he was issued with a British passport by Lord Curzon of Kedleston.

The Passport Number 102812 states:

> We, George Nathaniel Curzon, Earl Curzon of Kedleston, Viscount Scarsdale, Knight of the most Noble Order of the Garter and Member of His Britannic Majesty's Most Honourable Privy Council, Knight Grand Commander of the Most Exalted Order of the Star of India, Knight Grand Commander of the Most Eminent Order of the Indian Empire etc. etc. etc.
>
> His Majesty's Principal Secretary of State for Foreign Affairs.
>
> Request and require in the Name of His Majesty all those whom it may concern to allow
>
> Master Herbert Thomson Kienzle to pass freely without let or hindrances and to afford him every assistance and protection which he may stand in need.
>
> Given at the Foreign Office, London the 7th day of April 1920.
>
> Signed personally 'Curzon of Kedleston'

The 'Description of Bearer' states that Bert was Age *14*; Place of Birth *Ovalau Fiji 19/5/05*; Height *5 ft 3 inches*; Forehead *Low*; Eyes *Hazel*; Nose *Straight*; Mouth *Full*; Chin *Round*; Colour of Hair *Brown*; Complexion *Tanned*; Face *Oval*; National Status *British Born Subject*.

Proudly clutching this precious document, Bert continued his journey across to the Hook of Holland, The Hague and then by train to Stuttgart, Germany – the home of the Kienzle relatives. He was met at the station by his grandparents Gustav and Emilie Kienzle and taken to their impressive home at

22 Kanonenweg, where he would reside for the next three years. This Neo-Renaissance style five-storey mansion, designed by well-known local architects Hummell and Foestner and built in 1907, was in the wealthy part of the flourishing industrial city of Stuttgart. Similar to Bert's Fijian home, his grandfather's house was perched on a hill reached by over 100 steps from near the main town square. It had views all across the city, which was built on the hills around the Neckar River, with vineyards interspersed among many stately homes. Gustav owned a ladies' fashion and tailoring business in the König Wilhelm II Building on the corner of Tübinger Strasse and Eberhard Strasse, with the name Gustav Kienzle emblazoned in large steel letters across the top of the building.

By the 1920s, Stuttgart's status was growing as an industrial hub of Germany. Such famous names as Daimler, Porsche and Bosch started their industries in the region. But what a volatile time it was to be arriving in Germany.

The armistice had been signed on 11 November 1918, but right up until that day, the German people had been led to believe by their government that they were winning the war. They thus had trouble accepting their defeat and ultimately blamed weak politicians rather than the military exhaustion and overpowering by a stronger enemy that were the real reasons. In the space of two months, they had gone from a fighting nation to a defeated one. The German Empire had collapsed and the Supreme Command had informed Kaiser Wilhelm II that the field armies no longer stood behind him and advised him to abdicate and go into exile. Unfortunately, there was no organised government structure in place to take over and run what was now a republic. An uncomfortable alliance was formed between the major socialists and the independents but the gap between their ideologies was too great for this ever to be a successful partnership.

Food shortages had pushed the populace to the brink of starvation and farmers had no labour to harvest what little crops there were. Lack of food made the people susceptible to disease and it is estimated that a combination of influenza and starvation killed over 750,000 German citizens in the years immediately after the Great War.

A more official republic was established in February 1919 when the National Assembly met in the ancient picturesque town of Weimar, north-east of Stuttgart, to draw up a constitution, which was adopted in July thus commencing the reign of the Weimar Republic, which survived, often precariously, until 1933. This was a republic with very few vigorous supporters but with powerful enemies both left and right and its struggles were to influence Germany for decades – the open clashes between the republic and the right-wing radicals, and the covert struggle between these right-wing radicals and the conservative, responsible members of the German general staff.

Bert may have been relatively unaffected by all this upheaval as he commenced his studies at the Trotzendorf technical college, but he was certainly not immune to the effects of the chronic shortages of food and funds his relatives in Stuttgart were experiencing. Despite Gustav's apparent relative wealth, Bert recalls those years as being 'hungry, lean times with deep depression, no money and escalating inflation of incredible proportions'. In 1922, a loaf of bread cost 163 marks – by September 1923, this figure reached 1,500,000 marks and by November, 200,000,000,000 marks. Understandably, the impact of this was huge, but the blame for it as far as the German populace was concerned was the Treaty of Versailles and the Weimar Government for ever agreeing to sign such a document.

This treaty, which had been drafted by Britain, France and the USA, placed humiliating conditions on Germany. They were required to yield territory – Alsace–Lorraine to France, the Polish Corridor and Silesia to Poland and other areas to Denmark and Belgium. In addition, they were forbidden to unite with Austria and barred from the League of Nations. Apart from the strict restrictions the treaty placed on the redevelopment of the German Army, the heavy penalty it incurred for reparation of damages during the war meant Germany would be in debt for many years to come. By 1922, the Weimar government had reached the position where it simply could not afford to pay another instalment on its debt, a claim that the Allies, particularly the French, refused to believe. As a result, in that year French and Belgian troops invaded the Ruhr, Germany's industrial hub, and took over the iron and steel factories, coal mines and railways. The fact that in doing this France and Belgium were breaking the rules of the League of Nations, of which they were both members, did not seem to bother them. They even imprisoned any Germans who resisted. The Weimar Government responded by calling on all workers of the Ruhr to strike and to passively resist the foreign soldiers. Violence ensued and around 132 people were killed and over 50,000 Germans chased out of their homes.

The impact of this operation was disastrous for Germany as a whole. The cost of recovery added further to the burdens of the war debt and the government's solution was to print more money, resulting in the hyperinflation mentioned earlier. People literally needed wheelbarrows full of money to go shopping. The rich land owners managed but the poor became poorer and the middle class suffered proportionally even more, making them ripe for attraction to orators like Hitler who had the ability to express their fears and give them someone to blame. As early as 1923, Hitler's Nazi Party had established quite a stronghold in Munich and in the spring and summer of this year, Hitler's storm troopers (SA) and other right-wing paramilitary groups held a series of mass demonstrations calling for a national uprising.

One rally led by Hitler resulted in him being tried for treason, and it seemed his career had reached an ignominious end. Unfortunately, not so. He used the resultant publicity as an opportunity to establish his name and spread his message outside Bavaria. Fortuitously for him, Hitler received only the minimum sentence for treason and took advantage of his time behind bars to learn from his mistakes and plan his future attack, the consequences of which we all know.

The Weimar Republic managed to survive this upheaval. By November, their new chancellor Gustav Stresemann had started to establish some sort of control and, with the help of the US, the economic problems began to be addressed. A new currency, the Rentenmark, backed by US gold, was introduced and a plan by American Charles Dawes to restore stability was announced.

The remaining three years of Bert's time in Germany were therefore relatively stable politically. His life so far had been one of many contrasts – from the colonial life in tropical Fiji, to the hardships of internment in the harsh environments of Bourke and Canberra, and now to the softer environs of this ancient German city with its medieval buildings and strong cultural heritage. Despite the shortages of the time, Bert still loved to visit the local *marktplatz*, a bustling market square since the 1830s, with its ornately decorated town hall surrounded by attractive old townhouses with pointed gables, bays and turrets, situated very close to his grandfather's shop. The austerity of the Depression years meant it was often virtually deserted, but close by was the market hall and this was the place to come to get what limited fresh produce was available from the once rich surrounding countryside. Bert heard tales from his grandfather of what this market hall had looked like in better times. Cleverly designed by a local architect to blend well with the older buildings around it from the exterior but with an interior that was highly modern and functional for its time, this huge hall was made of reinforced concrete girders with a curved glass roof, meaning that all the fresh produce was clearly displayed in the natural light from above. In fact, Stuttgart was famous at the time for its adventurous architects and architecture and Bert was fascinated with the many magnificent buildings, most of which would sadly be destroyed only two decades later. From the rough and tumble of life in Fiji and internment camps, Bert adjusted well to the culture that now surrounded him. He developed a love of fine wines, Riesling being his favourite, as this was the best known product of the local vineyards. He learnt to appreciate classical music, opera and ballet, all of which had a strong base in Stuttgart, and although the lavish productions of earlier years were not performed during Bert's time in the city, diehard performers still produced regular shows in both the Grosses Haus, an Opera House, and the Altes Schauspielhaus, the smaller, more intimate Old Playhouse.

Bert completed his time at technical college in 1922, achieving the equivalent of Australian HSC standard. While at college he had done some part-time work in a bank, and on finishing was fortunate to obtain employment in a jewellery factory, Berg & Co, in Stuttgart, owned by Alfred Schoeffel's father, Albert. He considered those two years, 1923 and 1924, working in the factory as serving what he called his 'apprenticeship in the business world', but they were also to be the start of a lifetime fascination with jewellery and precious metals.

At the age of only 66, his grandmother Emilie Kienzle passed away on 23 October 1923, leaving behind her husband and six offspring who were by now spread all over the world. Gustav Jnr was in Switzerland, Alfred in Australia, Hans in South America, leaving only Egon, Oscar and Johanna in Germany. During his time in Stuttgart, Bert got to know some other members of the extended Kienzle family, a well-respected dynasty that had been involved in the clock-making industry in the Black Forest area for several generations. Kienzle is a name renowned internationally for timing devices of all kinds, and until very recently, their clocks and parking meters could be found throughout the world, including Australia. It is believed by the family that the timers for the buzz bombs that landed on London in World War II were produced at the Kienzle factory outside Stuttgart.

Soon after arriving in Stuttgart and before starting at college, Bert had taken the opportunity to visit his uncle, Alfred's brother Gustav Jnr, who operated a retail business in Bern in Switzerland only a short journey away. Stuttgart is ideally located for visits to many countries, being only three or so hours from the borders of Austria, France and Switzerland. It is also close to the now famous ski fields of the Swabian Alps and Feldberg in the Black Forest, well known for their cross-country skiing facilities. Feldberg, the highest peak in the Black Forest at 1,500 metres, has been popular with skiers since the 1890s. It is at the centre of a region that claims to be the birthplace of skiing in mid-Europe. Feldberg had the first ski club; the first wooden skis were carpentered here and the first ski lift was built. Its relatively mild winters that still generated plenty of snow, and its abundance of suitable trails through woods and hills, made it a favoured destination for ski enthusiasts. During his years in Stuttgart, Bert was a regular visitor to the fields and became an excellent skier, particularly cross-country.

In late 1924, following in his father's footsteps, Bert accepted a position as a clerk in an import–export firm called Robinow & Co, in Hamburg, north-west Germany. This was a city that moved at a much faster pace than Stuttgart. In the 1920s, it had a population of more than one million and, being the main North Sea port for Germany, was called the country's 'Gateway to the World'. Hamburg is not actually situated on the sea but near the mouth of the River Elbe. The city had been created as a free port in the 1880s and even then was one of the biggest warehouse locations for coffee, cocoa and spices – tropical products from those far-off lands to which Bert was longing to return.

While employed by Robinow & Co, Bert learnt some Spanish and Portuguese in order to correspond with clients in South America, as well as attaining a valuable knowledge about freighting of agricultural produce all over the world. He also had the opportunity in October 1924 to visit London, where he spent a month, once again staying with the Butterworths. For some unfathomable reason, Bert, despite his unpleasant World War I experiences at the hands of the British, became a staunch royalist in his adult life. Perhaps it was the time he spent with the Butterworths and the indelible memories of his visit to Curzon of Kedleston; perhaps it was a new respect he developed for Britain and its allies for overcoming the formidable enemy it met in Germany, or maybe it was a stance he chose to adopt, along with his father, to ensure their loyalties were never doubted again. Who could say for sure – but in future years he proved to be a devoted and loyal supporter of Queen and Country and the Australian Flag with its Union Jack.

While in London, Bert attended the British Empire Exhibition, which was held at the famous Wembley Stadium, then called the Empire Stadium, and less than one year old at that time. It had been officially opened by King George V and Queen Mary on St George's Day, 23 April 1924, and was a post-war exhibition with the stated aim: 'To stimulate trade, strengthen bonds and bind the mother country to her sister states and daughters, to bring into closer contact the one with the other, to enable all who owe allegiance to the British Flag to meet on common ground and learn to know each other'.

Wembley Stadium was the centrepiece of the exhibition and when Bert visited in October, the Prince of Wales, later to become King Edward VIII, was in attendance, and Bert's strongest memory seems to have been of being in the presence of royalty. It was at the reopening of this event the following year, 1925, when the Duke of York produced his infamously embarrassing stammer-filled speech that put the world on tenterhooks when he later became King.

The exhibition was quite an amazing event for its time – a veritable Expo '24! There were fountains, lakes, gardens and many pavilions, each representing the architectural style of the countries exhibiting. Most were later dismantled but the magnificent stadium with its famous Twin Towers and 39 steps to the Royal Box remained as a British icon until being demolished for rebuilding in the year 2000. Bert's passport states that his trip to England was for business reasons, so no doubt Robinow & Co were allowing him to combine some business, including attending the 'trade expo', with the first holiday he had had since starting his working life.

Bert remained in his position in Hamburg until early 1925, when Alfred arrived in Stuttgart to collect Elsa and Laura and take them home to Australia. Germany's politics and the news Alfred was hearing out of his homeland concerned him enough to want to get his family out. Bert also did not need much encouragement to make the decision to leave. He wanted to return to warmer climes too and hankered to get back to the Pacific, and so he resigned his position and joined his father and sisters on the trip to England.

4

CALL OF THE
SOUTH PACIFIC

The return journey from Germany to Australia meant first a train and ferry trip to London, then a P&O liner that took the family via the Suez Canal, Aden, Colombo, Fremantle and Melbourne before they disembarked in Sydney in late 1925.

During Bert's absence in Germany, his father had progressed from working for an import–export company to setting up his own business called Australia Pacific Trading Co based in Kembla Buildings, Sydney. On his journey to collect Bert and his sisters, he had incorporated developing agencies in the UK and the Continent. With his son's experience in the same industry in Hamburg, his father was willing to take him on as a salesman and Bert was happy to have a job and be back around the South Pacific.

By the time of their return to Australia, Bert was 20 years old, Laura 17 and Elsa 15, and they all moved into the house at Bexley where Hally and young Wallace, now aged 11, were already established. Once again, Hally's orderly life was disrupted by the return of the three stepchildren, but her health was much improved and of course the children were older and very mature for their ages after their overseas experiences.

All contact with the Fijian side of the family appears to have ceased during these years. Captain Wilson maintained his hatred of Alfred and all things German, and refused any relationship. In February 1916, in order to follow the path his favourite son George had taken, he travelled to England then on to visit his grave in Ypres. From the time he returned home at the end of 1916, George's medals hung by the captain's desk until the day he died. Despite remaining active running his plantations and doing relief work as a ship's captain, W. W. W. developed diabetes and other health problems. In January 1924, he was rushed to Auckland, New Zealand for an urgent operation; he did not wake from the anaesthetic and died on 24 January 1924. He is buried in Hillsborough Cemetery.

Because of her dislike of Suva and plantation living, Lizzy had moved back to 'Qima', the 'house on the hill' in Levuka where she lived mostly alone, only sometimes joined by the captain or visited by Tom and his wife and Laura with her husband and young family, who would journey across to the island for special occasions like Christmas. Tom continued serving in the Royal Australian Navy throughout the war, and by 1917 had become chief engineer of the SS *Aramac* and was living in Sydney. Laura also had left Fiji by the end of 1924 and was living in Sydney with her husband, although they soon returned to Suva. In his will, W. W. W. had left most of his assets to Tom and Laura, but he did direct them as executors to 'Pay my dear wife Lizzie Wilson the sum of £10 every month for her own use during her lifetime. I give to my wife absolutely all my household furniture plate linen glass and other goods and chattels and effects (except my library) in upon or about my dwelling house in Levuka aforesaid. I give to my said wife the free use of my said dwelling house during her lifetime.'

As time went on, Lizzy's loneliness, self-imposed though it was, resulted in depression and what at the time was labelled 'slightly odd' behaviour. She had outlived four of her six children; her husband, for whom she had uprooted herself from family, friends and country, was dead; and her only two surviving children were mostly many miles away. She had lost contact with her *aiga*, the extended family, identification with whom is vital to the Samoan concept of 'self'. Family and the land they live on are deeply embedded in the Samoan way – and are basic to the way Samoans view themselves in relation to the rest of the world. Lizzy's state of mind should hardly have been surprising.

By the early 1930s, the family had insisted that she could not live alone anymore so they brought her across to Suva to stay with some distant Samoan relatives. This did not work out, so she moved in with Laura and her family. She had not been there long when one morning very early, Laura was woken by the yells of the garden boy. Hurrying after him into the backyard, she was horrified to see Lizzy hanging from the mango tree. She was attempting to take her own life. Laura, the gardener and Laura's young son Billy managed to get her down before it was too late, but while examining her, the doctor found she was in the advanced stages of cancer and must have been in agony for some time. For the next two years Lizzy endured painkilling injections several times a day. When she finally passed away in 1933, it was a blessed relief for her and all who knew her. Her family remembers her as a loving person, full of fun and jokes but with an inner sadness fuelled by loneliness and loss.

§

Bert took the first opportunity not long after his return to Australia to join the Kosciusko Alpine Club and ski whenever possible from their base at Hotel Kosciusko. It is noted in their diamond jubilee publication that new members in 1926 included Herbert Kienzle, 'a young Australian back from skiing in Germany', and that he had brought back from Europe with him the first stick-on skins (strips of a special fabric attached to the bottom of skis to improve traction) ever seen at Kosciusko. The club was by this time developing quite a reputation for its social activities, so no doubt this tall, handsome, rather exotic young man would have been a centre of attention among the fashionably dressed young ladies at the traditional annual club dinner.

As with most things in his life, Bert took his skiing seriously. One of the biggest challenges available to Australian skiers at the time was the return trip from the Hotel Kosciusko to the Summit, and Bert, like quite a few before him, was inspired to reach the top of Australia at 7,312 feet above sea level over the cross-country route of 35 miles. Not satisfied with just making the overland trip, he decided to attempt to break the record, the contest for which had first occurred in 1914. In late July 1927, he succeeded in doing just that – he broke the previous record of 9 hours 46 minutes, which had been held by Dr Ashleigh Davy since 1925, despite numerous attempts to break it in the interim. His feat at the time was called 'sensational' because he was the first person to complete the trip in under nine hours. The event was written up by both the *Sydney Morning Herald* and the *Sydney Mail*, the latter stating:

Mr H T Kienzle . . . decided to make a trip to the summit of Kosciusko on Wednesday last. When halfway, he got into a blizzard and had to return. He then arranged with Messrs [Fred] Pentecost and [Arthur] Stone to leave the Hotel for Bett's Camp at 12 o'clock on Thursday night in order to prepare things and have breakfast ready for him on his arrival at the camp on Friday morning. Mr Kienzle left the Hotel at 6:52 a.m. on Friday and after passing Dainer's Gap in 23 minutes, arrived at Betts' Camp in the record time of 2 hours 3 minutes. After a rest of 35 minutes at Bett's Camp, he continued on his way to the Summit, and arrived at Charlotte's Pass which is half way from Bett's Camp to the Summit, at 10 a.m. Although the sky was heavily clouded he decided to keep going. On arrival at Etheridge Range the fog was so thick he could not see the top of the Summit. The snow on the Rawson Pass side was very deep and soft. He climbed the Pass and reached the Summit at 11:30 a.m. After a short stay, he set out on his return tip. With favourable snow conditions and a moderate wind, he reached Bett's Camp half an hour ahead of time. After resting 25 minutes, he continued on his way and reached the Hotel at 3:38 p.m. having made the trip in a record time of 8 hours 58 minutes. The weather conditions change very quickly on the Kosciusko plateau and Mr Kienzle was fortunate in having much better weather on the return trip than on the forward journey.

Although Bert's record did not stand for long, he was awarded a Summit Badge for his efforts. Interestingly, in historical records the badge shows 'Summit 7,312 ft' but the badge that is among Bert's possessions shows 7,305 feet and is engraved on the back with the date July 1962. One can only assume they were reissued when the correct altitude of Australia's highest mountain was accurately established.

A discrepancy of 7 feet not withstanding, it was not an easy journey he undertook. *Diamond Jubilee of the Kosciusko Alpine Club* describes the pattern of the venture as follows:

Breakfast in the kitchen of the Hotel at 5 a.m. and a start at 6 a.m, in the frosty, star-spangled darkness of early morning: the fascination of the dawn light on the run to Pipers Gap: the long climb to the Perisher Gap: tea and canned fruit at Betts' Camp: the thrill of the view from Charlotte Pass (all uninhabited) and the sight of the objective of the journey on the skyline: the final difficulties of the seventeenth mile to the Cairn: then the run back, as fast as possible to Betts' Camp, and the interminable and exhausting climb to Dainers Gap: and, finally, down the road to the Hotel and the triumph of success.

Many a party who attempted this journey was forced back between Betts Camp and the Snowy River and it was noted in Kosciusko Alpine Club records that Bert took more than a few 'bad tosses' on this leg of the trip.

Bert's feat was recorded in the *Sydney Morning Herald* on 25 July 1927, and then on 9 August 1927 a small article titled 'Alpine Record' stated:

Mr HT Kienzle of Bexley, who, a few weeks ago broke the record for the climb from the Hotel at Kosciusko to the summit of the mountain but whose time was subsequently beaten, will shortly make an attempt on a new record. Mr Kienzle's time was 8 hours 58 minutes but this was reduced to 8 hrs 56 minutes by a party of two who essayed the journey a few days later. As Mr Kienzle did the climb unaccompanied, his was a particularly meritorious performance. If conditions are favourable, it is expected he will do even better at the second attempt.

The same issue of the *Sydney Morning Herald* reported the heaviest falls of snow for years at Kosciusko that week and bad weather prevented Bert from making his second attempt that month. By August 1927, his life had taken yet another major change in direction that took him well away from the snowfields and his record was broken twice that season. By 1938 the record had been lowered to 6 hours 1½ minutes, and this time remained until 1964 when Ross Martin completed the trek – obviously with the advantage of much more modern equipment – in 4 hours 55 minutes.

Bert remained a member and loyal supporter of the Kosciusko Alpine Club for many years, taking up 20 £10 debentures in the club's fundraising for their first lodge, built in 1952, and donating his investment back to the club when the debentures were repaid in 1963. Many years later, in March 1969, he would be a special guest at their jubilee dinner at the Wentworth Hotel.

§

As the Kienzles carried on their lives in Bexley, not far away at Huntley's Point, Balmain, the life of a family that was to become inextricably intertwined with theirs was unfolding.

George Hubert Stanfield Holliday, eldest son of the Rev. Henry T. Holliday, had married Evelyn May Jones in 1906 in St Stephen's Church of England, Penrith, where the reverend was rector from 1902–1907. Their eldest daughter, Meryl Elma, was born on 7 January 1907 at Snails Bay, followed by Ailsa Mary on 4 August 1909, Audrey on 17 April 1911, then Hubert Stanfield on 28 October 1915.

Meryl grew into a vivacious but diminutive young girl, always the life of the party and with a delightful singing voice. She attended the local public school, where she did not really excel academically, unlike her sister Ailsa, who earned a position at Fort Street Girls' High School, which even at that time was acknowledged as an institution of academic excellence. By all reports, Ailsa was a model student in every way except her application to her studies. Every day she would carefully iron her uniforms and sharpen her pencils. Her desk was always immaculately tidy and efficiently organised and her notebooks were filled with copybook writing – but she never actually did much work. So she did not really take advantage of the scholarship she had won to this prestigious school. Ailsa opted to leave and study to be a nurse at Sydney Hospital, and here her attention to neatness and cleanliness held her in good stead and her natural intelligence carried her through the theoretical work so that she became an excellent nurse.

Meryl's skills were as an entertainer and singer and because of this she won a place at the Albert Street Conservatorium in Melbourne, soon to be renamed the Melba Conservatorium, a private music school in East Melbourne that she attended from 1927 to 1929. The director of the conservatorium at the time was Fritz Bennick Hart FRCM, an English-born conductor and composer who was a graduate of the Royal College of Music, London. The world famous Australian opera diva Dame Nellie Melba had joined forces with Hart to rescue the conservatorium in 1916 when it looked like collapsing. They became firm friends and business partners. Melba made a habit of visiting the conservatorium at least once a week, always arriving in style in her chauffeur-driven car promptly at 9 a.m. She would either randomly select one of her 'singing girls' to accompany on the piano, or pace the back of the room, hands in coat pockets, head down, concentrating on their every note. Her praise was sparing but her criticism was never cruel and her reputation as a bully did not extend to the classroom. Students certainly never forgot her lessons.

In a letter to the conservatorium magazine in 1945, Meryl recalled those carefree days when a visit by Dame Nellie was the highlight of the week and her memorable lectures and sheer exuberance filled them all with glee. She particularly remembered the day the Dame planted a kiss on Fritz's forehead in front of a most amused class of young would-be prima donnas.

Another unforgettable interlude was when Dame Nellie returned from her 1927 'Farewell Tour', one of several such tours, and strode into the first floor gallery of the conservatorium where Meryl and the other singing girls were gathered. It was 19 May and she announced, 'Well, I am sixty-six today.' Of course, the gathering responded with the requisite 'Congratulations!' and 'You don't look it', to which she replied 'I certainly don't feel it!' and promptly swept from the room – ever the one for making dramatic entries and departures.

Meryl was apparently one of Dame Nellie's favourites and would often be invited for musical weekends to her home 'Coombe Cottage' at Coldstream near Lilydale about 42 kilometres from Melbourne. The house incorporated a prominent clock-tower with the clear inscription 'East West, Hame's Best' and here, in her haven away from the city, Melba kept mementos of her many triumphs and accumulated a valuable collection of the works of Australia's best painters. The butler and footman served tea on the lawn or by the billiard room fireplace and Melba would take the opportunity to give the girls lessons in deportment and the social graces. Meryl would later often cite the many tips Melba gave on what she considered acceptable manners during those visits. Sometimes, she would invite the whole school out for a 'chop picnic' where she would don a chef's cap and brandish a long barbecue fork, while singing light classical favourites in her powerful voice.

Entrance to the conservatorium was much sought after and involved a strict selection process. Dame Nellie expected students to work hard and attend classes in a rather plain white tunic uniform with an 'M' embroidered on the bodice. Melba openly stated, 'I am a damned snob', although it was more of a cultural than social snobbery, as she often spoke in a derisory manner of Australians and their lack of appreciation of the finer things of life. She is recorded as saying to fellow artists at a time when she was disgusted with the lack of support for top European performers touring 'down under', 'Sing them muck', implying they wouldn't know the difference anyway! Thereafter, Meryl loved to quote Melba's 'Sing them muck' whenever the occasion suited.

Meryl passed the first year of her diploma in 1927, and in 1928 made her first public appearance in the students' concert in the assembly hall at the conservatorium on Tuesday 30 October. She performed an aria by Bizet titled 'O Dieu Brahma!'. At a similar concert in July the following year, she performed another Aria, this time 'L'amero' by Mozart.

The highlight of her time with Dame Nellie, however, was when she was selected to play Despina in the first performance in Australia of Mozart's comic opera *Così Fan Tutte*. The opera was produced by the conservatorium director Fritz Hart at the Playhouse. The production ran from 17 to 24 November 1928 and the troupe was accompanied by the Melbourne Symphony Orchestra. Meryl interchanged in the part with her close friend Margaret Casey and another good mate with a starring role in the production was Dawn Harding.

Unfortunately, by 1930 the Depression had set in and Meryl's father said he could no longer afford to keep her at the conservatorium so she reluctantly left and joined her sister Ailsa at the Sydney General Hospital to train as a nurse. Meryl missed the excitement and culture of the conservatorium life and always regretted not being able to further her career as an opera singer and performer. In later life, just listening to a Joan Sutherland or Pavarotti recording would bring tears to her eyes.

§

Meryl's younger sister Audrey was also a very artistic soul but her life panned out rather tragically. She was a lively, highly strung redhead who became an actress and artist after leaving school. She fell in love with and became engaged to a doctor whom she met in drama classes. His family did not approve of the relationship and ultimately convinced him to cancel the wedding and marry someone else. Audrey was the love of his life and not long after this arranged marriage he committed suicide. Audrey's heart was broken too, and she became a recluse, locking herself in her room, not interested in socialising and ultimately driving herself into an early grave.

Young Stanfield Holliday, called Stan, was also very musical, and was a chorister at St Andrew's Cathedral as well as achieving the position as their assistant organist at the tender age of 14. His education as well was cut short by the Depression and so he did the thing he believed he did best, and that was play the organ for a living. He started playing for various churches around Sydney but achieved most recognition when he played for Capitol followed by Hoyts Theatres, where he was on staff for over 20 years. In these cinemas, he played on the mighty Wurlitzer organs and established a reputation for technical skill combined with a rare sensitivity. Apparently one of the tactics of such a job was to select the appropriate music for the particular time in the program – most important was a fast tempo and strong theme to keep patrons moving out of the theatre at the end of the movie. Stan continued in this position until organ music in cinemas was dispensed with in 1961 whence his expertise on this instrument led to radio recitals in Sydney and for 3AR in Melbourne and even to the cutting of several successful records.

Their father George Holliday, or Pop Holliday as he came to be called, had had a strict religious upbringing, with both his father and his Uncle Billy being Anglican ministers, and he is remembered by some of the family as a tough and rather cold-hearted patriarch. He apparently did not really support his children in their various artistic pursuits, believing they were frivolous occupations. Despite their obvious successes in their performing arts endeavours, he did not congratulate or encourage them, something for which they never really forgave him over the ensuing years.

§

While in the camp at Molonglo, Bert had met several German families who had been planters on the island of New Guinea. This country, with its similar history to Fiji, its Melanesian people and its reputation as a wild, untamed land, had always fascinated him.

The newspaper reports of his Kosciusko feat had attracted the attention of the directors of the large pastoral company of Clarke & Whiting. A well-known company established by Sir Rupert Clarke Snr, in partnership with R. S. Whiting, at the time it owned Isis Downs on the Barcoo River in Queensland. This large sheep station covered an area of 2,430 square kilometres, carried 230,000 sheep and employed around 150 staff. Clarke, grandson of one of the most successful graziers of the Western District of Victoria and acknowledged as one of the richest men in Australia, was known for his flamboyance and willingness to take risks. In February 1907, the company had ventured into Papua New Guinea, registering a company in Victoria called Papua Rubber Plantations Pty Ltd (PRP). They leased 5,000 acres in Clarke's name on the western and northern sides of Galley Reach, which is along the coast north-west of Port Moresby, and a further 3,800 acres on the Veimaru River in the same vicinity. PRP developed these two properties for rubber and copra respectively. The Galley Reach property, called Kanosia Plantation, was experiencing some difficulties and the directors were looking for an energetic, adventurous young man with obvious leadership qualities to take up an assistant's position on the estate. Herbert T. Kienzle fitted the bill and from his perspective, it was just what he wanted – a challenge in a Pacific Island country on a plantation, his strong and fond memories of Fiji still clear in his mind.

He accepted the position enthusiastically, and in late August, boarded the SS *Morinda*, a Burns Philp vessel sailing from Sydney to Port Moresby. His excitement was palpable as he first sighted the island of New Guinea – at last, he was back in the tropics! As they entered Moresby Harbour, he was surprised by the bare, dry, rolling hills in the foreground, contrasting with the obviously thickly jungled, menacing looking mountains behind. He gazed at these dark grey – almost purple – ranges, their sinister peaks reaching to the sky through shrouds of floating mist. For someone like Bert, they beckoned with the promise of mystery and adventure, danger and hope.

Bert was fascinated by the village of Hanuabada, meaning 'great village' in the local language Motu, which sat in the Fairfax Harbour – a scrambled collection of thatched roofed huts, half-in, half-out of the water. Behind Hanuabada, memories of Levuka were rekindled by the mish-mash of ugly corrugated iron shacks shimmering in the midday heat, some single, some two-storey, all scattered on the hillsides with no apparent sense of order. This, then, was Port Moresby, the administrative centre for Papua – a small, poor place with only about 500 European residents, which reflected the lack of investment in the Territory by the Australian Government at the time.

Pulling up to a rickety timber wharf, the *Morinda* was superficially inspected by slovenly quarantine officers. Once this formality was completed, Bert was met by Mr G. A. Loudon, general manager of the British New Guinea Development Co Ltd as well as of Clarke & Whiting's Papuan interests. Loudon, known as 'Gal' and called 'the uncrowned king of Papua' by expatriates, was quite a local identity and had his finger in several pies. Owner of Eilogo Plantation at Sogeri outside Port Moresby, he imported the first motor car into the Territory and also the first soda-fountain. He had recently set up his own company, G. A. Loudon & Co, which was involved in retail, mainly trade stores that were run by his wife, Winifred, an ex school mistress known to most as 'Peg'.

Loudon instructed Bert to stock up with essential supplies of tinned foods in Port Moresby, no doubt from one of Peg's trade stores. His first visit to one of these retail establishments was truly an experience. Inside was shelf upon shelf of tinned versions of everything from meat to fruit, vegetables to milk, butter to matches – every conceivable necessity and even luxury for the nourishment of a plantation gentleman. There was no time to visit any of the infamous drinking establishments that had varying reputations in the capital at the time. Ribaldry and drunken stoushes were so common at the 'bottom' pub that it was called the 'slaughter house' or 'dead house'. The 'top' pub was patronised by a more gentlemanly type and a certain amount of decorum prevailed. Then there was the Papua Club – the Territory's equivalent of the Ovalau Club, the planter's haunt in Levuka that Bert's father and grandfather had frequented.

Once stocked up with necessities, Bert boarded a small launch that plied twice weekly between the capital and Kanosia. He was met at the plantation by the general manager Mr J. B. McKenna, who assigned him a very basic, rough-hewn timber house and a servant. His job was to take charge of a line of rubber tappers and a section of the plantation covering an area of around 100 acres. He was one of seven plantation assistants when he arrived, most of whom were Australians. Nearly all of the expatriate residents in Papua at the time were Australian or from the UK, as opposed to New Guinea, which had many German residents. The reason for this takes us back to a similar situation to the one in Fiji, a time when the usual suspects of European nations – England, Holland, Germany and Britain – vied for territory in the Pacific.

The island that we now call New Guinea, made up of Papua New Guinea and West Irian and the second-largest island in the world, was first sighted by the Portuguese in the 16th century. It was during a visit in the same century that explorer Jorge de Meneses gave it the name 'Ilhas dos Papuas' (Island of the Fuzzy Hairs), but it was not until 1848 that the Netherlands Indies Government laid claim to West New Guinea, the area now called West Papua or Irian Jaya. In 1884, the Germans raised the flag in the north-east part of the island, naming it Kaiser Wilhelmsland. The British had been under pressure from the London Missionary Society since 1876 to extend the jurisdiction of the Fiji-based commissioner of the West Pacific to New Guinea. It wasn't until Germany made its move that the British, this time also under pressure from the still unfederated Australian colonies, claimed the south-eastern quarter of New Guinea, until then called Papua, as a British protectorate. Commodore James Erskine formally took possession of the protectorate of British New Guinea on 6 November 1884.

Most of the European incursions in British New Guinea up to the 1880s had been restricted to gold seekers and the ever eager messengers of the London Missionary Society. Several fortune hunters had sailed their ships up the various rivers from the coast looking for signs of potential instant wealth. One such visitor in 1873 was Captain John M. Moresby, on the HMS *Basilisk*, sent by the British Admiralty to survey New Guinea waters. He named the outer reaches of a major waterway he navigated on the south side of the island 'Port Moresby' and the inner reaches 'Fairfax Harbour', both after his father Admiral Sir Fairfax Moresby. A year later, the Rev. William G. Lawes and his wife, missionaries from Australia, became the first permanent white settlers to arrive in the area, setting up residence in what soon became the town of Port Moresby.

By the early 1880s, cedar and rosewood were being indiscriminately and often wastefully harvested and exported from the south coast of New Guinea along with ebony, sandalwood and massoia. Resourceful merchants had encouraged local natives to extract rubber from the latex-producing jungle trees and harvest copra from the abundant coconut trees and sell them to the various trading ships that plied the coastline. Whaling, bêche-de-mer and pearl shell brought an assortment of other traders to the island.

In 1888, Britain extended its powers further, proclaiming British New Guinea an annexed possession and appointing an administrator to this new British sovereignty. This Scottish gentleman, Dr William MacGregor, coincidentally had served as chief medical officer, then colonial secretary and ultimately administrator of Fiji, and would have been in that position when Bert's grandfather Captain Wilson was establishing himself in Levuka. His experience under Sir Arthur Gordon in Fiji was to stand him in good stead in his new position and the influence of the Fijian police he brought in to train the locals would become entrenched in the local force. MacGregor was an imposing physical specimen, short but solid, bald and bearded, with high moral fortitude and a genuine respect for the natives of uncivilised regions. His desire to protect them from the potentially destructive effects of white settlement was to set the tone for much of what happened in Papua in the ensuing years and to contribute greatly to the reputation Australia ultimately earned as a benevolent colonial power. At the proclamation of Papua as a British protectorate, what some called 'an oddity of the Empire', MacGregor stated: 'The Queen's Sovereignty here will be a guarantee that every effort will be made to educate the native race, to impart to them the great sublime truths of the Christian religion, to teach them to value and respect law and order and to appreciate justice.'

Certainly, history has shown that European settlement of Papua was far less violent and destructive than in many African nations, for example. In 1906, the royal commissioners proclaimed: 'Australia has the opportunity to show the world that it is possible to introduce civilisation to a backward race without destroying it.'

MacGregor set out climbing the highest mountains, navigating the longest rivers and exploring every bay and estuary of his adopted country. Although he had no objection to white settlers taking up land in this undeveloped sovereignty, he was determined to put controls in place so that any such progress would be of benefit to the native population. To that end, soon after his arrival he enacted the Land Regulation Ordinance of 1888, which he called the 'palladium of Papua' because of the unprecedented protection it gave 'a diverse, primitive and fragmented population without a common body of law or the attributes of a state'. This first ordinance controlled the acquisition of land from the natives and was followed in 1890 by the Crown Land Ordinance that provided a comprehensive framework to allow fair and equitable white settlement and development of Papua

To MacGregor's frustration, his promptness in setting up these frameworks did not result in any influx of enthusiastic developers. Most attempts at establishing a plantation industry had been foiled by the lack of knowledge of the planters and the poor quality of administrative support they received. Unfortunately, in these early years Papua was somewhat of a dumping ground for those who could not find gainful employment elsewhere. It was not until 1905 with the passing of the Papua Act that things really started to happen. This Act put control of British New Guinea firmly in the hands of a now federated Australia and changed its name officially to Papua, which is correctly pronounced 'pah-poo-ah'. This fact, combined with an international boom in tropical agriculture, meant that by 1908 several other investors besides Clarke & Whiting had plunged into plantation enterprises in Papua and in the same year, another gentleman who was to play a long and significant part in the development of this territory had been appointed as administrator.

John Hubert Plunkett Murray, later to become Sir Hubert Murray, was promoted from chief judicial officer in Papua to administrator then lieutenant governor, a position he held for 32 years. Murray was an Oxford graduate, a previous lieutenant colonel of the NSW Mounted Infantry and a proud Australian nationalist with definite ideas about the future development of Papua. He was called a benevolent autocrat by some but still managed to achieve the affection and respect of black and white men alike. Murray was determined to be a positive influence on this civilisation and strongly believed that Australia could develop this country of what he, in the vernacular of his time, referred to as 'ignorant savages', without injury; indeed, to its 'lasting benefit and permanent advancement'. It was later said of his tenure that he probably achieved the best that could be done in a period of stagnant capitalism, Australian indifference and racial prejudice. He had arrived in a large territory, much of which had still not been explored, inhabited by approximately one quarter of a million Melanesians and only a few hundred Europeans. The native Papuans were a hugely diverse population, separated by geography, language and tribal hostilities. Operating a plantation, especially something as intensive as rubber, was indeed a challenge when suitable labour in any area was unreliable and bringing workers in from other areas was fraught with problems.

Despite all this, by 1910, a man very significant in the development of rubber throughout the world was encouraging investors to consider it as a plantation crop worth promoting in Papua. Henry Alexander Wickham, by then residing in the Territory, was involved in securing the original rubber seeds from Amazonia that were taken to the Botanical Gardens in London and grafted to develop more resistant varieties. These varieties of para rubber trees (*Hevea brasiliensis*) were to become the basis of the entire rubber industry throughout South-East Asia. Until their propagation, rubber had mainly only been used by the indigenous people of the Americas, particularly Brazil, for its elastic properties. With Goodyear developing vulcanisation in 1840 then Thomson inventing the pneumatic tyre in 1845, demand for increased worldwide production was high. By 1907, when Henry Ford started the first production assembly line for motor cars, a boom in demand for rubber resulted in Papua joining in the rush to plant acreage, but the expansion was cut short by the outbreak of World War I in 1914. One other impact of this war on the island of New Guinea was the occupation of German New Guinea/Kaiser Wilhelmsland by Australian troops, with the result that in 1920, the League of Nations conferred that region to Australia to administer as a mandated territory.

By the 1920s, when Bert arrived in the country, the acreage of cultivated land in the Territory of Papua was still limited, and Kanosia was one of the few properties whose planting exceeded more than 1,000 acres. Murray had never wanted Papua to become a pure plantation economy like Malaya and many South Pacific Island countries, but even he was disappointed about this situation. The problem was that Papua was a small player in an industry dominated by South-East Asia, labour was unreliable and not nearly as conscientious and efficient as its competitors to the north, and it seemed always to be the last to benefit from price rises and the first to suffer when they fell. The fortunes of rubber planters in Papua therefore also rose and fell constantly and often quite speedily – 1921–22 saw a post-war slump, 1925 and 1926 were two good years, but by 1927 things were on the downward slide again.

§

No expense had been spared in the initial establishment of Kanosia, with only the best rubber plant stock being imported from Malaya and planting supervised by an expert Ceylonese planter. Bert quickly established that the greatest challenge to operating an efficient plantation in Papua was in management's relationship with the indigenous workers. Communication was the first step, and he deliberately set out to learn the local language. He did this in three months. Police Motu, as it was called, had by this time had become the lingua franca of Papua. It originated in Hanuabada where the Motu tribe was based. The people around Port Moresby were mainly from two tribes, the Motu and the Koita. The Motu were a nomadic people who travelled and traded all along the south coast of the island overland or by sea in their catamaran sail boats called *lakatoi*. Their language, or close adaptations of it, was therefore spoken by the vast majority of Papuans, so it became the obvious basis for the means of communication for the police and European settlers as they moved throughout the region.

By overcoming the language barrier, Bert soon developed a good understanding of the local people, their customs and way of life. One of his workers, Robo Robo, years later talked of him 'striding around the plantation with his revolver in one hand and cane in the other' – an image most likely exaggerated by the passage of time but demonstrative of the awe in which he was held. Any initial fear of this gentle giant soon turned to respect and admiration. Back in the first decade of the century, Clarke & Whiting had been one of the first operators to submit a scheme to the government to allow whole native families to settle on their estates. There was considerable expense involved in this plan in setting up accommodation and other facilities but the long-term benefits outweighed the difficulties. This move had made it easier to keep labour once they had been recruited but shortage of manpower was still always a problem and Bert realised the importance of looking after the families already settled on the estate.

Conscientious as he was, Bert also very quickly learnt about all aspects of production and processing of natural rubber, from plant husbandry, maintenance and production of the raw latex, through collection and processing into a transportable form, and ultimately its export to Australia, mainly for the tyre-making industry. To this day, this whole rubber production process is very labour intensive, so the greatest challenge to any supervisor is keeping wage costs down.

As mentioned, Bert was in charge of a line of rubber tappers, which at that time would have been between 40 and 50 men. Each tapper was allocated a 'task' of about 300 trees that had to be tapped each day, six days a week. Tapping a rubber tree involves using a tapping gouge to slice a fine sliver of bark, half the circumference of the tree, angled 22 degrees down from horizontal. Care must be taken not to damage the cambium layer, which lies just below the tappable bark. Removal of this paper-thin piece of bark results in droplets of liquid white latex oozing from the 'wound' and eventually running down the gutter created by the cut, into a cup that the tapper attaches to the tree at the end of the cut. Having performed this procedure on all the trees in his task, the tapper then returns to where he started and collects the cups of latex, pouring them into buckets that he normally carries on a pole across his shoulders. These he takes to a central staging point where he pours them into 50-litre milk cans, which are collected by tractor and taken to the rubber factory. At the factory, the latex is poured into large vats and mixed in a solution of formic acid; then a series of slats are placed into the vat so that the latex sets in sheets. These thick, white, jelly-like sheets are then removed and put through a battery of rollers that squeeze the liquid out and flatten them into strips about 120 cm x 60 cm. The final roller ribs them and indents the company brand on them. They are then hung and dried in smokehouses. This whole process takes seven to eight days and the resultant sheets of rubber, called RSS (rib smoked sheet rubber), are a coffee brown colour and are compressed into self-wrapped 50-kilogram bales for transport.

One of the problems that rubber planters were always trying to address was the fact that, compared to their competitor producers in South-East Asia, in Papua more supervisors per tapper were needed to maximise production. As mentioned, Papuans had actually been trading rubber that they tapped from wild rubber trees that grew in the jungle for some years. This trade had not lasted long for two main reasons. Their abuse of the trees in their method of tapping resulted in the trees' death or at least in a fast drop in production. Secondly, the traders who bought the raw latex, which was sold to them in 'balls' that were purchased on the basis of weight, got sick of receiving complaints from the processors that the balls of rubber were more often than not just a thin layer of latex surrounding rocks or sticks – anything to bump up the weight.

These bad habits soon cropped up in the plantations as well, and rough treatment of the trees, failure to tap every tree each day, failure to collect every cup each time and to correctly attach cups to trees all affected production. Papuans needed to be monitored on this continually. In particular, they did not understand the need for conscientious plant husbandry to improve output and extend the productive life of the tree. They were used to growing consumable vegetables where garden plots are cleared, used for a few years, then moved to a new area. A plantation assistant's job was thus not easy; keeping the workers onside while trying to control costs and improve outputs was a continual challenge.

It was therefore very difficult for Bert when, with the onset of the Depression in 1929–30, one by one the other assistants at Kanosia had to be retrenched until he, as chief assistant, was the only one kept employed. In addition to overseeing the whole 1,683 acres of rubber, he was asked to take a cut in pay to one-third of what he had previously earned. Bert persevered in this position for nearly two years and learnt to run a lean and efficient operation.

In 1932, Ernest Trevor Ward and his wife Vera purchased Veimauri Plantation from Clarke & Whiting. Vera was a planter in her own right and also managed nearby Veiya Plantation. Soon after taking over the business, they offered Bert a job, on significantly better terms than his current position, managing Veimauri. Although this plantation only had about 450 acres of rubber, it had quite large plantings of coconuts and as Bert had fond memories of his experiences on his father's copra plantations in Fiji, he was keen to extend his knowledge of this crop.

Ernest and Vera Ward were fast becoming Territory identities, Vera for her business acumen and abilities as a planter, Ernest more for his forays into the Papua Club in Port Moresby and in particular, for his elegance and snazzy dress sense. He and 'Gal' Loudon apparently were the trendsetters at the club and in the Moresby social set. The club had been set up in 1912 by Loudon and some other 'silvertails' as a gathering place for selected members, mainly planters and businessmen, so that they could avoid the riffraff at less inviting watering holes in the capital. The club offered supper, alcohol, a game of billiards plus opportunities for singing, dancing and getting to know fellow expatriates. Even the local missionaries were welcomed and felt safe there. As with all such clubs, members had to adhere to a strict code of behaviour and dress and it was apparently Ward and Loudon, by all reports a bit of a ladies' man, who set the standards. Fellow member Percy Robinson wrote of 'Gal' and Ernest:

In dull or cool weather and in the evening they wear trousers of either gabardine or mohair of a khaki colour, socks to match and brown shoes, a shirt of a colour to go with the rest & tie likewise. Shirts are always plain . . . In hot weather, duck pants, white shirt and heavy twill with two breast pockets – gauntlet cuffs are an anathema. Loudon had his made with wide, short sleeves but this is his specialty and no one likes to copy him though they approve of the idea. Black tie as narrow as possible . . . anything in the nature of 'handkerchief' ties would cause the wearer to be tarred and feathered.

It would seem that Vera Ward, like her friend Peg Loudon, kept the home fires burning and the rubber trees earning while Ernest enjoyed life as the quintessential colonialist, spending much of his time in the elaborate home he had built in a prime position in Moresby. Perhaps this is why Vera needed the services of a well-trained and reliable manager like Bert to substitute for her often absent husband. Certainly, Bert recalls that he had to work very hard to keep the operation going in the Depression years and that he only succeeded by cutting costs to the bone.

Copra or coconut production was not quite as complex and labour intensive as rubber but it presented a whole different set of challenges. The most difficult aspect of the copra production process, after collecting of the coconuts, which fall to the ground when they are ripe, is the removing of the husks, which has to be done manually. The soft white flesh has to be scooped out of the brown nut and dried before it goes off. Weather obviously played a big part in this operation and ensuring the workers wasted no time in transferring the copra to the drying racks was a supervisor's greatest concern.

Bert continued in his position at Veimauri until the end of 1933, when the opportunity arose to start a whole new career that appealed to his pioneering spirit. He was offered a position as an assistant on a recently reopened goldfield in the Yodda Valley, near the government outpost at Kokoda just over The Gap through the Owen Stanley Ranges. A new and adventurous life was about to open up to Bert as a prospector and miner.

5

THE YODDA VALLEY

Since man first valued wealth and precious jewels, he has dreamed that every new frontier will be his 'El Dorado', and the island of New Guinea was no exception in this quest. The Spanish navigator Álvaro de Saavedra Cerón in 1528, on sailing along the north coast of the island, was moved to call it Isla del Oro, the Island of Gold, although there is no evidence he actually found any of the yellow metal.

A Theodore Bevan, one of the few travellers who recorded his impressions of New Guinea at the time, in 1872 wrote:

> . . . a land of gold, yet where a fig of tobacco would buy more than a nugget of the precious metal had power to purchase; . . . a land containing fertilizing streams, and millions of acres of glorious grass capable of fattening multitudes of cattle, yet where neither flocks nor herds are known . . . a great rich summer land 'where the skies drop continual fatness', yet but sparsely inhabited by a few inferior coloured races engaged in the sanguinary work of mutual extermination.

When Moresby arrived in Fairfax Harbour in 1873 and explored the estuary of the Laloki River, he made the error of sending word back home of seeing promising traces of the precious ore. Considering that he made a statement at the time that he was so impressed with the people he saw on the island that he lamented disturbing their peace, he would have regretted that his actions resulted in a disastrous but initially very short gold rush to the area. What occurred was to become the pattern of gold exploration in British New Guinea (Papua) for years to come. The fever, the rush, then the bitter disappointment followed by abandonment.

In 1888, a party of prospectors making their way up the Mambare River from the north coast of the Island reached a small tributary that the local natives called the Yodda. They found what they considered to be evidence of payable quantities of gold in the creeks in the area and over the next 10 to 15 years the Yodda find expanded into a goldfield spreading across creeks and gullies over a distance of nearly 50 kilometres. Place names like Finnegans, Prospect, Klondike and McLaughlins became familiar to the several hundred miners who came and went from the area.

Prospectors approached the region from both the north and south coasts. In 1896, they arrived en masse from Queensland in steamers, schooners and Chinese junks. One unfortunate party of 50 men set off to cross the Owen Stanleys from the south, a distance of over 160 kilometres through dense jungle, unfriendly native tribes and steep mountain ranges. Not one of them reached their destination.

Even if they had got there, as many others did, life in the Yodda was hard. If they survived the exhaustion and exposure of the journey, death from dysentery, malaria and just plain neglect was common. The natives were hostile and camp after camp was raided. They took perverse pleasure in lying in wait for passing miners, ambushing them from the trees above or the surrounding dense undergrowth; even hiding under the overhangs of the creek banks and attacking the prospectors as they tested the creek beds for any sign of 'colour' – a euphemism for the specks of gold found in the dregs of the panning dish.

Supplies had to be carried all the way from the mouth of the Mambare through swamps and rapids and treacherous native territory. Because a carrier would consume most of a normal load himself on the long journey, loads were increased to over the recommended 25 kilograms. Illness and desertions were frequent and relations with labour were continuously strained. Alcohol was a means of escape and statistics showed that the miners in the Northern District consumed more grog per head than any other Division of Papua at the time. Of the Europeans, only the tough survived, and it was often those with doubtful pasts who made it to the area, far away from the long arm of the law.

By the start of the 20th century, interest had extended to the search for gold in German New Guinea, which did not prove to be any more rewarding. In the Yodda Valley, however, some determined miners persevered and new areas opened up proved to be more productive. Word spread of encouraging results and miners from other sites started drifting to the valley so that by 1900, around 100 European miners and more than 600 native labourers were working in the Yodda area. These miners extracted an average of 2.5 kilograms of gold each, making it one of the most successful mines in Papua at the time. The problem was, the cost of production was very high and attempts by various government employees and miners to find a better track from the north coast to the Yodda were continually thwarted by the natives who lived en route. Resident Magistrate Armit, who made one attempt to forge such a trail, said of the Papuans he encountered on the way: 'They are certainly not destitute of courage, but on the other hand, they are treacherous, truculent, aggressive, cruel and cunning.'

The people he was referring to were the Orokaivas, who are the tribe that occupy the land virtually from the Yodda to Buna on the north coast. They were undeniably a violent and troublesome crew who had until recently actively practised cannibalism and who trusted no one, nor could they be trusted – a reputation they maintained right through World War II. This tribe was a dark-skinned, lanky, naked people with hair worn in long tags. Armed with long deadly spears, they liked to attack en masse. The sad truth was that after his initial violent meeting with these locals, Armit seemed to adopt the approach of 'shoot first, ask questions later' and as enthusiastic practitioners of the payback system that is ingrained in Papuan culture to this day, the people of the Kumusi, the large river on the route to the coast, killed two white miners, as they attempted to reach the Yodda. Armit's actions had caused long-term damage to the relationship between the Orokaivas and Europeans.

On his journey, Armit identified an area near the village occupied by a group of Orokaivas called the Koko (meaning 'skull') people as an ideal place for a settlement and recommended in his report that a government station should be established there. This could not occur until a safe course could be found from the coast but before they could achieve this goal, both Armit and his immediate successor Walker passed away from malaria-related diseases. They were followed in 1904 by a resident magistrate who was to have a similar impact on the history of Papua to William MacGregor, a Charles Arthur Whitmore Monckton.

Monckton commenced in the position in September 1903 and was an efficient, energetic and courageous operator who quickly saw a need for a government outpost close to the Yodda goldfields. He agreed with Armit's choice of site for this station, and so *Kokoda* – '*da*' meaning 'place of' – 'place of skulls', was established. By late 1904, a house, office, police barracks and store rooms had been constructed on the plateau at Kokoda and extensive areas on the flats below were cleared for gardens. In a report he wrote in 1905, Monckton stated:

> The station is situated some 13 miles from Mt Victoria and 70 miles from the Coast: it is the farthest inland government station in British New Guinea . . . Kokoda has from the first laboured under peculiar difficulties, for it must be remembered that nearly every ounce of food consumed by Armed Native Constabulary, prisoners and officers, together with building materials, ammunition, and the hundred and one requisites

necessary for a large government post have to be carried in on the backs of carriers for six days' journey from the coast.

For this reason, Monckton continued to apply pressure to improve the road from Buna to Kokoda. Six months before the final stretch of the Buna–Kokoda roadwork was completed in June 1905, another walking track, this time from the south coast of the island at Port Moresby to Kokoda, was opened – a track that was to substantially follow the now famous Kokoda Trail. This took over as the means of mail delivery to the goldfields, but supplies still had to be brought from the north coast. As time progressed the natives along the way realised there was more benefit to them in bartering with and selling their produce to the porters and miners than in attacking them. In 1907, they even cooperated in the construction of a wire rope footbridge across the massive Kumusi River, which until then had to be forded on foot – not an easy task. To this day, the Papuans call this locality 'Wairope'.

The annual report of the Kokoda outstation noted in 1908: 'Considerable difference of opinion exists as to the permanence of the Yodda Goldfield, some declaring that it is worked out, and others maintaining with equal confidence that only the surface has been scratched and that a field of unparalleled richness stills remains to be discovered.'

One problem that even the few remaining miners seemed reluctant or unable to address, and that negatively impacted their profits, was the conditions under which native labourers were expected to operate. The Orokaivas, and the other local tribe in the area, the Biagis, refused to work on the goldfields, so most of the workers came from other regions and were not accustomed to the conditions. The humid, water-laden locale was full of malaria-carrying mosquitoes; the days were hot and steamy but the nights were damp and cold with rain falling like clockwork at just before sunset almost every day; nutritious food was in short supply and accommodation was of a very poor standard. This situation was exacerbated by the fact that the method of alluvial gold mining being used involved the use of sluice boxes and spending much of the day up to the knees in the ice-cold water that came straight down from the mountains. The labourers' job involved cutting the races, erecting flumes across the gullies, removing the top soil called overburden, tossing big stones out of the alluvium and shovelling it into the riffle boxes. Desertions were common and the death and illness rate of native employees was unacceptably high, reaching as many as 10 per cent of the workforce in 1904–05, and in those two years alone around 10 Europeans perished from malaria and other endemic diseases. Death was very much a part of life at the Yodda and when traces of gold were found while digging a grave at the goldfields cemetery, the whole graveyard was dug up and the human remains moved so the area could be mined.

Other problems arose when dry spells occurred and there was not sufficient water to feed the races. Astute miners were careful to protect their water rights as well as their mining rights. There was a saying on the Yodda at the time: 'The more the rain, the less the law', as disagreements that often broke out over water usually dissipated once the rains fell.

Despite all these problems, by 1906 Yodda had produced nearly 24 per cent of all the gold produced in British New Guinea to date.

In a disappointing twist of fate, just as the problems of transport and troublesome natives were being addressed, productivity of the Yodda area dropped rather drastically. The number of miners steadily declined until 1909 when news of a new find at Lakekamu River on the south coast of Papua caused a mass exodus, leaving only a handful of stayers in the Kokoda district, and by 1910 only one long-suffering miner hung in at the goldfields.

Not a lot happened in the Yodda area for the 20 years from 1910 to 1930, and Kokoda Station lost its position as a prominent outpost in the Northern Division of Papua. With the decline in gold production, officials at Kokoda turned their thoughts to agricultural pursuits as having better potential for the future provision of gainful employment for the local people.

The Kienzle family (*left to right*) at Cronulla, NSW, in 1919:
Elsa, Wallace, Laura and Herbert

Captain WW Wilson,
Bert's maternal grandfather

Mary Kienzle (nee Wilson),
Bert's mother

Bert (*leading*) setting off to break the Mt Kosciuszko summit record, 1927

Bert with the steam boiler he assembled for the Yodda goldfields in 1934

Gold mining at the Yodda was very labour-intensive

Bert supervising his rubber tappers while still in the Army

The impassable road near Buna–Gona, 1943

The Trail wasn't any easier on foot

Captain HT 'Bert' Kienzle, MID MBE CBE

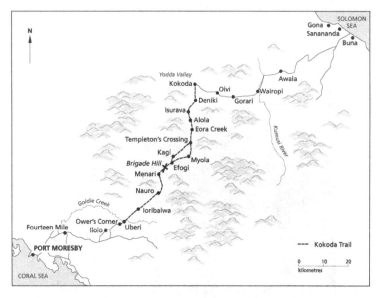

The Kokoda Trail

At least nearer the coast there were vehicles to help transport the wounded, 1943

Bert buying vegetables for the
troops from villagers, 1942

Bert (*centre*) with Colonel Arthur Bell
and other US troops near Popondetta

General Vasey (*left*) and Captain Bert Kienzle address the fuzzy wuzzies
on the Kokoda airstrip, 6 November 1942

Sergeant (later Major) Wallace A Kienzle (Bert's brother)

Bert (*rear, with white belt*) with US and local mates at the Tropical Paradise Tavern

Following the success of trial plantings, the government went ahead with establishing around 60 hectares of rubber in the hope it would prove to be a beneficial crop for the local region.

By 1930, however, with the disappointing extent of investment in agriculture in the Territory, Administrator Hubert Murray remained hopeful of discovery of a major goldfield. Murray liked the idea of gold as a source of wealth for the Papuans, backing up his reluctance to see this developing country become entirely a plantation economy. Having studied the history of the area and been a regular visitor to Kokoda on his patrols, he encouraged the reopening of the Yodda fields. By 1931, three miners had returned to the area and were employing about 30 natives, but they extracted only 31 ounces and as with their predecessors, paid highly for the cost of transport of supplies and poor living conditions.

Onto this scene in 1932 stepped Ward Williams, a highly professional American mining engineer with a wealth of theoretical and practical knowledge. James Sinclair, in his book *Wings of Gold*, says of Williams: 'For perspective, imagination and endurance over a considerable period of time, few prospectors in New Guinea have approached the record of J. Ward Williams . . .'

Williams believed in using the latest methods and the best equipment, including radio communications and air transport. In 1931 he visited the area to carry out scout borings and thought it had potential, so that by 1932 he was established at Yodda and putting pressure on the administration to build an airstrip at Kokoda. Under supervision of ARM Mac Rich, using Papuan officers and prison labour, a small, rough strip was built below the station and on 28 September 1932, a Guinea Airways Junker F/13 flown by Orme Denny made the first landing at Kokoda with a load of supplies for Williams. The Junker landed but unfortunately Denny decided he would not risk an attempted take-off, as the surface was too soft and sticky.

Rich came up with a rather ingenious solution to this problem. He lined up all the policemen and prisoners and recruited any miscellaneous villagers who had gathered around to wonder at one of these strange noisy birds that flew overhead regularly, but until now they had never seen so close up. He proceeded to march them all up and down the centre of the aerodrome. On the soft spots, he had them mark time, and after an hour or so of this Denny was able to get the Junker back in the air!

Over the next 12 months, when weather permitted, up to three flights a day were made into Kokoda carrying mainly freight for Williams, one of them bringing in his wife, who was treated with a great deal of curiosity by the local people for whom a white woman was a very rare sight. Drainage of the airstrip continued to be a problem, and flights during the wet season often had to be cancelled. It was also a one-way runway on this strip, meaning the planes needed to take off to the north and land to the south; otherwise they were too close to the mountains. After take-off it was necessary to circle over the Yodda Valley in order to reach around 1,500 metres before turning towards the infamous Kokoda Gap, which peaked at over 2,100 metres. Failure to reach the required altitude before heading into The Gap was a recipe for disaster, as many pilots would learn over the ensuing years. If the valley was 'socked in' with cloud, this was a dangerous exercise. These problems with the airstrip meant that the postal service was fairly unreliable, so that mail sometimes still had to be sent overland via the old mail trail. Guinea Airways complained that the Kokoda leg of their air service was extremely unprofitable, but they persevered in support of Williams in the hope that in the future their losses would be recouped.

By March 1934, Williams was well established at Yodda and had floated a company called Yodda Goldfields Ltd with a nominal capital of £25,000, 12,500 shares of which were offered to the public at 5 shillings a share. Ward Williams was the managing director and it was at this point that he employed three assistants to manage the fields – F. T. Moates, Noel Hides and Herbert T. Kienzle.

Williams had started to address the transport problems of the past; now he wanted to address the labour problems. Fortunately for his requirements, in 1933, to facilitate the needs of the mining industry, the rules restricting employment of natives more than 160 kilometres from their village were rescinded. The first job he gave Bert was to fly to Wau and then to Garaina in the Mandated Territory of New Guinea to recruit 100 or more labourers. From Garaina, Bert walked through the Waria district where he met up with some of his old workers from Kanosia and convinced them to join up. He continued on down through the Boera–Eia and then the Gira goldfields, over horrendous terrain and through tribes of ferocious warriors, on to the lower Mambare areas of the Ioma District and the beaches of Gona and Sanananda. At Buna, he picked up a group of Gosiago labourers who had recently been brought across from the Goodenough and Ferguson Islands specifically to work on the goldfields of the mainland.

In order to carry out this recruiting drive, Bert would have had to obtain a licence. These were normally issued to official recruiting agents, but a limited licence could be obtained for a particular enterprise to recruit for itself alone. It was traditional for recruiters on arrival at a village to sit down with the *luluai* (head man) and get the natives travelling with him to hold forth about the virtues of working with this *masta* (master in Pidgin) or *taubada* (Motu) and the benefits of life away from the village. Bribes of beads, machetes, *laplap/rami* cloth, jew's harps and mouth organs, salt, tobacco and newspaper were normally offered to the *luluai*. After a few days he would manage to convince a few of the young men to give it a go and they would join the caravan of the recruiter and his men to the next village. Although they were usually paid about 10 shillings incentive money to get them going, often as these recruits got further away from their village some would lose their nerve and run away home. Many considered this indenturing of labour a thinly veiled excuse for slavery but the reality was that these men were paid wages and in the majority of cases were well cared for, well fed and protected and given medical treatment they would not have got at home. Most 'contracts' were for three years and many would come back for seconds after having some time back in their villages. For Bert, the whole exercise was made more worthwhile by the newly introduced Mining Ordinance employment conditions, which allowed labour to be recruited for 12 months without a written contract of service and with no limit to the duration of their indenture.

It was stated in administrative reports at the time that a patrol like this took tremendous personal energy and physical endurance, mental and moral stability as well as courage and strong nerves. This epic recruitment drive took Bert nearly two months, and he arrived at Kokoda in early March 1934. He and his 'troops' picked up food and other supplies that Williams had had delivered to the station, and carried them the 13 kilometres to the Yodda campsite. Here he met Ward Williams for the first time, along with Tom Moates.

Williams's priority, which Bert fully supported, was construction of native-style accommodation for the newly arrived labour force of over 100 – not an easy task, particularly as it needed to be done as quickly as possible. A whole new village was created virtually overnight so that workers would at least be able to get warm and dry after toiling six days a week in the cold streams.

On Bert's arrival in Papua seven years before, one of the first reading tasks he was given by his boss was a 1926 publication of the government press of the time, *The Feeding of Native Labourers in Papua*, by Walter Mersh Strong. Historically, the habit had been to feed the natives a staple diet of rice and tinned meat but experience had shown that after two or three months on such a diet, many of them suffered from beri-beri and scurvy. The solution to this problem stated by Strong, obvious to us all today, was the provision of fresh fruit and vegetables. His booklet's summary states:

> I would have cod-liver oil always available and would do my
> best to persuade the labourers to come and ask for a dose
> from time to time. I would also have quinine, salts, soap,

simple dressings and a place where they can come and wash any trivial injuries always without ceremony. I would make every possible effort to grow native vegetables, especially sweet potatoes, pumpkins and papaws . . . I would also make every possible effort to get extras for the boys as opportunity occurs e.g. fish, shellfish, native roots, coconuts and sugar cane.

Because of this knowledge, Bert always placed a priority on giving his native workers land to cultivate their own gardens, and as soon as their houses on the Yodda were completed, he allocated garden areas to each of his men and encouraged them to plant up their basic vegetable needs without delay. This caused them some consternation, as gardening was mostly women's work back home in their villages.

Bert's next big project was construction of an airfield much closer to the goldfields than Kokoda, where drainage problems continued to limit flights and cause delays. Williams was looking to bring in some heavy equipment that he did not want to be carried any further than absolutely necessary. A site was chosen on a slightly raised area of land above the Ebei Creek, a small river by Australian standards on the southern side of Yodda Creek.

Choosing the site was the easiest part: clearing dense jungle entirely with manual labour, including large trees that had to be hand grubbed, was a real challenge for Bert and his band of workers. The big advantage Bert had over most other Europeans trying to work with Papuans was that he now spoke Motu fluently – not just basic phrases for barking orders but social Motu, so he could have a joke with the boys and jockey them along. *Tok Pisin* (Pidgin English) was never a language to which Bert gave much credence and he certainly never used it with Papuans. He believed it was a language used by the Germans and others in New Guinea to keep the local population 'dumbed down'. This belief was backed up when he heard of natives who had learnt to speak proper English being called 'upstarts' and 'trouble makers'. He told even those recruits he had collected from the Mandated Territory to learn

Motu within three months or they were on the next plane out, and out of a job. He had learnt it in that time and believed they could do the same, such was his respect for their natural intelligence and ear for languages.

The completed Yodda 'drome was 700 metres long and 80 metres wide with a gradient of approximately one in 20. The approach was one-way east-north-east, and the well-drained surface was nice and firm. In April 1934, the first plane landed, a Fox Moth again flown by Orme Denny. On its return flight, it took Williams back to Port Moresby, where he took delivery of a radio transceiver that had been especially made for him in Australia. When he came back to the Yodda, he registered as a public radio station and communicated daily with Port Moresby. Telegrams could even be sent, for two pence a word – a very rare facility in 1934.

From June 1934 W/34 Junkers commenced up to four flights a day into the Yodda and over 14 days, the bulk of the machinery Williams had ordered was delivered to the goldfields – the biggest operation since the Bulolo fields of New Guinea. Robo Robo, the loyal worker who had come with Bert from Kanosia, recalls one of the first flights into the Yodda, where a group of curious local women stood by the airstrip watching the aircraft take off, when the wind from the propellers sent their grass skirts billowing skywards causing peals of laughter among the men and children nearby.

The next job Williams gave Bert was to assemble the two steam boilers that had arrived in parts at the airstrip. This involved welding, which Bert had never really done before, and it was most important it was done properly or the boilers could explode. These boilers used steam pressure to move the skip that had been filled using shovels with gravel from the creek banks. The skip was on the end of the boom and it unloaded its contents into the hoppers. Bert also had to construct two of these hoppers, which are like giant funnels for directing the pay dirt (hopefully, gold-bearing gravel) into the sluice boxes, which he also had to make from local timber. Into these long flat rectangular boxes, he welded riffles, which were like a set of steel combs over which the pay dirt swirled. He had set up a mini-sawmill to produce timber for sluice boxes and the derricks to hold the funnels and water races. Bert was a fast learner, but years later avoided all things mechanical, so much so that his sons would tease him that they reckon these gold mining days must have been the last time he actually did any real work with machinery.

Within less than six months of Bert's arrival at the Yodda, Ward Williams was offered an opportunity to manage a large organisation called Oroville Dredging Company of London. This company was developing major operations throughout Papua, with vast reserves of funds and experience behind it and prepared to risk considerable sums of money to do the job of prospecting for gold properly. The offer was too good to refuse, so by October 1934 Williams had departed and appointed Bert manager of Yodda Goldfields. On investigation, Bert quickly discovered that the company was in a poor financial state. Once again, his challenge was to increase productivity while keeping costs to a minimum.

Early in 1935, Bert's brother Wallace, now a graduate of Hawkesbury Agricultural College, journeyed to Papua and joined him on the staff of the company. The deal was that Wallace would get £20 a month and 'keep' – not much even by the standards of the day, but Wallace was a hard worker not afraid of roughing it for the sake of some adventure. He arrived in rather spectacular fashion. With the usually reliable Orme Denny as pilot, they actually crash-landed at the Ebei airstrip. Both Orme and Wallace walked away unharmed but the same could not be said for the aircraft.

Bert also invited his father Alfred and stepmother Hally to come to the Yodda. Alfred's import–export business in Sydney had been hit hard by the Depression, and in 1930 he too had taken a job in Papua, managing the Commonwealth Hemp Company at Tavai. In 1933, with news of renewed discontent in Germany, Alfred had opted to change his name by deed poll to Kingsley. He suggested that Bert and Wallace follow suit but they declined. Alfred had not forgotten his experiences in

World War I and was determined they would not be repeated. Bert was proud to carry the name of Kienzle, and Wallace went along with him, although he held no love for the Germans and felt strongly that he was an Australian. The family was now the centre of what was a small but real community on the Yodda. Native-style, yet quite respectable and comfortable houses, had been built for each of them, and every residence was surrounded by gardens cultivated by loyal local workers.

Bert formed the Yodda Prospecting Syndicate to mine areas outside the leases held by Yodda Goldfields, and Alfred managed this company, which incorporated trade stores selling basic supplies to the natives, as well as prospecting for gold. Everybody worked hard to keep their heads above water in these difficult times, and in May 1935, with both Alfred and Wallace there to hold the fort, Bert decided to take his first leave after eight years of uninterrupted service in the Territory. He planned to meet the directors of Yodda Goldfields in Sydney, then to take a well-deserved holiday catching up with family and rediscovering a social life.

He obtained passage on the SS *Montoro* from Port Moresby to Brisbane, then flew by light plane to Sydney. Allowing for return travel to and from the Yodda, and meeting his bosses, he actually only ended up with about one week's holiday in Sydney, but in typical Bert fashion, he was to achieve a lot in that week.

The first person he contacted on arrival in Sydney was his younger sister Laura. Laura was now a nurse at Sydney Hospital, and had recently married Dr Harry White, a physician with the Public Health Department. Bert's other sister Elsa had returned to Germany in the early 1930s for what was actually her third visit. During this time she met and fell in love with a German Jew called Hans Levi. This relationship was eventually to cause a huge rift between the German and Australian branches of the Kienzle family, a rift that would never really be repaired. At one stage, grandfather Gustav wrote a letter to Alfred demanding that he instruct Elsa to break off the relationship or she would cause the family great shame and would have to be disowned. Alfred replied that his daughter could choose whoever she liked as her friends and marry whoever she wished, from which point all communications appear to have ceased. Hans and Elsa were wise enough to leave Germany, marry in London on 6 February 1934, and emigrate to America soon thereafter.

It would be many years before Bert would see Elsa again, but he enjoyed catching up with Laura and meeting her husband. On the second night of Bert's stay, Laura suggested he make up a foursome on a blind date with a friend of hers from work – Meryl Holliday.

Bert was smitten from the word go. This 6-foot-2 sunburnt man fresh from the jungles of Papua and this five-foot-nothing vivacious opera singer, reluctantly now nurse, seemed a bit of a mismatch, but it was love at first sight. Neither was very young – Meryl being 28 and Bert 30 years of age – and Bert had no doubt that this was the woman of his dreams. The lack of women in his life did not sit well with Bert. Apart from a short fling with a young Aussie lass in Port Moresby during his Kanosia days, his had been a celibate existence. He courted Meryl doggedly for the whole week of his stay, and on the last night, took her to the best restaurant he could find. On returning her to the nurses' quarters, he asked the taxi driver to keep driving around the block and would not let Meryl out until she said yes to his proposal of marriage. How could she say no to those intense hazel-green eyes and clear olive skin, those expressive hands that gesticulated incessantly as he told the tales of his fascinating life, and the chivalrous, old-fashioned character of this dashing pioneer! The combination of cultured European and intrepid adventurer was irresistible.

Reluctantly returning to the Yodda, Bert began preparing for his marriage and the arrival of his bride. Things were tough on the goldfields, and money was tight, so it was to be over a year before they actually wed. Those were a very long 13 months for both of them, and it would be unrealistically romantic to suggest that Meryl did not have her doubts during that time. Her friends and family were horrified that she intended to marry this man she had only known for one week, let alone disappear with him into the jungles of a land that to them was beyond the realms of their imagination.

Bert wrote to Meryl several times a week, describing life on the Yodda, the preparations he was making and the house he was preparing so that she would feel safe and comfortable. He continually reassured her of his love and that he would protect her, and Meryl believed this to be true. In the time she had spent with him, she knew he was a strong, honest and honourable person, different from any other man she had ever met and she knew that she would always feel safe with him.

Despite her family's misgivings, on 29 May 1936 Meryl set sail all on her own on the *Macdhui* bound for Port Moresby and on 4 June she and Herbert were married in St John's Church of England by Rev. H. Matthews. After the wedding, once again it was Orme Denny who flew Bert and Meryl out to the Yodda in a Guinea Airways Junker. The flight was a memorable one for both of them, taking off from the Kila airstrip at Moresby, Bert sitting in the open cockpit next to the pilot with Meryl on his lap. Quite serious turbulence over the infamous Kokoda Gap certainly put to the test Meryl's belief that Bert would always protect her, and the approach and landing on the Yodda strip tried her nerves to the limit.

Bert had arranged for his workers to be waiting at the airstrip with a sedan chair for Meryl: four Papuans with a seat perched on a lawyer cane platform. She felt like royalty as they gently lowered her down onto the verandah of the home Bert had built looking across to the goldfields and surrounded by rich vegetable gardens high with sweet corn and the broad, lush leaves of taro plants. Despite all Bert's letters of description, Meryl really had not been able to imagine what she was coming to and she was pleasantly surprised by what she saw. Her mind quickly started creating how she could give it a woman's touch with the wedding gifts she had brought with her from Sydney and with the addition of some tropical plants in the garden – bougainvillea and frangipanis, hibiscus and monsteria.

Their lives soon settled into a routine, with Bert rising early to work in the fields but always coming home promptly for lunch at noon. Meryl thought she might have trouble adjusting to this set of habits after nursing, where she had worked shifts and odd hours, but she soon adapted to being woken at 4 a.m. by the cookboy with a cup of tea to start the day. However, by the time her husband went back to work after his lunch break she was ready for an afternoon nap. This was a tradition she kept up for the rest of her life, and it served her well in the tropics, ensuring she stayed out of the sun during the hottest part of the day, thus protecting her fair skin and compensating for the enervating effects of the hot, humid days so different from Sydney and Melbourne.

The most difficult adjustment for Meryl was handling the native houseboy who had been Bert's cook and general batman during his bachelor days at Yodda. Meryl never really felt comfortable speaking Motu, and Bert had trained him in certain routines and habits that did not really fit with his new wife's plans. A certain amount of initial competitive jealousy was common in these situations, and Meryl was not immune to this but her cheerful and friendly disposition helped her to laugh off the problems and eventually win over the hired help.

Life continued relatively smoothly despite the huge learning curve for Meryl, until September 1936, when Bert suffered a bout of malaria from which he could not seem to recover. Treatment with quinine had no effect and the fevers continued unabated until he reached the stage where, tall and solidly built as he normally was, his weight had dropped to 45 kg, less than half his usual size, and he was excreting black fluid from almost every orifice in his body. He had blackwater fever. Meryl's nursing experience could not help in this extreme situation and to make matters worse, the weather had closed in and atmospheric interference was preventing any radio contact with outside help. In desperation, one of Bert's most loyal workers, Hosiembo, set off on foot to try to reach the government station at the mouth of the Mambare. Hosiembo ran non-stop for a day and a night, covering a distance that normally took five days, eventually reaching Ioma. The patrol officer in charge there arranged for a plane to fly into the Yodda and evacuate Bert to Moresby hospital. When the pilot saw Bert on arrival at Yodda, he whispered to his father Alfred, 'You don't want to take him out – he's had it.' As they crossed the Owen Stanleys, they had to climb to 3,300 metres to clear the high clouds, and when they struck quite a lot of turbulence on the way as the aircraft was slapped around the sky, Bert's mouth and nose bled severely. Bert was nursed lovingly by Meryl, despite this being only her second flight in Papua. No surprise that she quickly developed a fear and loathing of flying!

After initial treatment in Moresby, Bert recovered enough to fly with Meryl to Sydney and stay with his sister Laura and her husband Harry at their home in Emmaville. Having two nursing sisters and a doctor to care for him certainly helped in his recovery.

Blackwater fever is a complication of falciparum malaria, which is a parasitic disease carried by the Anopheles mosquito, at that time very common in the Yodda Valley. The symptoms of malaria are high fever, chills, sweats and body aches, but when it progresses to blackwater fever, added to this is abdominal pain, nausea, vomiting and jaundice. These extended symptoms are caused by enlargement of the liver and spleen, and ultimately the presence of haemoglobin in the urine results in dark almost black urine and even other secretions like tears go a dirty brown colour. The onset of blackwater fever can be very sudden and the death rate is quite high. There is now some evidence that it is actually brought on by the quinine used to treat the malaria, but the reality is they were lucky that this drug existed at all, and it remains the most effective cure for that disease.

Other illnesses like scrub typhus, amoebic dysentery, tropical ulcers, yaws and various unpleasant skin infections were not so easily treated, as penicillin and other antibiotics were non-existent.

While Bert was recuperating in Sydney, Wallace had been offered a job with Ward Williams and Oroville to join the prospecting party he was putting together to explore the upper regions of the Fly and Sepik Rivers. It was still a struggle for the Yodda Goldfields and syndicate to support all the Kienzles now living in the valley, so despite Bert being absent at the time he made the decision, Wallace felt it was an opportunity too good to miss, and a way of taking some financial pressure off Bert. Alfred and Hally were still there, although Hally was to head south soon after her oldest stepson was well enough to go back to work. Hally still remained closest to Wallace, and his departure to places unknown, for an unspecified time, made life at the Yodda less bearable for her. She was still a rather grim, hypochondriacal dowager who found Meryl's cheerful disposition and general *joie de vivre* irritating. Her departure meant Meryl was the only white woman at the Yodda, a situation that arose quite a few times over the coming years. Alfred, who had also become a little dour and sour in his old age, once wrote to Elsa calling Meryl a flibbertigibbet, or words to that effect. Their interests in and approach to life were completely opposite and they often clashed. Bert was fortunate to have found a woman like this to share his life or he too may have succumbed to the humourless and stern nature of his German heredity. Meryl brought out his lighter side, the traits inherited from his mother Mary, and would gently tease him whenever he started to take himself too seriously.

Wallace's expedition with Ward Williams was to be acknowledged as an epic journey and is considered as one of the most significant in the exploration of Papua New Guinea. It is well recorded in the book *Wings of Gold* by James Sinclair. One story not told therein, however, gives an insight into the man Bert's young brother had become.

While on the expedition, it was Wallace's job to keep the supplies up to the prospectors, including fresh meat, which he obtained in the form of wild pigs and Goura pigeons that he shot in the surrounding forests. He became an excellent marksman, and the story goes that at one stage when supplies were running low a group of natives raided the stores while he was absent from camp, threatening and scaring off all the expedition porters in camp. Wallace returned in time to see them disappearing into the distance, by now about 1 kilometre away. He was so incensed at their thievery that he took aim at one of the offenders – and hit him! Good shot or just bloody good luck? The thieves dropped the axes and knives they were carrying and hightailed it back to their village. Wallace followed them there, where he found the culprit was a fellow called Arfiengim. He was not badly hurt, with only a flesh wound in the back of his shoulder, but he literally did not know what had hit him! Even though they had observed Wallace shooting game, they had no idea the damage a bullet could do to a human, especially from so far away. Wallace applied first aid and the native soon recovered, and they never again had trouble with these villagers trying to steal camp supplies.

By the end of May 1937, Williams had to concede that there was no payable gold anywhere that he had searched. The expedition was abandoned, and he returned to his homeland, having expended in excess of US$100,000 of Oroville's funds – a lot of money in those days. To quote James Sinclair, 'The most ambitious and determined effort ever to find gold in the centre of New Guinea was over, with honour even if not with profit.'

Other members of the expedition dispersed back to the Morobe fields, while Wallace returned to the Yodda, no wealthier but certainly a lot wiser and having made a huge contribution to the opening up of western Papua and other areas never before explored by white man. He had traversed the steamy swamplands at the mouth of the Fly, scaled the multiple ridges and sheer cliffs of thinly covered white limestone of the Kaban ranges, on to the massive Hindenburg Range – an impressive wall of rock nowhere less than 2,700 metres and in places exceeding 3,300 metres. He had encountered Papuan and New Guinea tribesmen, most of whom had never seen white men before, some not so friendly, some very welcoming.

Wallace and Stuart Campbell prepared a report for the administration titled 'Notes on the Natives of the Fly and Sepik River Headwaters, New Guinea'. They comment on being particularly taken with the people they encountered in the Telefomin region, whom they called the Mountain People.

> '. . . they are uniformly dark skinned and short in stature with the women generally being even smaller than the men. They lead an idyllic life in the healthy, bracing mountain climate, with little work to do and lots of time to do it. Disease, especially the unsightly skin diseases so prevalent elsewhere in New Guinea, appears almost unknown.'

Despite these people being cannibals, Wallace and Stuart wrote that it had never before been their fortune to meet a more friendly, cheerful, happy and unsophisticated community of natives. After all, they only ate their enemies!

§

During Wallace's absence from the Yodda, eking out a living from the gold had become more and more difficult. A coffee plantation came up for sale near the north coast for £250 and Bert walked from the Yodda to the coast to check it out, but the reality was, as he had not a cracker in the bank at the time, and he could not be in two places at once, it was not a realistic option. With the success of the government rubber plantings at Kokoda in mind, combined with his knowledge of this crop, Bert decided he should establish his own plantation. While carrying on working for Yodda Goldfields Ltd, he applied to the government to lease land in the Yodda Valley and was granted a 99-year lease on 1,000 acres by Sir Hubert Murray. The Land Ordinance of 1935 prevented Papuans from selling or leasing land to anyone other than the Crown, and this was subject to the provision that 'no purchase or lease of land may be made until by sufficient enquiry the lieutenant governor has become satisfied that the land is not required or likely to be required by the owners'. Murray had remained keen to see controlled plantation development in Papua and he encouraged Bert in his endeavours, although he cautioned him on the risks of starting such a venture so far inland and dependent on air transport. The 80 acres of government plantings at Kokoda were now producing and the rubber had to be carried in 18-kilogram bales by native porters over 120 kilometres to the coast at Buna, from where it was shipped to Australia via Samarai. Murray's support could also be put down to his firm belief that Japan was becoming the major threat to Australia's survival as a European society in the Pacific, and he held that the success of Papuan industry was vital in the event of a Japanese blockade of the Pacific. Murray's enthusiasm combined with an international rubber agreement being put in place, plus the growing demand for the product worldwide, resulted in the area of rubber in Papua actually doubling between 1936 and 1942.

This first lease that Bert took out he named Mamba Estate after a creek called Mamba that flowed into the mighty Mambare River upstream from the Yodda. Seed was obtained from the Kokoda Government Plantation and from Koitaki Rubber Estates near Moresby. Other areas soon followed, the next major expansion being in 1938 when Alfred invited Dr Geoffrey H. Vernon to be his partner in an estate they called Komo Planting Syndicate, also named after the river that flowed through it. Doc Vernon, ex AIF World War I RMO 11th Light Horse Regiment, was GMO (Government Medical Officer) at Daru and, like many other Papuan MOs before him, had always had an ambition to become a planter. He had been carrying out experimental plantings of both kapok and rubber in the Daru area for some years and had recently taken out a lease at Oni-Oni, Port Glasgow in the same year, so becoming a partner in another enterprise at Kokoda suited his plans well. Before arriving in Papua, Vernon had been on Thursday Island, followed by Misima Island, and had become the foremost expert on the causes and treatment of beri-beri and many other tropical diseases. A capable and cultured man, Vernon's compassion and love for the native people was legendary and administering to their medical needs always took priority in his life to the extent that he could never in the years to come really claim to have been a very successful planter. Wallace had met him briefly near Daru on his Fly Expedition, and Bert had become a friend during his years on the south coast of Papua.

Bert describes those years from 1936 through to 1939 as very tough ones, consolidating their position by extending areas of alluvial mining in order to survive on the proceeds and finance their expansion into rubber. Daily life was arduous. Each morning he and Wallace would rise before dawn, get the labour and sluice boxes working on the goldfields, then tramp the 10 kilometres or so back up the valley to the site of their agricultural lease. Here, they worked with their labourers, felling, clearing and burning the virgin jungle in preparation for planting rubber. There were no open grasslands in the Yodda Valley, so every development had to be carved out of thick jungle. The afternoon meant tramping back to the Yodda to supervise the cleaning of the boxes. Somewhere in among all these jobs, the men had to find time to cut tracks, fix machinery, maintain the airstrip and, always, keep prospecting new country. Areas cleared for planting of the trees were interplanted with sweet potato, bananas, taros, yams and other vegetables to feed the growing population at the Yodda.

At the end of each day, as they headed back to camp in the fast-falling dark, it was the boys' final job to carry any felled timber suitable for milling back to the Yodda homestead. Up to 40 boys would hoist a massive log onto their shoulders and as they felt their way home through the pitch-black jungle, having this connection to their mates ensured they did not wander off the track. Their confidence was further boosted by loud singing to ward off any evil spirits they might pass in the dark. This ritual scene was one Bert and Wallace would remember with great fondness in future years. For Meryl, the increasing volume of their harmonious voices as they neared her home meant the end of another workday and the safe return of her husband from his sometimes dangerous duties in this untamed territory.

In a 1938 report, Bert noted that an average of 30 cubic metres of gravel wash had to be processed to retrieve just one ounce of gold. This compared very favourably to the Lakekumu field at the time where it took nearly 2,000 cubic metres for the same outcome. Despite this, with the expenses invested in equipment and the maintenance and supply costs to the remote Yodda region, the operation hovered very close to being uneconomic. In 1938, Bert had estimated the leases held by Yodda Goldfields and Yodda Syndicate probably had a remaining life of about seven years. In 1938–39 they extracted £7,480 worth of gold and in 1940–41 £12,053, being 43 kilograms. The fluctuating price and variable concentration of ore, however, meant the average value per cubic metre was declining fast. By mid-1941, Bert reported that 'if no further payable ground is found, the prospect for 1941–42 is anything but bright'.

The Ward Williams Company under Bert's management is reported to have gathered more than 8,000 ounces of gold in eight years, at a time when prices ranged from £8 to £14 an ounce and costs were high. Records show the company produced about the equivalent of $100,000 of gold from 1935 to 1942, with dividends being paid to shareholders for four consecutive years. In 1941, Yodda Prospecting Syndicate produced 425 ounces gold and had gradually bought out all the equipment and assets of Yodda Goldfields. Government annual reports at the time put the Yodda on a par with Woodlark Island for gold production.

§

For Meryl, gold fortunes or not, 1937 and 1938 were very productive years. On 18 May 1937, one day before his proud father's birthday, Carl Herbert Kienzle was born in Sydney. Meryl had remained at Yodda until her seventh month but then reluctantly boarded a plane for the dreaded flight over the Kokoda Gap and on to Sydney where her good friend from her nursing days, Eve Condon, was married to a highly respected and successful general practitioner, later obstetrician, Dr John Mutton. Carl was born just before Wallace came home from his Fly expedition. Wallace sent a telegram advising of his imminent return in which, typical of his humour, he jokingly wrote words to the effect that he liked the people so much he thought he might bring home a Telefomin bride. The same day a telegram arrived to tell Bert he had a new son. Apparently to two got garbled and the outcome was one radio message saying that Wallace was coming home with a new £10 bride and a new baby boy!

When Carl was only one month old, Meryl returned with him to the Yodda, and soon afterwards Ailsa made the journey to visit her 'big' sister. '*Sinana miraki, karu na huina be kakakaka lahi bamona*' – 'the aunt with the flaming red hair' as they called her – was a keen gardener and did her best to help Meryl establish a proper lawn at the Yodda. She brought with her many plants, including choko vine and morning glory that just loved the jungle and in the ensuing years would almost take it over. She also took the time to develop a strong interest in Bert's bachelor brother and when illness forced her to leave in early 1938 then aged 29, she began a correspondence with Wallace that continued for several years.

Within a short time Meryl was pregnant again, and on 16 July 1938, once again in Sydney in the safe hands of Dr John, Katherine Evelyn Mary Kienzle was born. Since his near-death experience with blackwater fever, Bert now insisted on leave every two years, and so this time was able to travel down south with his pregnant wife.

Back at the Yodda with her two young babies, life was full and busy for Meryl. As with most plantation wives of her era, her days revolved around the responsibilities of the household – ordering the food, preparing and designing the meals and managing the house staff. At least by 1938, the first form of refrigeration, the 'Icyball', had been invented. This apparatus used heat to vaporise ammonia and so freeze water to cool its contents. It was rather a temperamental device with a tendency to explode, so it was a relief when it was soon replaced by the kerosene fridge. Up until that time, fresh meat was only what could be shot by the locals or bred and killed on site, all having to be consumed within 24 hours unless salted.

Interestingly, in those days most of the house servants for married couples were males – 'houseboys' – mainly because the females were busy with all the domestic duties back in the village. Relationships with the planters' wives and these village men could sometimes be difficult. Mutual respect needed to be earned, established and demonstrated, and everyone needed to be aware of and not step outside of their place in this ordered society. For example, Papuan men were not allowed to wear anything on the top half of their bodies, and just a *rami* below the waist. The reason given for this is because they were inclined to wear shirts when they were wet and so expose themselves to chest ailments. Meryl chose to follow this tradition mainly because, if allowed to wear shirts, her houseboys tended not to wash them regularly enough and the odour soon became intolerable. She insisted they shower each day before entering the house, and this would have been pointless if they had then been allowed to put back on a smelly shirt.

Most of the visitors to any outstation in Papua in the 1930s were men, and so life for Meryl could be very lonely. At one stage, with Hally unwell and away in Australia, she was again the only white woman in the valley, this time for more than a year. She recalled her reaction when finally a female missionary landed at the airstrip en route to the Chirima region north of the Yodda. Missionaries, often single women, were sometimes a little wary of planters' wives. There was traditionally a hierarchy in the Territory, with planters at the top, government 'wallahs' next, and missionaries at the bottom of the ladder. They were, after all, there with different expectations of life and of the natives – planters were looking for profit, administrators for order and missionaries for conversions. Meryl was unaffected by all this and besides, it was not in her nature to be unwelcoming of anybody. She burst into tears and hugged the amazed woman, reluctant to let her go.

Meryl was sometimes called upon to use her nursing skills for the more serious health problems that arose in the valley. The natives loved to be administered to by the *sinabada* (Motu for 'big lady') and sometimes faked illnesses or cut themselves just to receive her attentions. But probably the most demanding role for any woman in the Territory at the time was motherhood – the continual fear, particularly of health risks and accidents, was always at the back of their minds. The reality of this situation was to hit Bert and Meryl in the most horrific way some years later.

6

KOKODA CAMPAIGN

The outbreak of World War II came as quite a shock to Bert and his growing family at the Yodda. Contact with his German relatives had virtually ceased after the furore over Elsa's marriage to Hans, and although Bert was aware of the problems brewing in his family's home country, he was not expecting it to result in war.

Despite Alfred's anglicising of his surname, again the Kienzles' loyalties were questioned. At least this time, once the authorities had established that Bert was a British-born subject and his father now a naturalised Australian, they left them alone and instructed them to keep operating their mines and plantations in the interests of the war effort.

For the rest of 1939 and early 1940, Bert, Wallace and Alfred continued to work hard mining gold and maintaining the rubber, very little of which was mature enough to be tapped. By this time, the Kienzle family had leased a total of 7,700 acres of good agricultural land, approximately 900 acres of which was planted with flourishing young rubber. Plantings of rubber in Papua had steadily risen to a total of 18,000 acres by 1940, and the price improved considerably with the onset of war, but it was too early for Mamba Estate to benefit from this, as rubber trees take nearly seven years to reach productive maturity. Sir Hubert Murray was now well into his seventies and a change of regime was imminent in the administration in Moresby. Bert had a great deal of respect for Sir Hubert but there were many, including 'Gal' Loudon, who firmly believed he had stifled the development of Papua. They looked forward to someone different and dynamic taking over the reins and maybe stimulating some real growth in plantation industries in this land of huge agricultural potential. To the frustration of many, the establishment opted for more of the same by appointing Sir Hubert's nephew Leonard to take over as administrator. Bert continued to do his own thing and forge ahead with his plans, supported by his family and his special relationship with the Papuans.

One interesting event that occurred during this time was the unexpected arrival at Yodda of two Japanese gentlemen, who wandered into the settlement claiming to be anthropologists. In their limited English, they related a tale of having walked from the north coast of Papua at Buna with the aim of crossing over the Owen Stanleys to Moresby studying the indigenous people of the region. They were rather unsuitably dressed for the environment, wearing their *zori* or what Australians liked to call 'Japanese riding boots'. A little reluctantly, and being careful what they said, Bert and Meryl showed them their usual hospitality for one night, but Meryl was adamant they were probably spies. Bert, well informed by radio of international tensions, made light of her concerns to allay her fears, but no doubt had similar suspicions. Events in the near future would cause him to ponder in retrospect that if indeed they were spies, they must never have got back to Japan with their information. It was poor reconnaissance and in particular a lack of understanding of the difficulties in crossing the mountains separating north from south that ultimately led to Japan's defeat in Papua in 1942–43. They would land with pushbikes and horses but limited food supplies, as they intended to live off the towns and cities.

Since Bert had built the Yodda/Ebei airstrip, the one at Kokoda had literally sunk into disrepair so that the Guinea

Airways Junkers and later Trimotor Ford aircraft that plied the airways from Moresby to Kokoda carrying mail, government and plantation supplies, and the fairly rare intrepid passengers, nearly all landed at the Yodda. Well-known identities such as Aubrey Koch, Ken Garden, Tommy O'Dea and of course, Orme Denny were the regular pilots on these flights. In early 1941, they flew in one most precious article as a surprise for Meryl – a beautiful little piano. Bert had ordered it for her birthday and it arrived out of its case, which would have made it too heavy for the plane, wrapped only in wheatmeal sacks. It took about 10 men to carry it up the airstrip and amazingly it did not have a mark on it, and soon took pride of place in the corner of Meryl's lounge.

In 1938, Assistant Resident Magistrate Sydney Elliot-Smith, who was now in charge at Kokoda Station, had decided the time had come to repair the aerodrome. Bert had met Syd on his first boat ride to Moresby on the SS *Morinda* in 1927. The two adventurous young bachelors, full of bravado and excitement, had been vying for the attention of a pretty lass on board whose uncle owned the Papua Hotel. Neither had any success, as she apparently had her eye on another fellow, Ivan Champion, a member of a well-established pioneering family in Papua. The two handsome and cocky mates couldn't work out the attraction to Champion as he was short and quiet with glasses, and they jokingly asked him what his secret was. Bert and Syd commiserated with each other over their apparent lack of lady-killer skills and became firm friends thereafter.

The jungle had begun to reclaim the edges of the Kokoda airfield and drainage remained a huge challenge, but with the use of prison labour and determination to do a good job, Elliot-Smith had the airstrip functioning again – what should have been a very timely result in the light of events of the near future.

With two operable airstrips and Bert's possession of the radio originally supplied by Ward Williams in 1934 and upgraded in 1936 to a portable AWA receiver and transmitter operated by a bicycle, communications between Kokoda and other posts were amazingly efficient for the times. Daily weather reports on the capricious Kokoda Gap were invaluable to the many aircraft now crossing the island between Moresby and northern stations and towns. Bert became expert at analysing and predicting the weather in the Kokoda Gap and the Yodda Valley. Although the pilots joked with him that the visibility from the cockpit of their aircraft was apparently proportionate to the urgency of the cargo on board, Bert seemed to know when, even if the valley was often 'socked in' at 7 a.m., by the time the planes arrived, all would be fine and clear.

Having taken a further lease of 990 acres that he called Amada Plantation, and needing to get 300 acres planted with rubber within two years to meet the terms of the lease, early in 1940 Bert continued with his policy of helping out family members by providing them employment and an adventurous life when he engaged Meryl's cousin David Marsh. David was a young man of 17 years who proved to be an enthusiastic and hard-working addition to the staff. Meryl's father Hubert Holliday had also landed on hard times, so Bert engaged him to assist with the building program. The only non-family European employees at the time were Gordon Chapman, a friend of Wallace's, and Bert Garbutt, an experienced miner who stayed at the Yodda until 1941.

In late April 1940, Wallace and Gordon were due for leave. On their way to Australia they decided, unbeknown to Bert, that they should enlist in the Australian Army. Wallace was allotted to the 2/2nd Machine Gun Battalion. Gordon would end up in the 7th Artillery Division.

After training at Ingleburn, then on to the facilities at Cowra, Wallace's fledgling battalion was given a few weeks leave before embarking for the Middle East. Dressed proudly in his AIF uniform, he decided to duck home to Papua and take Hally with him, as she had been away from Alfred for some time recovering from a string of illnesses. Also on board was the ubiquitous Robo Robo. With Orme Denny once again as his pilot, Wallace's unbelievable luck with flying continued when history repeated itself and they crashed on landing at the Yodda. Fortunately for Hally, she must have stopped off in Moresby, as she was not on board. Wallace and Orme again walked away unscathed but this time the aircraft was unsalvageable. Observing all this, no wonder poor Meryl hated having to go anywhere near planes in Papua. In later years, stories would be told of one particular native who had flown about three times and each time his plane had crash-landed. With the philosophical approach that Papuans have to such matters, he accepted that this must be the way it was done, and by the third time just grabbed his *kiapa* (billum bag), climbed out the nearest available exit and went about his business. It would not have been surprising if Wallace reacted the same way. He certainly seemed to shrug off any fear of flying when his experiences would surely have grounded anyone else.

Bert was disappointed that Wallace was leaving him when there was so much work yet to be done, but he understood and was very proud of his little brother for going off to fight for a country that had really not treated him that well during his life to date.

Bill Oakes's *Muzzle Blast: Six Years of War with the 2/2nd Australian Machine Gun Battalion, AIF*, tells the story of Wallace's battalion but it does not include the tales of some fairly harrowing experiences for this patriotic young man who his army mates affectionately called 'The Kokoda Kid'. These best left unprinted incidents no doubt contributed to his sometimes bitter moods and excessive drinking in later years.

§

If Wallace had known what was going to happen back in PNG during his time in the Middle East he probably would have opted to stay and help Herbert, as he always called his brother, and fight for his country closer to home.

In October 1941, Bert, Meryl, Carl and Mary headed down south for some overdue leave, leaving Alfred, Pop Holliday and David Marsh behind to manage at the Yodda. They travelled with the newly formed airline Carpenter Airways in a DH84, which had just begun a regular service from Moresby to Sydney. They spent a quiet holiday at Manly catching up with relatives and friends and savouring seaside living. On 7 December, they were enjoying lunch in a King Street restaurant in Sydney when the news was broadcast of the attack by Japanese fighters and bombers on Pearl Harbor. The broadcaster advised that war had been declared on Japan by America, Australia and the Allies. The enormity of all this and what it meant to her and her family was not lost on Meryl, who rushed from the restaurant, gagging from the sheer force of her terror.

Straight away, Bert contacted Carpenter Airlines to arrange return tickets for the whole family, but he was advised that women and children would not be allowed to travel. Meryl wanted to argue the point with the airlines. Memories of the tales Hally had told her of her internment in horrific conditions in Australia in World War I, despite being an Australian, just because she was married to a German, filled Meryl with fear. She would much rather take her risks back in Papua with Bert by her side. Eventually, with much trepidation and heartache, she had to accept that she should stay in Sydney with the children. Bert settled her in at Penrith with her Aunty Dinah Jones and boarded a plane back to Papua on 11 December 1941. Meryl recalled a few years later that the day he left to board the plane and she saw him disappearing around the street corner she said to herself, 'I shall never see him again.'

On his arrival in Port Moresby, Bert took it upon himself to report to Brigadier B. Morris, General Officer in Command of the 8th Military District, which had been set up as part of the Australian Defence System on 1 August 1940 and covered Papua and the Mandated Territory of New Guinea. If required, he would have joined up there and then, but Morris advised him to return to the Yodda and carry on operations awaiting further orders. Since mid-1939, Australia had been undergoing a slow, unfolding realisation of the threat posed by Japan, but all preparations in Moresby were based on the expectation of a seaborne attack. A paragraph in an article in the *Pacific*

Island Monthly in January 1939 noted: 'The topography is such that the port could easily be defended against approach from the sea. At the back are the foothills leading up into the high mountains – there could be no approach from there.'

Reliable maps of the Territory were hard to come by, and the authorities in Australia, and even the recently posted military in Papua's capital, had the false impression that, even if the Japanese should opt for an overland strike on Moresby, the site known as The (Kokoda) Gap was something of an obstacle at which any advancing enemy troops could be 'cut off at the pass'. The Gap is actually just an 11-kilometre-wide dip in the mountain range convenient for air traffic to bridge the Owen Stanleys.

Hence, in December 1941 when Bert passed through the capital, which at the time had a European population of less than 400, there was only a detachment of the 15th Battalion helping with public works around the town, two companies of the 49th Battalion, plus a detachment of the 13th Field Regiment who were manning the single gun emplacement mounted on Paga Hill – pointed out to sea of course – the lessons of Singapore yet to be learnt.

On the day Bert flew back to Yodda, Morris had ordered the evacuation of all white non-combatants to Australia, so his first duty was to put his stepmother Hally on a milk-run plane ride to Sydney. The flight out of the Yodda was initially in doubt because the wet season was in full swing and the strip was in a very boggy state. During Bert's absence, a Trimotor Ford VH-UBI flown by Captain Tommy O'Dea had bogged on the aerodrome and had to be pushed off the runway by Bert's labour force, under instructions from David Marsh. It had only just been repaired and flown out when Bert arrived home. Hally was lucky to catch a flight. As the number of expatriate women brought to Moresby for evacuation increased, most had to fly to Cairns and catch trains further south, or go on boats that wound their way through the islands hugging the coast of Queensland to avoid encountering Japanese raiders. Kokoda was now under the control of Claude Champion, one of the many members of the Champion family who worked in administration in the Territory at that time. Kokoda Station became the staging point for women and children being evacuated from the Bulolo goldfields. By New Year's Day 1942, the only white women left in Papua were a sprinkling of missionaries and nurses, and some isolated or recalcitrant planters' wives. At Yodda, Bert Garbutt had already departed and gone back to Townsville, where he intended to join up, following in the tradition of his well-known military family after whom his home town airport was named. His departure left only Bert, Alfred, Pop and David Marsh to carry on.

§

After the fall and occupation of Rabaul by invading Japanese forces on 23 January 1942, hostilities escalated quickly. The first bombs fell on Moresby on 3 February, killing only one person and inflicting very little damage, but causing a mass exodus of the natives who deserted their employment and headed for the hills or west along the coast to Daru. Port Moresby had at least established a blackout regime but the uninformed local people in their villages continued to light their evening fires, making them sitting targets for enthusiastic Japanese bombers. These enemy aircraft had to fly over the Yodda Valley and the Owen Stanley Ranges on their way to Moresby for their strafing and bombing missions, so Bert was able to use his radio to report to Moresby, giving them ample warning of air raids. This continued throughout the months of February and March. In early March, Bert observed about 60 planes pass overhead on their way to Moresby. On their return, one of them made a couple of runs over Kokoda Station and dropped four bombs. They missed their target but gave the locals a hell of a fright, to put it mildly. Despite these 'minor' obstacles, Bert continued to arrange charter aircraft to operate into the Yodda, stocking up on a good supply of foodstuffs. It was at about this time that he was instructed to sabotage Yodda airfield to prevent enemy aircraft landing, and so he strategically placed his old gold mining steel sluices and logs across the field.

When Japanese Zeros sank three Catalinas off the Papuan coast, Morris got serious about mobilising what forces he had. He instructed a small group of the Papuan Infantry Battalion led by Lieutenant H. J. Jesser to cross the mountains from Moresby to Buna in order to patrol the coastline between Buna and the Waria River. They had to pick their way over the old mail trail, last used around 1932 and now degenerated into a series of tracks from village to village, confused by intertwining native hunting pads and with fairly dilapidated shelters at the various resting points between the dozen or so villages en route. In January, two more militia battalions, the 39th and 53rd, had arrived in Moresby, raising troop numbers to Brigade strength. Formed in 1941, the 39th, comprising mostly inexperienced 18- and 19-year-old conscripts mainly from Victoria, had suddenly found itself in Port Moresby with little or no training. They were armed with World World War I era weapons and led by officers considered too old for overseas service. The 53rd were just as young, with even less training, having virtually been 'shanghaied' from the suburbs of Sydney and not even allowed to farewell their families. Morris had also drafted a plan for the administration of native affairs, setting up the Papuan Administrative Unit from which emerged the Australian New Guinea Administrative Unit (ANGAU), later sometimes called The Third Force because it ultimately played as vital a role in the New Guinea campaign as both the Australian and American defence forces.

One of the first major appointments he made in ANGAU was of magistrate Sydney Elliot-Smith to the position of captain and commander of the local Volunteer Defence Force. Elliot-Smith was a stocky, forceful but happy-go-lucky fellow with twinkling blue eyes and a laugh like the roar of a bull. Always considered to be a good man to have around in an emergency, he obviously had strong leadership skills. Until the cessation of civil administration, he acted as liaison officer between administrator and commandant. On 16 February, Morris advised all district magistrates by telegram: 'Elliot-Smith will issue you instructions in future. Carry on as usual. Vigorous patrolling to be carried out. Establishment embodies all into the Army.'

All other able-bodied white men had been called up on 25 January. Many older plantation owners had fled to Australia, leaving only their junior staff to keep production going, but the most infamous exit was what came to be known as the 'Daru Derby', where a caravan of mainly government employees made their escape via Daru on to Thursday Island then Queensland.

Thus, in February, despite the ever increasing threat of an onslaught of Japanese, and acknowledgment that a land offensive was increasingly likely, military authorities seemed more concerned with Bert's productivity than his potential as a soldier. Yodda Goldfields had started to experience some problems with desertion of their workers, particularly those Bert had brought in from other districts, as word travelled on the native grapevine of strange activities in New Britain and on the main island's north coast.

Claude Champion wrote to Bert as follows:

This morning I received a radio from the Military Authorities at Port Moresby and the following extract concerns the gold mining at Yodda:

'INFORM KIENZLE ALSO CARRY ON' . . .

I have sent a message down the road to all V.C.s to arrest deserters and within a few days I am sending out several RPCs to help with the colossal task. Kokoda Rubber Plantation is also to be reopened as soon as tappers can be engaged. If desertions continue at Yodda I will suggest to the military that when the RPC has been increased here that armed guards be placed on the goldfields to ensure that production of gold is maintained with an adequate labour force. I am also enquiring about the shipment of your gold and I will advise you on this matter as soon as I have had a reply on my radio.

On 24 February, he followed this up with a 'Minute Paper': 'Inform Kienzle ship gold as opportunity offers to ADM 8MD who will arrange shipment to district finance officer.'

Malaya, Singapore and other parts of South-East Asia had fallen into the hands of the Japanese, so Australia would soon be relying heavily on its own sources for vital raw materials. At this stage, although all agricultural produce including rubber was being shipped by the army, it was consigned to its owners or their agents in Australia and proceeds still went to these owners. This was to change in May 1942, at which time Morris issued the Plantation Control Order, which gave complete control of plantations and their produce to the senior officer for the time being exercising military command of Australian New Guinea, that being none other than himself. He also gave himself control of all plantation labour, which he administered through ANGAU's Plantation Production Staff Section. Extreme as this seemed at the time and as much as it alarmed the planters, it gave him what proved to be the vital ability to strip estates of their labour for the war effort.

On 5 March, Bert received another 'Minute Paper' from Champion that said:

Dear Sir, With reference to Military call up of men between the ages of 18 and 45 I have to advise of the following radio from HQ Port Moresby ... to magistrate from ADFM8MD Kienzle and Marsh are to be left alone provided they carry on with their jobs to mine inform them.

January 1942 found Japan in the midst of good war news in southern Asia and Tokyo was considering ways to protect these gains in a strategy called 'Fringe Outposts Campaign'. There were two such fringe outposts: Guadalcanal on the left flank and Port Moresby on the right, which guarded an entrance later called Hell's Gate. The left flank anchors on the south-east tip of the Solomons while the right flank was the only important port of the south-east shore of Papua, Port Moresby. Moresby was practically unknown to most Japanese and the Imperial Army had only one map of New Guinea, which they had located among their dusty files – a British War Office reference map dated 1915. However, on 10 March when a detachment of South Sea Corps was attacked off Lae by 60 Allied carrier planes, sinking several transports, the hot heads at Supreme HQ Tokyo were inflamed enough to give orders that Port Moresby should be taken with minimum delay.

Bert's continual reprieves could not go on forever and, sure enough, around the ungodly hour of midnight on 31 March, he was awakened by a loud knocking on the door of his home at Yodda and was confronted by a native police constable who handed him an important message from the new ARM Peter Brewer. The message stated:

> Radio instructions have just been received at this office that you are to cease operations and together with your staff proceed to Port Moresby immediately. I shall be over tomorrow to arrange with you about closing down of the mine and plantations and also to arrange transport of yourself and staff to Buna, at which place a vessel will be waiting to take you to Port Moresby. I will be obliged if you will treat this as a matter of extreme urgency.

The next morning, Brewer, who Bert had met several times both socially and on administrative matters, arrived at the Yodda as advised. Like all his fellow ARMs in the same position, in February he had automatically been given the rank of lieutenant in ANGAU; resident magistrates were made captains and patrol officers dubbed warrant officers. Brewer was operating at Kokoda under the command of Captain Tom Grahamslaw, OIC Northern District. It came as quite a shock to Bert when on addressing Brewer as Peter, he was curtly told, 'You will call me "Sir", thank you, Kienzle.' This was pretty typical of the latent animosity that continued to fester between public servants and those in private enterprise. Taken aback though he was, Bert acquiesced, but in a very short time he was also to reach the rank of lieutenant, then captain, promotions he earned through effort, not by nature of his pre-war position. Being the dignified gentleman that he was, when Bert later met Brewer again he just gave a wry smile when Peter was obliged to salute Bert and call him 'Sir'. Mind you, once he became a lieutenant he took great pleasure in addressing all correspondence to Brewer 'Dear Pete', despite the latter insisting on addressing him as Lieutenant Kienzle.

Brewer instructed Bert that he was to pay off all labour, of which there were about 200 at the time, and that this was to be done in his presence so that he could report that all was fair and correct and there could be no comebacks at a later date. Bert arranged for a skeleton crew of volunteers to remain as there were some goats, pedigree pigs, ducks and poultry that needed to be cared for. The one bull and five milking cows that David Marsh had brought from the coast in a tricky cattle drive only a few months earlier Brewer insisted on taking across to Kokoda Station. Bert quietly spoke to his most loyal boss-boys, Kordunga and Morso, telling them that he would be in touch as soon as he could and that they should carry on tapping as much rubber as possible. He asked 10 or so of his best tappers to stay at Yodda for this purpose. As the trees had only just started to come into production, output would not be a lot, but Bert figured every little bit would help the war effort. He instructed them to care for the acres of gardens planted at the Yodda that were flush with healthy sweet potatoes, taro, yams, sugar cane and pineapples. The plantation stores were also well stocked and he advised Kordunga and his two houseboys Simi and Jack to guard them and to ensure they did not get into enemy hands – to distribute them to all their families and other natives in the area before this happened.

He gave David Marsh the task of escorting Bert's father Alfred and his father-in-law Hubert to Buna, and as they said their farewells on the last day of March, they placed bets with each other as to when the war might end. Marsh said June 1942, Pop Holliday nominated January 1943 and Bert, December 1942 – all too optimistic as it turned out. On Easter Monday, 6 April, the two elderly gentlemen then boarded a coastal vessel and made a long, potentially dangerous and ultimately adventurous trip to Moresby via Dogura, Milne Bay, Samarai and Abau, arriving at Moresby in early May just after the Coral Sea battle. Of particular excitement on their journey was when they stopped at Abau on the south coast of Papua, east of Moresby, and had to take on board a captured Japanese pilot they believed to be the first such prisoner to be taken in the New Guinea campaign. The story goes that he was escorting bombers strafing Port Moresby but ran out of gas and tried to land on a narrow and hazardous beach fronting a coconut plantation. He came down at right angles to the beach, bounced in the air, lost one wing on a coconut tree, spun and hit another, after which the fuselage corkscrewed into the ground. He was uninjured apart from a scratch to the arm but gave himself up to the natives, who brought him to Abau. They last saw him in irons in a prison camp in Port Moresby but Pop Holliday kept his identification badge as a memento of the incident and he sent this to the War Memorial after the war.

In addition to this episode, they survived violent thunderstorms, raging seas, engine difficulties and overflights by both enemy and Allied aircraft to eventually reach Moresby, from where they were lucky to get transport on the MV *Taroona* to Australia, arriving in Townsville on 11 May. Safe at last on home soil, they caught trains to Brisbane then Sydney. Having put the two men safely onto the boat, Marsh reported to the nearest government station to enlist as was now expected of all able-bodied men.

Once Bert was satisfied he had done all he could at Yodda, he reported again to Brewer, who had changed his mind about him travelling to Moresby by sea and instead instructed him to take a number of the native deserters who had fled the capital, but been rounded up in the Northern Division, back to their jobs in Moresby. This entailed Bert's first land crossing over the Owen Stanleys and it took him and his troop of 64 deserters about seven days to reach Koitaki on the Sogeri plateau. Organising rations for this number of men at such short notice with no access to camping gear and limited portable food was a challenge in itself, yet Bert soon had his team ready to go, carrying their inadequate supplies in metal patrol boxes. These boxes were like a foot locker made of iron with long u-shaped handles so that they could be carried by two porters on a single pole. They were standard equipment for patrol officers in pre-war Papua and hidden in the bottom of his own personal box was the last of the gold Bert had extracted from his fields.

As with the Papuan Infantry Battalion group before him, Bert and his charges would have to try to select, from a series of tracks from village to village, the best route over the ranges. Most of the track from Kokoda through Deniki, Isurava and on to Alola was not too bad. This was Biagi country and Bert had a few of these people working for him and they knew him well. From Alola to the Koiari village of Kagi, however, was a no-man's-land, a place of darkness the Papuans called *vabula*. This was a buffer zone between two different tribal areas where by native custom any stray trespasser was fair game and where many a wanderer had disappeared without a trace over the centuries. Most of the track in this forbidden place was just a dark shadow hidden beneath the thickly matted foliage of intertwined creeping ground vines and stinging nettles that tugged at Bert's dungarees and tripped the unwary. From Alola to Eora Creek was one of the most dangerous portions of the journey, an almost vertical climb where one missed step could mean a long, painful fall to the raging torrent below. Once the track joined the fast-rising creek bed, it became a soul-destroying series of climbs and descents – up, down, up, up, down – along the dark, dank creek bed over slippery bulbous boulders and fungi-encrusted fallen trees, through the constantly dripping foliage where the springs ran along the track – often the springs *were* the track. Bert's boots and the boys' bare feet had no respite from the sodden, soggy soil and the ice-cold wind created by the rapids bit at their faces and ears as it whistled down the gullies. Bert was very fit from all the walking between the goldfields and the rubber plantings – there was no transport at the Yodda – but he had not done a lot of hill climbing for some years and this trek tested him to his very limits.

From the Eora, the track wound along the ridges to the ancient virgin jungle where the dappled sunlight was a high, distant tease. Even on the clearest day, the sun's rays didn't penetrate to the forest floor. At the Eora there were a couple of broken-down old huts that had been used by the mailmen as a mail exchange point many years before, but in most places sleeping shelters had to be hastily erected from pandanus leaves as protection from the rain that seemed to fall like clockwork just as they needed to make camp for the night in the fast-fading light. There is no twilight in this part of the world. One minute it is light and seemingly the next it is pitch-black. Only a fool walks in the jungle at night if he has a choice, so days had to be planned to try to arrive at a suitable campsite in time. And the rain! The Yodda valley and surrounds produce every type of rain, from days and days of drizzle to short sharp afternoon showers to big, fat thundery rain. Then there is the stuff that arrives by the bucketload with seemingly no air gaps at all among the sheets of water. Bert was used to all this but it was certainly not enjoyable when trekking a rough mountain track with a troop of somewhat reluctant charges.

Each day in this no-man's-land they had to clear the track, all the way straight up the face of Mt Bellamy until they reached the highest point of the trek at over 2,100 metres. From here the terrain became a little more undulating and the vegetation more open and alpine. Although much of the ground was still covered in moss, it was interspersed with thickets of bamboo. This the boys needed to slash with their machetes, leaving razor sharp edges that could slice through a boot with ease – one nick of the skin often quickly resulting in blood poisoning. Drinking water was a worry here too on this high ground, with few sources from which to replenish canteens.

It was such a refreshing moment for Bert when they finally stepped out of the forest and for the first time in nearly four days saw a horizon – looking down on Kagi with its surrounding vegetable gardens and in the distance, seeing the smoke from the cooking fires of other villages. They were now in Koiari country and Bert knew that they had broken the back of this mammoth walk but he could not afford to be lulled into a false sense of security. The Koiaris had a reputation as a ruthless tribe, and many a foreigner had disappeared while traversing their territory. The boys with Bert knew this and were very nervous. No one got much sleep during this part of the journey.

From Kagi on, the tracks were much more defined being often used by the villagers as they moved among their wantoks (members of the same tribe), at Efogi, Menari, Nauro and Iorabaiwa. Fresh food could be traded for salt or other special treats. The Biagis liked to swap for tobacco but being under the influence of the Seventh Day Adventists, the Koiaris were not supposed to smoke. Marginally more comfortable accommodation could be found in village guesthouses or missionaries' huts. From here on the air was a little less humid and the rainfall not quite so relentless, and as they dropped down to lower altitudes and got closer to their destination the vegetation became less intense. A few cabbage gums and other eucalypts caught Bert's eye and reminded him of his 'time before' on this south side of the range. A section of kunai on the dry ridge near the village of Iorabaiwa was most unpleasant in the middle of the day, with the heat radiating off the 2-metre-high blades of grass and no cool streams around to relieve burning brows and quench parched throats.

What a relief it was then for Bert when he reached his destination at the government station at Fourteen Mile outside Port Moresby, where he handed his charges over to the authorities and reported for enlistment. Little did he know at the time how vital this trail he had just navigated would become over the ensuing months, and what an important part it would play in Australia's war history.

§

Bert was immediately given the rank of warrant officer class II in the Australian Citizen Military Forces. He later received a written warrant to this effect addressed to P.461 Pte Kienzle, H.T. and signed by Major General Basil Morris GOC New Guinea Force. He was now Warrant Officer Kienzle PX177. He was initially posted to Itikinumu Rubber Plantation, Koitaki, where he helped the manager Colin Sefton and was involved in general administrative and organisational duties as well as search and rescue of downed Allied aircraft. One such plane that he located was the Kittyhawk shot down by Japanese fighters, inside which he found the body of Flight Sergeant Granville of Sydney. Granville of 75 Squadron RAAF was shot down by Japanese Zeros in an interception over Moresby. Bert and his boys brought Granville's body back for burial. As a memento of what was to be the first of many such unpleasant tasks of search and rescue, Bert kept a piece of canvas from the fuselage of the P40 Kittyhawk on which he wrote 'Sergeant R. J. C Granville, Empire Air Trainee KIA 18/4/42'.

He was then sent back to his old stamping ground at Kanosia, where he was instructed to open up the rubber estates at Doa and Lolorua and produce as much rubber as possible. Bert would rather have been at Yodda doing just that, but he appreciated that Kanosia was in a much better position to contribute significant quantities of the needed resource to the war effort. Most of the labour at Kanosia had joined the swarms of people fleeing Moresby for Daru in February, but RM Mick Healy, an old mate of Wallace's from the Fly River expedition, had managed to re-recruit a lot of them by the time Bert arrived on the scene.

On 4 May, Bert received instructions from Captain Brian Molloy of ANGAU to report to headquarters, New Guinea Force, for attestation and medical examination and then to return to Yodda and commence tapping the rubber both there and at Awala, a plantation about 8 kilometres the other side of Kokoda. With no vehicle available to travel between the two plantations, this in itself was a big ask: the first of many to be made of Bert. The letter even instructed him to tap the rubber at '20 inches up and at 20 inches round' – a case of 'telling your grandmother how to suck eggs', which really got Bert's goat! Probably as a result of the implications of the Battle of the Coral Sea, where the American navy successfully intercepted the Japanese fleet headed for Port Moresby, this directive must have been rescinded.

Bert was back at Kanosia when on 29 June he received an urgent message to report to HQ Port Moresby immediately. The telegram addressed to J. B. McKenna at Kanosia stated: 'Instruct Kienzle return Moresby quickest available means stop bring gear.' On 2 July, a RAAF crash launch under the command of Lieutenant Commander Hunt came to Kanosia to collect him and delivered him to Moresby. There he met a Lieutenant Pomeroy and was immediately ordered to report to Major Elliot-Smith. His old mate Syd welcomed him and after lunch at Military District HQ he was taken by staff car to Koitaki where, along with Lieutenant Thomas, he spent the night. Somewhere in among all this Bert fitted in an unexpected but enjoyable round of golf on the local 'course'. This would prove to be his last chance to relax for a very long time and he would later often ponder how much better it would have been if they had called him up sooner to begin the gargantuan task they were about to hand to him.

Back in May, American code-breakers intercepted and deciphered a Japanese message that clearly indicated their next operation would be over the Owen Stanleys. MacArthur chose to virtually disregard this one. He was preoccupied with his plans to mount an offensive based at Milne Bay to advance along the north coast of New Guinea and on to Rabaul and the Solomons.

Bert was immediately promoted to lieutenant then handed a copy of New Guinea Force Instruction No. 13, which advised that Elliot-Smith, now a major, was chief supervising officer of Bert and 14 other ANGAU personnel plus surveyor Lieutenant Owers. Their duty was 'the construction of a road from McDonald's to Kokoda and the maintenance of supplies to the forces of the Kokoda District'. Bert was to take control of 1,000 native labourers on this line of communication to Kokoda from Ilolo, which was otherwise known as McDonald's Corner, being the site of old timer P. J. McDonald's plantation. The road was to commence construction no later than 29 June and be completed by 26 August 1942! Knowing well the terrain involved, Bert's comment at such a ludicrous request was: 'I have heard of superman but I have yet to see him in action!!' What he later said about the directive was: 'Some twit at headquarters had looked at a map and said "We'll put a road in there". Had it been possible it would have ranked as one of the most colossal engineering feats of the world!' With one small bulldozer, a few packhorses and mules of the 1st Independent Light Horse Troop and a few picks and shovels the only equipment available, it was a mere pipe dream. Only just over 11 kilometres of the road was ever completed from McDonald's Corner to Owers' Corner, wide enough for jeeps and to take, with some difficulty, the 25-pounders that would eventually arrive on the scene.

Bert's friend, Doc Vernon AAMC, had most recently been medical officer at a native hospital at Sapphire Creek and was in the process of setting up a new hospital at Ilolo staffed with medical orderlies from Sapphire. Bert quickly requested that he be appointed MO in charge of native carriers, with all medical personnel, both European and native, under his orders. By now, Doc was 59 years old, tall and gaunt looking but still fit, even though a World War I concussion meant he was deaf as a beetle. He was determined to stay in Papua to serve his country. Earlier attempts to send him back to Australia with others considered past serving age had been unsuccessful. At one stage he was virtually a wanted man – on the run from authorities who had him listed for repatriation. In keeping with the character that won him a Military Cross for Conspicuous Gallantry in the Great War, Doc dug his heels in, ignoring the disrespect and slights thrown his way by several officers at HQ who called him too old and a nuisance. Eventually they reneged and put him to work in native health where his expertise was legendary and would soon prove vital.

On his arrival at Ilolo, Bert was handed a copy of a letter Doc had written to the Commanding Officer Native Medical Services, Captain Jensen, expressing deep concern about the potential for an outbreak of dysentery because of poor hygiene and bad accommodation. In particular, the habits of native cookboys and the ignorance of officers with regard to construction of proper latrines meant that the environment was ripe for fly breeding and hence dysentery. In addition, the 600 or so natives who had been seconded from among the indentured plantation labour of the area's estates were sullen and unhappy. Illness was rife and desertions were common. Intertribal conflicts and fears bubbled ominously beneath the surface.

Bert first gathered all the men together and addressed them in Motu, explaining what was happening and why they were being required to work together and do these different jobs of carrying supplies and building a road. The resultant understanding produced a boost in spirits and a much improved attitude to the job. Bert then set about ordering them to construct new huts, for themselves as well as the Europeans, and better located, deeper latrines using local materials, as there were no army supplies available for such a purpose at this time. This rare rapport of Bert's and his ability to communicate with the natives in their own language and explain as best he could the reason for their tasks was to prove vital for cooperation and morale over future months. One of his most significant and admirable skills was his patience and his willingness to listen, something the Papuan people valued greatly in their *taubada*.

Having considered the enormity of the tasks given him, Bert had concentrated on getting his priorities right and decided that only after local labourers were appeased and accommodation improved could roadwork commence. The natives' main job was clearing the road of trees, which involved grubbing the roots in preparation for the oncoming bulldozer. Like much of the jungle in this area, the predominant trees had no real tap roots, so this was not too difficult a task.

No sooner had he commenced this project than he was advised by Captain 'Ned' Kelly of the 39th Battalion, now, OIC of the Line of Communication (L of C), Ilolo to Kokoda, that a Captain Sam Templeton CO of B Company of the 39th Battalion had been waiting for some days for someone to guide him across the Owen Stanleys to Kokoda. A site had been chosen at Dobodura, inland from Buna for an airbase to carry the war closer to the Japanese, now firmly entrenched at Rabaul, licking their wounds and regrouping. New Guinea Force was instructed to supply a rifle company to secure Kokoda then move on to protect the American Engineer Regiment assigned to the construction of this forward base. Templeton and his men were chosen for this job. They were to march to the site over the mountains, with their supplies to be shipped by sea to Buna.

Having recently traversed this route himself, Bert was the obvious guide for these troops and he arranged with Templeton that they would depart on 8 July, giving him four days to get things organised at Ilolo. In no time, he had two large grass-covered shelters completed and had placed WOII J. Rae from Ubiri in charge of this base camp at Ilolo. He then put Private Wainwright in control of the native labour for the road works that had commenced on a stretch from Ilolo to Uberi, ultimately reaching Ower's Corner which was named after the surveyor who worked on the project. WO Jack Wilkinson, ex AIF Middle East and Greece, now an ANGAU Medical Officer, was to accompany Bert to Kokoda.

Bert then put together a group of 140 carriers made up of a mixture from about 15 different tribes from all over Papua – mainly Tufi, Kapakapa, Orokaiva, Goaribari and Kiwai – to escort Templeton and his troops. He intended to carry out his assignment of commencing establishment of an efficient line of communication across the Owen Stanleys even as he led B Company to Kokoda. The Japanese were now regularly flying low over the Trail area, especially around Iorabaiwa. They had obviously been ordered to recce the region on their way back from their bombing forays over Moresby, and it was surely now fairly obvious that they did have plans to cross the Owen Stanleys.

Throughout this journey, Bert seconded the village people, Koiaris and Biagis, to improve the Trail in their area and to build, improve and extend the accommodation facilities at the various staging camps along the way. This, along with the numerous other tracks he cut as the campaign progressed, is why many people contend that Bert really blazed much of what was to become the war trail. Wilkinson called him a wonderful physical specimen and a tower of strength as he worked with demonic energy organising labour, establishing camps and food dumps at the same time as he guided the troops along the track. Another young digger in the Company, Lieutenant Arthur 'Judy' Garland, wrote in his diary that Bert was a man for whom they quickly developed respect and admiration, and that they were destined to hear a lot of him in the ensuing months. To many of the young men of B Company he was a rather forbidding character with a powerful presence and a confidence in his environs that had them in awe.

Traditionally, Papuan villages include at least one rest house, and other shelters had been set up over the years when the trail was used for mail deliveries; but with the exception of Ubiri, no camp or staging place had sufficient accommodation for a company of men and their attachment of native carriers. Despite the fact that on this journey the natives carried the soldiers' packs for them, a luxury that soon had to be forgone, by the time they reached Nauro they were exhausted and Templeton ordered a day of rest. The men were amazed at the speed with which the local boys could erect quite substantial and comfortable shelters, and they were also most appreciative of the baked sweet potato (*kaima*), bananas (*biku*) and pawpaw Bert arranged the villagers to supply to supplement the limited army rations B Company had been able to bring with them.

By the time Bert and Templeton's mob reached Kagi, camps were established, or well under way to being so at Ilolo, Iorabaiwa, Nauro, Menari and Efogi. Once at Kagi, Bert sent back his carriers who had come with him from Ilolo with instructions to build up supplies at the various depots. He believed it was best to have native labour based at each of these stations, supervised by ANGAU personnel, so that they could carry between stages. They seemed more content with not having to travel too far from a set point and, of course, it was physically less demanding. This policy was not always possible as the war progressed, but it worked well in this initial phase of establishing supply points.

From Kagi, Bert and the others breached The Gap, back on through the horror area of *vabula*, with its leeches, stinging nettles and miles of oppressive jungle, before again reaching Biagi country and the descent to Kokoda and the Yodda Valley. What seemed to stick in the memory of the troops were the little native bees, commonly called 'sweat bees', which stuck in large numbers to any bare skin, tickling more than stinging but extremely irritating all the same. Then there was the prickly creeping vine with small pink flowers similar to the infamous lantana that is a pest in Australia, but fortunately for the jungle ecosystem, the native vine is not as voracious or as woody and thorny as the Australian version. Despite this misclassification, the name 'lantana' would become synonymous with the track for the boys of the 39th and was adopted as a symbol of their service on the Trail. Worse than this vine was the lawyer cane, otherwise known as 'wait a while' for obvious reasons, and which some diggers also seemed to call 'razor wire'. Various theories circulate as to the reasons for the name 'lawyer cane', but one popular one is because once a lawyer gets you in his clutches, it's hard to get away.

About six hours from Kagi they passed through Eora Creek, which is the narrowest part of the trail when approaching from the north and provides an excellent water supply. Always on the lookout for potential defensive positions, Bert considered this point but soon discarded the idea because the area suitable for a camp was far too small. Further down the mountain at Isurava, the rest houses and shelters were filthy and the track in a pretty bad state, so they pushed on to Deniki where they rested for one night while Bert and Captain Templeton continued on to Kokoda. The boys of the 39th followed the next day and set up camp, 10 and 11 Platoons on either side of the airstrip, and 12 Platoon in the rubber plantation south of Kokoda. All was quiet there, the area being relatively unaffected by the hostilities to date. How quickly this was about to change. Wilkinson later wrote:

> Kokoda suited us well while we were there. There was plenty
> of native fruit and vegetables and the men were in good shape.
> The climate was good. Mosquitoes were few. Housing was
> good. We had radio communications. Life looked sweet. For
> a full week.

The three men then walked on out to Yodda where Bert checked on his home and the men he had left in charge. Kordunga and Morso had protected his stores reasonably well, although some tools and batteries were missing. Now, as there was nothing available at Kokoda, he had to take as many of these supplies with him as he and his men could carry. B Company were badly in need of provisions to be able to continue their journey to the coast, and Bert himself needed food for his return trek. Ever the businessman, he made a list of everything provided to Templeton and his men – cod-liver oil, sugar, tea, hard biscuits, cans of beetroot, carrots, peas, parsnips and mixed vegies, tins of salmon, pilchards, sausages and tomatoes, lamb and green peas, minced collops [sic]. He also grabbed shovels, picks, knives and axes, benzene, kerosene and lubricating oil – even his faithful typewriter. The boys of B Company realised how lucky they were to get these stores and to have Bert there to get them the best food they had eaten for over a week. Cec Driscoll and a few of his mates experimented with a brew of hard biscuits and freshly chopped pawpaw mixed with a bit of powdered milk, all mashed up and heated to create an inimitable porridge. Then there was the green pawpaw, sliced and fried in their dixies in the oil strained from the tins of bully beef – the closest thing they could create to match potato chips.

Bert had been thinking hard as he trudged over the mountains, working mostly with natives he had not met before. He had been thinking that he should have the best of his own men from Yodda with him. Furthermore, he did not want them to be overseen by just any other European because he felt many of them did not respect the Papuans. So, he had Kordunga appointed to the police and Gagamu, Jighetti, Pogimo, Hitolo, Umbuta and Huika either joined the Papuan Infantry Battalion (PIB) or stuck close by him as his 'shooting boys'. All of these men would still be with him until the day they died or the day he finally left PNG 38 years later. None were killed during the war.

Having checked on his other properties on the way, on arrival at the Yodda, Bert again asked the ever reliable Morso to stay behind and keep an eye on things and continue to oversee tapping of as much of the rubber as possible. Amazingly, Morso and his men would manage to keep producing for several months, carrying the scrap rubber around enemy lines and on to Koitaki. On his way home, Morso would then catch up with Bert wherever he was along the track and give him a report of events at the Yodda and quantities of rubber tapped. It was rare for expatriate men in Papua at the time to be able to claim such loyalty and devotion from their boys. Bert's formative years in Fiji were standing him in good stead in this Melanesian land he had chosen for his home and the respect he received from his workers was the envy of many a pompous patrol officer.

Bert wrote to Meryl a few days later saying that when he had paid this hurried visit to their home he found most of their belongings still intact but her precious piano covered in dust. He instructed her houseboys, Simi and Jack, to dust and sweep out all the houses. As he lunched at the Yodda with Sam Templeton and Lieutenant Graham, Bert said a silent prayer that it would not be long before he could return to his rough but beloved jungle home. With a heavy heart, he handed the keys to Lieutenant Graham, who was to be left in charge of all plantations and buildings in the Kokoda district.

Back at Kokoda Station, Bert spent some time catching up with Captain Grahamslaw, who then left on 16 July, accompanying Templeton on his way to take over stores from the *Gili Gili*, now supposedly docked at Buna, and to supervise the transport of these stores from the coast to Kokoda. Bert then set about recruiting 62 new carriers, Orokaivas from the Kokoda area along with some Tufis. On 17 July after a delayed start due to heavy rain, they set off on their return journey – Bert's third trip along the overland route to Moresby. He was eventually to traverse the route eight times in four months – more than any other white man at the time. His new carriers were from flat and coastal areas and they were not as physically robust as the first group; they had difficulty handling the steep ascents and descents and the extreme cold at high altitude. From Kagi to Ubiri there are six steep ridges, a real test of endurance.

In his second letter to his 'darling sweetheart', he wrote:

> Have learnt to sleep on bare boards, fall across slippery logs and bruise the old chest – must be made of tough fibre. Acting as mountain guide and leader to large parties is a responsibility and at the same time do a number of other jobs keeps me busy . . . wish I could tell you lots more about the journey but I can't. Have had lots of experiences since I left the last plantation.

On his arrival at Kagi this time, Bert wrote to Captain 'Ned' Kelly, currently the officer in charge of the Kokoda Line of Communication, and advised him that he had just returned over the range and that the track was a different proposition this time. Bad weather had started the day he left Kokoda, and as the track from Kagi to Kokoda had been badly neglected it was wet and slippery, with hazardous tree roots and rocky slabs of schist meaning every step had to be taken with care.

On this trip, distances, which were measured by time here, grew longer – a one-hour distance became a two-hour distance; a one day walk became almost a two-day slog.

Bert wrote further:

In my official letter you will note that I am trying hard to tie up worst stretch of the road or track i.e. from Kagi to Kokoda and that with no European help and poor native material. We require urgently 2 Europeans, one at Kagi and the other at Eora Ck Camp. Both camps over 4000ft . . . cold and wet . . . Stores are beginning to pile up here for Kokoda and Eora camps. If I should send my bunch of carriers numbering 90 odd to Ubiri there won't be any for staging from here unless Kokoda should come to light with 200–300 carriers. I know they are short of carriers for their work now greatly increased with incoming vessels. It will be a mistake to take carriers away from the various stations to carry forward a large quantity of stores in one batch – much better to stage stores from station to station and build up the number of carriers allotted to each station.

On 22 July, Kelly replied:

Your report and letter to hand. The position here is this. We may be required to move 600 troops through to Kokoda any day. One company of 120 men should have moved two days ago only for a change of plan. Carriers are not coming forward from ANGAU as expected. I have been making a lot of noise about it and have been promised men daily from today. We are placing rations at each stage and are using all carriers available for the job. I have just heard that troops will not move till after 26.7.42 so I think that by then we will be able to handle them alright.

In his official report, Bert had commented:

The establishment of small food dumps for a small body of troops was now under way as far as Kagi. This ration supply was being maintained by carriers over some of the roughest country in the world. But with the limited number of carriers available maintenance of supplies along this route was going to be impossible without the aid of dropping by plane. A carrier carrying only food stuffs consumes his load in 13 days and if he carries food supplies for a soldier it means six and a half days supply for both soldier and carrier. This does not allow for the porterage of arms, ammunition, equipment, medical stores, ordnance, mail and dozens of other items needed to wage war carried on the backs of men. The track to Kokoda takes eight days so the maintenance of supplies is a physical impossibility without the large scale cooperation of plane droppings.

All these theories and concerns would soon be put to the test when, unbeknown to Bert as he trudged over the mountains, the battle-trained Japanese Nankai Shitai landed at Buna on 21 July with over 2,000 troops and hundreds of press-ganged and enslaved Rabaul natives. Interestingly, in a conversation with Bill Guest of A Company 39th Battalion around this time, when asked where he thought the Japanese would make their landing, Bert said he felt it was most likely they would deliver their troops to the beaches at Buna, Gona and Sanananda. This they did, advancing virtually unopposed, across the bridge over the Kumusi at Wairope on up the Kokoda–Buna Road, engaging Templeton's B Company at Awala through Gorari and on to Oivi only three days later. Just over 90 men of 'Maroubra Force' – against just under 900 – yet the Japanese believed they were outnumbered two to one! 'Uncle Sam' Templeton, who Bert had come to like and respect as they crossed the mountains together, was killed in this battle when he set off on his own from Oivi back towards Kokoda to warn the rest of 16 Platoon that the enemy were approaching fast. Templeton's men reported hearing two shots ring out soon after he left them, but his body was never found.

Having walked from Kagi to Ubiri in one day, a fantastic effort in itself, in order to relay the message of the Japanese landing, Bert hurried on to Ilolo to meet with the 'brass' and pass on his report and urgent request for more carriers, a telephone cable to be urgently laid along the trail to the front, and arrangement of air drops to suitable staging points along the L of C. Ilolo was now the main base for supplies, with jeeps and pack animals as well as native porters being used to transport stores to Ubiri, the start of the carrier line.

The next day, Bert set off for his fourth traversing of the Kokoda Trail, this time with 500 carriers to follow on with supplies for A Company of the 39th Battalion. Several problems became apparent on this trip. Pilfering by villagers had been occurring at various staging camps along the way, and many of the camps still could not cope with the quantity of personnel arriving and needing accommodation at any one time. Some parts of the track, through kunai grass and over bare ridges, left troops and carriers exposed to enemy aircraft fire, so crossing these areas had be timed for early or late in the day. Communications had to be handwritten, or in Bert's case sometimes typed with his trusty typewriter on Australian Comforts Fund paper and carried across the track by faithful native 'mail boys'. He was meticulous about keeping carbon copies of all his correspondence and writing in his diary daily. Communications began to gradually improve with the telephone cable, or 'sigline' as it was called by army personnel, eventually being laid through to Efogi by 31 July. Once this cable was in place, Bert then also kept copies of every telegram sent and received.

As the campaign progressed, these siglines sometimes served a second purpose as a guide-line along the pitch-black track when the troops formed caravans of men carefully holding the scabbard of the bayonet on the back of the soldier in front. Occasionally the men would even collect handfuls of the phosphorescent fungi that lit up the tropical forest at night, and put it in their back pockets to make it easier for the bloke behind to stay in contact.

In the meantime, on 29 July, the Japanese had attacked Kokoda with overwhelming strength forcing Maroubra Force, now led by Majors Watson and Cameron, to retreat to Deniki. The troops straggled in to Deniki dumbfounded, disillusioned and in disarray. They had lost two leaders – Templeton then Owen – the latter being killed by a sniper in a skirmish at the end of the plateau. They felt orphaned and abandoned. Since the first encounters at Awala, they had operated on instinct and adrenalin. Their escape from Kokoda had been a shemozzle of small groups of men scattered through the rows of rubber trees and surrounding jungle. As they regrouped at Deniki, the enormity of what they had been through and what was ahead of them began to sink in. There was no feeling of being heroes, no real feeling of relief or satisfaction at their escape. The strongest emotion that these mostly raw and inexperienced young men recalled from those days was of fear. All they could do was turn to their fellow soldiers for support. From this point on, the fight became more about looking out for your mates than some burning desire to defend your country. Courage, mateship, endurance, sacrifice – but the greatest of these was mateship.

§

Reports were received of an enemy patrol being seen at Yodda. 'The Front' was now a perimeter defence at Deniki, and Bert was advised not to proceed any further forward from Isurava, but to pull back a distance and organise the supply line from the rear for rations and ammunition. The next staging camp at Eora Creek was not a suitable dropping ground for air supplies, and drops carried out a few days before at Kagi and Efogi had resulted in a very disappointing collection rate. One problem was that most pilots had very little experience in air dropping techniques. The defence forces had not yet developed effective methods of dropping stores, especially into jungle. Wallace Kienzle's 1936 expedition up the Fly River was one of the few where experiments were made with different methods. In 1942, the air force was using fighter planes to carry the stores, which were enclosed in two or more sacks, using the theory that the inner one would shatter but hopefully the looser outer one would remain intact. The Japanese were actually having more success using wicker baskets. Unfortunately for the Allies, target accuracy was poor and the bundles often completely disintegrated or were hard to find. Thus the types of provisions that could be delivered this way were limited.

On 29 July, Bert wrote to Meryl:

> I am fit and well after the fourth journey on this track towards home . . . Our home is in for some hot fighting and I am going to see what I can do. Don't worry about me dear – I'll look after others and myself to the best of my ability . . . All I have with me is a change of clothes, 2 blankets and one boy. The rest of my gear is back at the end of line. Every carrier is precious . . . Wish this business could only end soon but fear it will last for years. Hope we never lose this country. It would be a big loss. But Australia must have a bigger population and the breed must be better. – bigger, brighter, better and more of it will be the motto . . . This fight is going to be tough. Old Doc Vernon is an old tiger. As soon as he heard of it he made straight for the Valley – he is attached to my unit . . . Never thought I would have to not only help build and organise a big job in the army but also fight for my own home and properties. Wait until that day comes to a number of Australians in Australia. Hope it never comes to pass, but some people need shaking up. Trust my brother Wallace is safe.

One can only assume that by this stage he was already becoming frustrated with the sluggish response of Australian HQ, which seemed to have no concept of the supply problems ahead and no idea of the multitude of difficulties the diggers were up against in this jungle terrain. He remained baffled as to why HQ had not used the two airstrips at Kokoda to build up supplies on the north side of the Owen Stanleys, rather than sending them by sea, then overland, where they were accumulated too far from where they were needed.

Bert summarises his situation in his report as follows:

The period 2–31 July ended with the fact that I together with my carriers had taken across the Owen Stanley's Range 3 Company 39 Bn safely, who were now in action against a well prepared and equipped enemy who was making a determined effort to press forward to Port Moresby, via the 'Gap'. Our problem of supplying these troops in addition to carriers in the forward areas with food and ammunition was a real and serious one and had to be overcome by establishing a base closer to our Forward Defence Line. We did not have sufficient carriers for the job to keep supplies flowing along the long and arduous mountain trail from Moresby and the immediate prospects of securing additional carriers were not bright. The period had opened with the prospect of quietly building a road from Moresby to Kokoda with a time factor that was an impossibility from the start but as already stated above, ended with the fact that we were at war and at grips with a determined and ruthless enemy. Road building was a matter that I could not worry about for the time being but had to concentrate on keeping the carriers together and willing to play their part in this struggle and to find a dropping area which could be used closer to the line.

7

A TACTICAL RETREAT

Bert had now traversed the Kokoda Trail four times by foot, but before the war had flown over the area countless times more. During the flights on clear days he had noticed to the south-east of The Gap two apparently flat, treeless grassed areas, one larger than the other, which were obviously ancient lake beds now drained dry. As he racked his brains for a solution to the problem of successful air drops of vital supplies, he decided that if he could clear a route to one of these lakes it would be an ideal dropping zone.

On 29 July he had received a note from WO Jack Mason, friend and fellow planter from Awala, now also with ANGAU and currently at Deniki, about to head to Isurava.

The pencil-scrawled note read: 'Dear Bert, A note received from Deniki with message for you in it reads as follows "Message for Kienzle from Watson. Have one days supplies only for party here – send more urgent". Am sending this with a boy immediately.'

The problem was, where in God's name would these supplies come from when air drops into camps so far established were not a success? During this period of the campaign one ANGAU officer had his leg broken by falling tins of bully beef and one soldier was killed by the base plate of a mortar dropped from a supply plane. Another unfortunate incident, where tins of biscuits crashed through the roof of a kunai hut at Menari killing Private Jim Dynan and injuring five other hapless young diggers, earned the DC3s the nickname of 'biscuit bombers'.

Carrier lines from Moresby could not possibly meet the demand. A better drop zone was vital. Bert immediately advised Major W. T. Watson, CO Maroubra Force, of his idea to use the dry lakes, and requested permission to reconnoitre the area. On 31 July 1942, he received a scribbled note from Watson that said: 'Thanks for information per Sergeant Evenson. Food situation acute need all we can get. Investigate dry lakes and report if suitable for landing stores from planes in view of Kagi. Rush food through.'

On the first day of August, Bert trekked from Isurava to Eora, where he was surprised to find Elliot-Smith, who had just walked in from Moresby and with whom he also discussed his idea about the dry lakes. Syd was on his way to Deniki with his entourage of about 20 carriers carrying all his gear, including his treasured shower bath that he still insisted on having with him, as when on patrol before the war. This did not go down too well with the troops and he had to give up this luxury only a few days later. Bert at least had restricted himself from an early stage of his travels to one Kapakapa cookboy/batman who he tells Meryl does a pretty good job making army rations palatable, always adding the proviso in his letters of how much he misses her cooking.

Syd gave his enthusiastic support for Bert's plans, and so, permission granted, on 2 August Bert gathered together V. C. Sasi, R. P. C. Orama and five Koiaris from Kagi village – Laba, Siuli, Lavai, Lobe and Ligo – and at 8.40 a.m. they set off from Eora Creek camp in search of a track to the lakes.

In his official report of the campaign, he wrote of that day:

Left Eora to locate the dry lakes for a suitable dropping ground. Heard the bombing of Kokoda and Yodda by our planes about 0900hrs. There were many loud explosions. At 1200hrs I passed the signallers laying down the telephone lines right on top of the Main Range and at 1345hrs I sighted the dry lake due south by east of the track from Kagi. I descended east through very heavy jungle and followed a native hunting pad . . . guides were reluctant to show me the area. A taboo existed on the area except for a few who used it as a hunting ground at certain periods of the year. The hunting pad had not been used for some time – therefore most difficult to follow, although being flat the country proved good walking.

Being the geographical phenomenon that they are, combined with their strange and eerie presence as they loom through the mists at the top of the Owen Stanleys, the lakes were, and indeed still are to some, *taravatu, jilava garbuna* (forbidden, place of ghosts). Many legends about the evil spirits who inhabit the area instil fear into the Koiari people to this day. They took some convincing by Bert to go that last mile. After shivering through a cold, wet night, they broke camp early and, only about 20 minutes later, stepped through the end of the jungle onto a treeless plain. They had reached one of the dry lake beds. To the knowledge of Bert and the local people, no other white man had ever visited this area, and what a magnificent site it was both aesthetically and practically. A large patch of open ground with the look of a Scottish heath, about 1,200 metres long and 500 metres wide, perched right on the top of the Owen Stanley Ranges. A creek meandered through the middle of it cutting a shallow channel, and either side of this creek the ground was reedy and swampy. On the higher portions, the grass was short and tufty, and among it could be seen the tracks of quail and wild bush pigs. After the oppressiveness of the interminable jungle, to walk out onto the edge of this treeless 'plain' and behold a visible horizon was a soothing balm to tired eyes and claustrophobic minds.

The Koiaris with Bert were still very nervous about standing on this *tabu* ground and when he asked what the area was called they just hung their shaking heads and indicated that such evil places have no name. As he stood on the edge of this picturesque, potentially life-saving discovery, the sun was just rising, looming up over the ranges to the east and he thought of his good mate Major Elliot-Smith, who had supported him wholeheartedly in this quest. Syd's wife, who Bert and Meryl had met at Kokoda several times before the war, was called Myola, a pretty name that Bert knew meant 'dawn of day' in the Aboriginal language from which it originated. He thought this was an ideal choice, doubly suited to the scene that he saw around him and as a mark of respect for Syd. Of course, when Meryl heard of this choice, she was not very impressed that he did not opt to call the lake after her! In contrast to her somewhat larger-than-life husband, Myola was a tiny, genteel woman, who had obviously left quite an impression on Bert. To add insult to injury for Meryl, in one of his letters later that month he exhorts his darling wife to write more regularly, pointing out that 'Myola writes to Sid 3 or 4 times a week'. For some years after this, the mention of Myola's name would elicit a good-natured snarl from Meryl's lips.

In his diary entry for that day, Bert notes the area is swampy in the centre but good for dropping stores and paratroops, but that even though it is a bright clear day, being at 1,800 metres it is very cold. After reporting back to Elliot-Smith, he decided to rest and erect shelters while awaiting further orders.

The shelters were erected using pandanus leaves that his helpers collected from the surrounding jungle. This find of Bert's was fortuitous in every way, and his discovery is credited by Raymond Paull in his *Retreat from Kokoda* as being 'the key to the success of the Kokoda campaign', and by Peter Brune in *A Bastard of a Place* as 'the logistical turning point of the campaign'.

When Bert had stood on a high point the day before, locating the lake and seeing it to the east, he also noted to the north-east another ridge running back along the range in the direction of Eora Creek. He believed there would be a quicker route back to Eora if he followed that ridge and, pursuing his policy of keeping tracks up on high ground as much as possible, he intended to blaze a trail this way. Anywhere, but particularly in jungle country, it is better to walk along the tops of ridges rather than on their sides or in the valleys, provided the jungle provides cover from visibility from the air. The ground is usually drier, vision is better and defensively, ridges are much easier to hold than hollows.

On Tuesday 4 August, he set off to blaze this new trail. Along the ridge as far as the first Eora Creek crossing, the going was relatively easy, but from there to the junction with the Kagi track it was very rough and in parts quite treacherous. Late that afternoon, as Bert and his men slipped and slid along the side of the ridge carrying heavy packs, he lost his footing and fell into a deep ravine, landing heavily and badly hurting his hip. He carried on in quite a lot of pain. The boys' remedy to ease such discomfort was to rub stinging nettle on another part of the body away from the painful area – this supposedly distracts from the sore knee or aching head. For Bert, this was no solution to such a severe injury, but he never complained or even recorded the event in his diaries or reports. His inability to have the injury tended to meant permanent damage was done. After the war, he would endure several painful and ultimately fairly unsuccessful operations and be forced to walk with a stick for the rest of his life.

This new track eventually joined up with the Eora Creek–Kagi track, the old mail trail, which was now being walked by the troops downstream adjacent to Eora Creek. This junction of two tracks – one old, one new – he called Templeton's Crossing in memory of Sam Templeton. As he and his boys hacked their way through the virgin jungle to reach the established trail, Bert had been pondering how much had happened in the less than a month that had passed since he had led 'Uncle' Sam and B Company over the track. He thought of how well he had admired this man who, despite badly blistered and battered feet, had kept pace with him on that first trip, and whose first thought throughout the journey had always been for the safety and comfort of his men. The news of his death so early in the campaign greatly saddened Bert. Some days later, he established a camp at this intersection of his new track and the old mail trail, adjacent to Eora Creek. Templeton's Crossing would soon earn tragic infamy, as well as immortalising the name of his mate Sam.

As Bert continued on to Eora Creek camp where E Company was resting, and learnt that D Company were at Kagi awaiting instructions to move forward, he realised how acute the food shortages and lack of general supplies had become and how vital it was to start air drops at Myola. He had already instructed Sergeant Hylton Jarrett at Efogi to proceed to the lake and commence construction of a camp there without delay. He had telephone conversations with both Captain Kelly and Major Cameron over the newly completed phone line and advised them of the necessity for urgent air drops at Myola. The first experimental drop occurred on 5 August. Unfortunately, the follow-up drops were not as timely or efficient. On the 7th, Bert made his way back to Myola accompanied by four signallers to lay a line connecting Myola with the main line, but they ran out of wire before reaching their destination. Jarrett, who was held in high regard by both Bert and Doc Vernon, had done a great job starting the camp, and the next day they all waited in anticipation for air drops to begin in earnest. Owing to yet another army 'snafu', the reasons for which vary according to which history book tells the tale, no more drops occurred for five wasted days. In the meantime, the Japanese had won the second battle for Kokoda and attacked the troops at Deniki.

Word had filtered back to Bert of damage to his home at Yodda. He was to learn later that Australian troops and some natives also looted his home when they knew the Japanese arrival was imminent. This information was confirmed when, not long after the war, Bert and Meryl were invited to a battalion function on a quick visit they made to Melbourne. As they sipped their cups of tea, Meryl noted that the crockery was the same as the set she had received for a wedding present. When enquiries were made as to where it came from, one digger confessed he had got it from 'some planter's house' near Kokoda. Imagine his embarrassment when Bert said it was his home. The digger was most apologetic but Bert in his usual forgiving manner just said to forget it but to be aware that if ever there was an invasion of Melbourne, he would be volunteering for the 'raping and pillaging squad'.

On 8 August he wrote to Meryl:

I am fit but feel the loss of our home very much – I am confident we will recover it ere long. Wish I could get a few of the yellow blighters, didn't think I'd have to fight for my own home, like this, well, as long as we pull through.

Four days later he told Meryl:

Morso is coming to me today and I will get further reports on the recent activity and setbacks around our home. From all accounts our home has been occupied by the yellow curse and all our treasures, effects and belongings looted and ruined, so be sure to list every little thing you can remember and make 2 copies so that full compensation can be obtained. Furthermore I hope that one of these days we will get assistance to rebuild our homes which have taken me years to build out of virgin jungle. They should pay for this ruination. What a wicked thing war is. To think that twice in my life I have had to feel the effects of war in no mean way. I have a wild desire to go right into it and get even with a few Japs, but have to hold myself back as there is a much bigger job depending on me in supplying even though it is right up to the front.

§

For four long days of frustratingly good weather, the men waited at Myola for planes that did not arrive. Then suddenly on 12 August they appeared unannounced and began disgorging their cargo. Bert had sent an urgent telegram to Captain Kelly ordering:

Rice 10 Ton

Meat 2500 tins
Biscuits 100 tins
Tobacco 6 caddies

He requested this order be repeated each week. He also ordered urgent supply of 600 blankets, 100 groundsheets, 100 pullovers and emergency rations of 500 shell dressings and 100 field dressings.

All went well for four days and they began to accumulate a good body of supplies at Myola, although there were still problems with target accuracy and parcels being dropped from such a height that they buried themselves in the swampy ground, some never to be found again. Percentage return from the 'biscuit bombers' was certainly far better than when dropped into the jungle, but wastage was still high. And it was still a two-to-three-day carry to the front. The staging points Bert had established on the route became even more important as the large quantities of ammunition, rations and medical supplies arrived at Myola and had to be distributed to troops all the way to the enemy action point.

The strain started to show in Bert's letters to Meryl. On 15 August, he wrote:

Am still within a day's walk from home. Brewer has just come in worn out and fever-ridden – just done in and he tells me he saw huge fires at our home, everything destroyed, also at Kokoda not a thing left standing not even coconut trees. So far the weather has been shocking and not at all an easy matter. The yellow curse is a determined swine and certainly has the numbers. I wonder when we will have him worried and chased out of his illgotten domains . . . Peter did a good job of work – is very tired and ill. Some even do just as big a job – if not bigger and get through – others can't take it physically. It is worrying to see some of our chaps perforated and hurt – but that is war. We have inflicted heavy casualties on the rising sun but not nearly enough to stop them . . . We can win through if only everybody would pull together and not just look out for their little selves all the time. Some of the worst offenders are the big monopolies and firms – I still believe in a fair deal.

Two days later, on the morning of 17 August, he writes that he is only an hour's walk from the front line, that he is fit and that he has just been advised that he is to be attached to staff HQ, which may mean a promotion. He details a little of what he is doing, explaining that he is expected to be road builder, guide, explorer and supplier. With 60 Europeans under his command and over 2,500 natives, it was a worrying and responsible job and one that would normally warrant the rank of brigadier. That same afternoon at 1 p.m. he scribbles a note to tell his darling:

> I am moving hurriedly to meet a 'big gun' and to get further orders, so this is just a short note to let you know sweetheart that you may not get a letter for a few days, but I will write as soon as I can. You do your bit by writing as often as you can. Look after the kiddies Darling and keep your chin up. I may be going back to the place I discovered but I'll let you know as soon as possible.

On the same day, the skies over Myola went silent again. Another of the litany of disasters that dogged this Kokoda Campaign had struck in Moresby. The tale of this particular catastrophe is well documented but worth the retelling as it demonstrates the stupidity of some of the 'powers that be' at the time.

The day before, Lieutenant General Rowell, on returning to his headquarters in Port Moresby, noticed as he passed the 7-Mile airfield that the US 5th Air Force had parked all their aircraft neatly wing-tip to wing-tip along the edge of the airstrip, a sitting target for Japanese bombers and fighters. He immediately contacted Brigadier Ennis Whitehead, Deputy Commander, and suggested he disperse the aircraft forthwith. Whitehead said he would act on the matter the next morning

– alas, too late! At 10 a.m., Japanese bombers, accompanied by several fighter escorts, appeared over Hombrum's Bluff and had a veritable sideshow alley duck-shoot with all these perfectly positioned planes. Two Dakota transports, full of fuel and supplies to go to Myola, and three Flying Fortresses were destroyed. Five more Dakotas and five Fortresses were badly damaged. The Americans had made the very same mistake at Pearl Harbor, giving the reason that positioning the aircraft this way made them easier to secure against sabotage.

News of this disaster did not reach Bert immediately as he was busy keeping what supplies had already arrived moving along the line to Templeton's Crossing. The Japanese had now captured Deniki and many of his carriers had to be transferred to carrying the wounded to the Advanced Dressing Station set up at Templeton's. This junction of two tracks was by no means the ideal place for a field hospital; in fact Brigadier Potts himself described it as 'a dark gloomy place, perpetually wet with a general air of depression'. Even worse was Eora Creek, which Bert had always said was not a suitable camp site or defensive point as it was a small, cramped area of flat land in a valley surrounded on all sides by high mountains, yet it briefly became one of the busiest field hospitals on the Kokoda Trail and the scene of the longest battle of the campaign, with the most Australian casualties.

As the pace of the battle picked up, so did the need for carriers. It took eight boys to carry one wounded soldier, four at a time with four to relieve or help over difficult terrain and the hazardous creek crossings. Demand far exceeded supply. Stretchers had to be hurriedly constructed using poles, vines and blankets. In addition, the natives had become more and more terrified with the proximity of the fighting and confused by why such brave, strong young men as the Australian troops were being brought back wounded and appeared to be losing the fight. The white man and his gun had seemed almost invincible to the Papuans in the past and this turn of events baffled and frightened them and sent their morale plummeting. Much of Bert's time was spent geeing them up and trying to minimise desertions. He gave permission to some of his Koiari boys whose wives and families were hiding in the bush on adjacent ridges to leave their posts and go to check on their safety as he was concerned they would soon be surrounded by the enemy. The boys appreciated this but Bert joked with them if they did not come back or they ran with the enemy, he would come and shoot them himself! They moved their families further afield and all returned to remain his loyal carriers until the end of the campaign.

In reality, these 'fuzzy wuzzy angels', as the troops would come to call them, were being pushed to the limit physically; they were cold, hungry and just plain exhausted. Bert and Doc Vernon, also stationed at Templeton's at this point, continually argued for improvement of the conditions for these 'angels' and expressed deep concern for their welfare. Bert ensured they received a daily ration of rice or wheatmeal and biscuits, and a weekly issue of sugar, salt, tinned meat, tobacco and matches. Despite all his efforts, the pressures on them were horrendous – the wounded had to be carried out, and the ammunition and rations had to be carried forward.

When Bert did hear of the supply problem at Myola and calculated that the collection rate of what had been delivered was only 70 per cent, he made up his mind to locate the second dry lake bed that he knew was bigger than Myola and could perhaps fit an air strip, which would allow supplies to be safely landed and wounded to be flown out. Once again he sought permission from his superiors to take some time to find this bigger site. On 21 August he set off on his quest, while back at Myola the 2/14th and 2/16th AIF Battalions were due to arrive any day with nowhere near sufficient stores on hand to meet their requirements.

Bert set off early on the morning of 21 August and climbed the small range between the two lakes by following a native hunting pad. At the top of the ridges he sighted the second, larger lake. He decided to call this new lake Myola 2, and so the first one became Myola 1, although in his reports he normally refers to it simply as Myola and his later discovery as Myola 2. What impressed Bert about this larger lake, apart from the potential benefits of its size, was its even more striking natural beauty. Spring was on its way here in the mountains and the scene was alive with alpine flowers – masses of tiny violets and yellow buttercups interspersed with primroses and forget-me-nots. It brought back memories for Bert of the Alps of the Black Forest outside Stuttgart in summer. It seemed so incongruous to him here in the middle of the jungle, in the middle of a war. In the far east corner of the lake were two cascades tumbling from springs and feeding into the creek that meandered across the middle of the lake, the headwaters of the Eora Creek. As at Myola 1, as he walked through the short tufty grass he disturbed multitudes of quail and snipe and saw the evidence of many wild pigs.

He immediately sent a telegram to New Guinea Force for attention of Brigadier Porter as follows:

> Reconnaissance of area east of Myola found suitable for possible landing ground. Level surface covered with short grass and reeds. Rough with tussocks. Approach 295 degrees first 700 yds soft but could be improved with steel matting. Last 500 yards ground hard. Northerly winds prevail. Foxmoth Junker or Ford with wide tyres can land with safety.

In a note sent the next day, he asked for some indication of when a plane might be able to be sent to check out his find and advised he would prepare and mark out the landing ground.

Unfortunately, the Japanese, after holding at Deniki for several days, were now swarming fast up the northern side of the Owen Stanleys, and Bert's plans for better use of this new site were put on hold. Moresby was finally getting mobilised with supplies again, and on approximately 22 August 14 plane loads were dropped at Myola, where the two AIF battalions awaited orders to attack the advancing enemy at Isurava and Abuari. These men were itching to get into battle and said to Bert when he first came across them that they were looking forward to 'stringing a bunch of Jap navels'.

On 24 August Bert was excited to receive a long letter from Meryl, the first response since he had written telling her of the destruction of their home. He writes back immediately:

Yes, my dearest one, what a shame I didn't get a chance to get that photo album of our kiddies and many other treasures which no one can replace. I know how you feel about it – just the same as I did. We were so innocent about it all – kidding it couldn't happen at home and it actually did – complacency is a disease – a very dangerous one. We should have buried or hidden a lot of our treasures. That little album meant a lot to you and me – so did my stamp collection, your piano, books, those beds and many other personal effects. Suppose Dad and Mother felt it too – they both had a lot of treasures at home. A damned shame – there is only one way to look at it now – to get compensation and to look forward to rebuilding our homes and pray our productive rubber trees will be left intact, and that we will be safely together when all this is over.

He continues with more about his duties:

. . . kept busy with all sorts of jobs for the Army and I may say that it has been appreciated and one of these days I may be able to tell you all about it. Have one of the most responsible jobs of the whole set up and glad to be playing such a vital part in the scheme of things. Our lads have done an excellent job of work. I feel confident of the ultimate regain of our home and properties and driving the yellow curse out.

As always, he finishes his letter reminding Meryl to write often and to keep sending those parcels containing cakes and lollies.

Bert's optimism was soon to be shot to bits with the disastrous battle for Isurava, where 1,800 Australians – 600 of them from the inexperienced and untrained 53rd and 39th Battalions, the balance being battle-hardened men of the AIF – faced 6,000 crack Japanese troops. The struggle for this position raged on for five long days, and by the end of it Australia had lost 75 men. Japan's casualties reached 142 dead with many more wounded. Many soldiers from both sides remember this as the defining battle of the campaign. The enemy thought they were facing far greater numbers and now realised they were fighting a formidable force with a willingness to struggle to the death they had not seen to the same extent in the British, Philippine and American troops they had confronted in the past. The Australians realised that the Japanese soldier was smarter, braver, bigger and better trained than they had been led to believe in briefings. The reality was that Australia had been outfought and outmanoeuvred, their officer numbers had been severely reduced, and they had lost one of the most bitterly and closely fought infantry battles of the Pacific War. And to top it off their uniforms were the wrong colour. The khaki of their issued outfits was designed for fighting in Europe and the Middle East. It provided little disguise in the speckled greens of the rain forest. In comparison, the Japanese were properly kitted out and had learnt the art of jungle camouflage.

The men scattered in all directions as they made their escape from Isurava. As one group headed east towards the village of Misima, led by some terrified carriers, it seems that the officer pointed across to a ridge that was most likely occupied by the enemy and asked the boys the name of the place. The boys thought he wanted them to go over and recce the area so they shook their heads and said '*Ai sia gari, taubada*' ('We are scared, Sir'). The officer duly noted on the rough map he was using that the area was called Asigari – and henceforth a non-existent village of that name appeared on war maps of the Kokoda Trail.

By the first day of spring, the Japanese had converged on Eora Creek to find only an abandoned hospital hut, pits full of destroyed weapons, and scattered and spoiled food rations. As the first week of September progressed, the damaged and demoralised Australians made up a sorry sight of stragglers along the Trail from Templeton's Crossing to Myola, where they were hastily fed, had their wounds dressed and their blood-soaked stretchers renewed, then were sent on their way to Efogi through Menari and Nauro on to Uberi.

In his official report, Bert says of this period:

We had planned to attack on the 3rd September but were ordered not to before we had built up dumps with sufficient food and ammunition to maintain the troops and carriers. Every article from ammunition, mortars, bombs, food, Aust. rations, native rations, blankets, medical supplies etc were carried forward by natives to dumps at Templeton's Crossing. Eora Ck, Alola and Isurava. At each of these stations ANGAU men were in charge of the carriers and up until AIF arrived, stores also. They all did a grand job. Woollen coats and sweaters had been ordered when I first contacted Brig Porter on 17/08 and were issued to all carriers at Myola and forward areas.

Period 24th August to 4th Sept was the most trying time as carriers who had already done such a sterling job in continuous carrying were being pushed to the extreme limit. Some desertions taking place owing to these enforced conditions and I had a worrying period when they were further called on to carry back the wounded. As each stretcher case took up to 8 bearers they were depleting our carrier lines quickly The largest single batch of stretcher cases – 42 – took up 336 carriers. The decision was quickly made to get these men away to Moresby and evacuate the ADS at Myola.

The decision to evacuate Myola was not an easy one. Its discovery had raised the morale of all at New Guinea Force HQ even though they still had no real understanding of the terrain of the lakes or their surrounds. Brigadier A. W. Potts, Commander 21st Brigade, saw Myola potentially as his HQ, with Menari as the main supply base, and on 4 September he had arrived at the lake to make plans for defensive positions. He went on a reconnaissance with Bert and Lieutenant Colonel

Cameron to the hills overlooking Efogi and Kagi from the north. Surveying the topography of the area, they concluded that should the enemy break through The Gap, defending Myola would be impractical and, indeed, impossible. The decision was made that the only area that could be defended was on the ridges to the south of Efogi and that all personnel at Myola should be evacuated to Menari. Potts instructed Bert to cut yet more tracks, one from the south-east corner of Myola as direct as possible to Menari as well as an escape route from these ridges to Menari, just in case the enemy tried encircling and cutting off withdrawal. As he and his men hacked their way through the jungle creating this new route, officers arrived to advise that Myola was already being abandoned, so Bert was to speed up his work and wait at Menari to prepare for arrival of evacuees. Of all the stopping and staging points on the Kokoda Trail, Menari seems to be the one remembered most kindly by the troops for its natural beauty as well as the luxuries and comforts that awaited them there, particularly at this stage of the campaign. They recall arriving at this pretty mountain village to find everything from salmon, cheese, bully beef and chocolate, tobacco, new boots and foot powder all laid out for their selection.

Back at Myola, troops and injured were given a hot meal, extra rations and fresh clothing, then told to destroy the rest of stocks that could not be carried to Menari. The men set about with gusto destroying food rations by breaking open bags, puncturing tins and burying or exploding ammunition. Trouble was, they were making such a racket they had to be reprimanded for fear the Japanese would locate Myola even more quickly just by following the noise. At about 7 a.m., destruction was completed with the firing of the buildings, and the troops departed leaving behind a trail of battered bully beef tins, rain-sodden rice and broken biscuits.

Potts set up his headquarters at the defensive position they had chosen in a clearing on a steep hillside, later to become known as Brigade Hill. Bert was back and forth from there to Menari for the next few days directing the ever increasing traffic of troops, wounded and supplies. In Menari on 8 September, he was pleased to meet up again with Doc Vernon, who had just been in to Moresby. Doc always brought a smile to Bert's face as he loped into camp, dressed in a most unregimental manner that had nearly got him shot for lack of recognition several times in the past. Jack Wilkinson paints the picture beautifully in his diary:

> Vernon had shorts which were actually long strides rolled up, a blue pullover with the arms tied round his neck and hanging down his back, a felt army hat, worn as no hat should ever have been worn, and a long newspaper cigarette in his mouth. A small dilly bag had some army biscuits and tobacco in it.

As the two men chatted over their bowls of soup, Doc asked after Bert's health. When they last spent any real time together, it was at Templeton's Crossing, where Bert had had to call on Doc's surgical skills to solve a rather delicate problem. Bert was a stickler for a regimented ablution schedule, a habit developed working on plantations where 'fall-in' was at daybreak and there was no time from that point on to disappear for a major call of nature. The result of these years of forced regularity had finally caught up with Bert at the worst possible time and when he had arrived at Templeton's one day in August, Doc Vernon had commented how pale and tired he looked. Bert confessed that he was losing significant amounts of blood from very troublesome haemorrhoids. Doc volunteered to solve the problem forthwith. This involved Bert straddling the root of a giant jungle tree allowing Doc to have light where the sun normally 'don't shine' and give easy access to remove the offending 'piles' with a couple of dexterous nicks of his knife. No painkillers of any strength were available to help Bert through the procedure, and the risk of infection would not have been insignificant, so it must have been a case of the lesser of two evils, to opt for the op. Despite the fact that there are probably still teeth marks in that tree root, within hours of this excruciating procedure, the battle at Isurava had gone pear-shaped and Bert had been required to give of his best. As with his hip damage, Bert never wrote of this in his diaries and reports, only telling it to his family years later.

Doc was actually on his way back from reporting to GHQ in Moresby and replenishing his supplies. On his return, Bert had originally intended for him to set up a central hospital for carriers at Myola. Too late for this now. From this point on it was hard to plan anything from day to day. The two men were now in the thick of it, and the danger of being outflanked by the enemy was high. Potts had insisted that Bert and at least 100 fuzzy wuzzies stay with him at this HQ. Once or twice during this period, Bert and his carriers had to duck sniper bullets and the occasional random friendly fire. At least once already, Bert and his men had been fired on by small groups of Japanese who had calculated that Australia's troops were better supplied with food than they were, and if they could just get around behind the front, they must find carriers toting rations. As Bert had not been issued with any arms personally, his only protection on these occasions was his own Webley 44 revolver backed by some of his men like Indiki, Harika and Kordunga, who carried weapons in order to help protect the carriers. Bert had issued bolt-action 12-gauge shotguns to a number of his trusted shooting boys from the Yodda as well as to a few chosen new ones. These were temperamental firearms at the best of times, and to make it worse, often in the excitement and heat of battle, the boys could not always remember which end of the rifle the bullet exited! There was sometimes more danger from friendly fire than the enemy. Everybody now lived in a permanent state of fear, and at night Bert always stationed two of his most trusted police boys to guard the carriers and keep them calm.

Bert convinced Doc to go back to Nauro and take care of his much-loved natives and the wounded there. He was lucky that Doc followed his orders. He had a bit of a reputation for doing his own thing using the excuse that when he received the orders second-hand, he reckoned he was sometimes better to follow his instincts and what he had learnt in World War I, in particular, that it was an MO's duty to stay at the rear of a retreating army to be able to treat the wounded without delay. The result of this approach was that he often turned up in places where he was not expected or supposed to be, causing confusion and concern, especially for the likes of Jack Wilkinson, who always felt he had to protect this 'old' but valuable mate.

The speed of the retreat was such that they would all be at Nauro soon anyway. From 5 to 9 September, the battle had raged at Brigade Hill, and Bert's and Potts's belief that it would be a good defensive position proved wishful thinking. Against all odds, the Japanese traversed seemingly impossible terrain to outflank the Australians, inflicting horrendous casualties and leaving a trail of dead and wounded from Efogi to Brigade Hill. On 8 September alone, 51 men met violent deaths in this most horrific confrontation, one of the worst of the Campaign. Bert's escape route, cut less than a week earlier, proved a lifesaver for many members of the 2/16th and 2/14th. Along with the 2/27th, these troops were cut off from HQ at Brigade Hill by the enemy and had to beat their way through jungle south-east from the main trail until they came across Bert's rough track, which led them to temporary safety at Menari. The boys of the 2/27th and some stragglers of the 2/16th who had been assigned the role of rearguard with the added burden of carrying the wounded, got left behind. Wandering in the dark, they missed a vital fork in the track and ended up hopelessly lost and missing in action for what would be two tragic and terrible weeks. Anxious for their return, Potts and Bert sent off WO Preece with every available carrier to help with the wounded. Eventually the survivors of these two groups of men, bedraggled and starving, rejoined their mates at the end of the Trail near Sogeri – except for two heroic medics, Alf Zanker and Johnnie Burns, and their surviving patients, who would not reappear until October.

Within two days of this disaster at Brigade Hill, with increasing and more accurate enemy gun fire, Menari also had to be abandoned. This escape is the one where Bert recalls his life was most at risk. He, Potts and Smith were pinned to the ground under enemy fire, and years later he painted the picture to his family by describing how he ate a lot of dirt and eyeballed quite a few worms that day. At the time he described it in letters: '. . . haven't been closer to the ground than I was that day . . . have you ever seen a small puppy spread eagle itself on the ground when it gets a lashing for something and it can't get close enough to the ground and starts peeing itself!?' In the middle of all this, to top it off he was cursed with an attack of dysentery.

The Japanese had hauled two of their large mountain guns over the Trail, quite an amazing feat in itself, and with their range of about 5,000 metres, combined with the high-speed output and impressive accuracy they were achieving, the damage they were inflicting was quite demoralising to the withdrawing Australians. In a letter to his Meryl on 15 September, Bert makes the understatement, 'Within firing range of the Japs and the constant thud of bombs, mortars and firing is a little disconcerting and at times uncomfortable.' In fact, they were so close to the guns that they felt the explosion before they heard the sound of them firing.

While all this was happening, Bert did some quick reconnaissance to try to find a spot overlooking the area to observe and report on enemy movements but had no luck, so he pushed on quickly to Nauro. Here, the 3rd Militia Battalion took up defensive positions near the river to try to waylay the enemy while Bert and his men loaded what stores and equipment they could onto available carriers and destroyed the rest.

Although the troops did not have much choice in the matter, Potts insisted that this apparent high-speed retreat was a planned tactical withdrawal. As it turned out, this was a very wise move on his behalf, but one that ultimately cost him his job. Blamey and his henchmen, always on the lookout for someone to blame, were under pressure from the egomaniacal MacArthur and the subsequent parade of scapegoats that came and went on the Trail is the subject of consternation and anger in every history of this campaign. The US general actually made the statement, 'The Australians have proved themselves unable to match the enemy in jungle fighting and aggressive leadership.' Blamey took pleasure in passing this opinion on to Potts, who saw red. He never wanted this move to be called a retreat. His troops would withdraw fighting all the way, resisting at every opportunity, drawing out then strangling the enemy's supply lines. A successful fighting withdrawal takes surgical precision. Pull out too soon and you achieve nothing; pull out too late and you will be annihilated. The aim is to make the enemy pay dearly for every metre of their advance, and by always destroying any rations left behind there were no free lunches for the enemy. A tin of bully beef goes rotten very quickly in the tropics but the Japanese were often so desperate, they ate the spoiled food anyway with dire consequences.

Of course, to the average observer, it did appear very much like a retreat, indeed a rout, and Damien Parer, the famous wartime journalist who was caught up in the scramble back over the mountains, is reported to have commented to one young soldier who asked what he thought was happening, 'An Army in retreat, my boy. Not very pretty, is it? I have seen many retreats. Greece was a picnic compared to this.'

Potts was called to 7th Division HQ at Bisiatabu, where he attempted to explain his reasons for a withdrawal that should have been obvious to any military tactician. Bert was an avid supporter of these tactics and would later say in a letter to author Raymond Paull that Potts's fighting withdrawal was one of the 'finest epics' in the wonderful record of Australian military history, and that Potts was one of the 'finest high-ranking officers' he had had the privilege to meet.

Potts began by pointing out General HQ's refusal to even accept that Japan had any land invasion plans until they were practically at Kokoda, their underestimation of enemy strength, and their complete ignorance of the terrain where the campaign was being fought. This, he said, was then compounded by being given inexperienced troops coupled with catastrophically unreliable supply lines. It made no difference. He was to be the fall guy, and so was unceremoniously dumped and replaced by Brigadier Porter, who arrived at Nauro on 10 September.

Porter very quickly summed up the situation and concurred with Potts's tactics, fast realising that Nauro was no more than a short-term delaying position and immediately ordering a withdrawal to the higher ground of the Maguli Range then Ioribaiwa. Bert and his men established this camp on the Moresby side of Iorabaiwa Ridge at Ua-ule Creek. From here, once again Bert set off on a recce, this time as far as possible along the old Kokoda track back towards Nauro to try to observe enemy movements. With all this track making, trail blazing and route reconnaissance, is it any wonder they called him 'the Architect of the Kokoda Trail'?

The new camp south of Iorabaiwa was now the most forward carrier camp and Bert called it Station 44 in a system of naming stations that he introduced apparently for clarity of radio communication. Because the telephone lines only had a range of about 13 kilometres, at which points signallers had to be based to pass on the message, information could often be distorted by the time it reached its destination. Using repetitive numbers – four, four, six, six – was a recommended way to reduce these errors.

In his report of the period from 11 to 18 September, he wrote:

I paraded all carriers – 310 natives – and we remained at Station 44 until 16th Sept. I had previously sent back the rest of the carriers to Ubiri, now totaling 860, and they were able to keep up supplies to us with the shortened line of communication but many were going out sick for treatment to Bisiatabu and Hanuabada, and others were deserting. Despite those setbacks it was indeed gratifying that so many natives had stuck to us loyally. The Japs had pushed on and taken Iorabaiwa by the 16th September and by 1030 on that day an order was received to evacuate the camp in 2 hours. We moved back towards Ubiri and established a camp south of Imita Ridge to be known as '66'. It was a very wearying day, as 2 trips had to be made and the track was crowded with troops going forward and carriers coming back with stores and wounded to safety. Rain set in heavily towards evening and some carriers could not get back into camp. At '66' we established a camp, shelters, latrines, hospital in 24 hrs and in addition continued with the normal routine of carrying supplies forward to troops. I also established a forward camp [Ack-Ack] near the top of Imita Ridge with WO Davies in charge of 60 carriers. They were to carry forward to units and bring back any wounded.

Throughout all this, Bert was continually having to reassure the natives and to reduce the number of malingerers and deserters. Doc Vernon wrote in his diary: 'Desertions from the force were frequent, but wherever Kienzle happened to be they died down; on his arrival in a camp, the boys bucked up and went about their work as if General MacArthur himself were among them.' The carriers tried every trick in the book, and then some, in order to be invalided out – overdosing on Aspros stolen from medical supplies, faking dysentery and vomiting by concocting weird-looking brews out of bully beef and heaven knows what else to look like the resultant excretions, tales of woe about wounded dying wantoks back in the village. The worst offenders were those who came from the Moresby side; they were now close to home and some had been away for nearly five months, so the temptation to shoot through was understandable. Not quite so for those from the Kokoda side who had no relatives (*tumbuna*) around Moresby and would have to sneak back through enemy lines to get home.

Despite this, Bert's continued admiration and concern for his native charges comes through repeatedly in his letters:

> . . . [despite] the roughness of the country when the tracks are so steep, through jungle and almost impassable it is marvellous how the carriers get them through. Our personal touch and supervision has a lot to do in keeping them together . . . the natives get rice, meat, meat extract, sugar, salt, biscuits,

wheatmeal and tobacco so they are not doing too badly. It behoves people to look after them as they have done and are doing a marvellous job. Doc Vernon is with me and he is a great old scout.

The huge load Bert had now been carrying for nearly 120 days of continuous active service involving 10- to 15-hour days was starting to take its toll, and on 21 September he was bedridden with a severe attack of fever and dysentery. With Doc Vernon hovering by his side, he recovered enough by the 25th to follow orders to report to 7 Aus Div HQ at Bisiatabu where he was advised that he was now seconded to the AIF and attached to this HQ, and was to give all assistance regarding carrier organisation, tracks and intelligence reports received from natives regarding enemy movements.

He wrote to Meryl on 24 September:

Feeling ever so much better, a little weak, after that second attack of dysentery and fever, thanks to a rest and Dr Vernon's care. I know what I do need – a complete change & rest away, preferably in your care my dearest. I have been in this campaign longer than any other man in the forward area & in this sort of country as tough as I am, must admit that it has played up with me. Pray that I come through this all safe & sound as I am living only for the day when I can be with you and the children again. Do take care of yourself my dearest. My life with you is the happiest period in it & it has a long way to go yet God willing.

Having met Major General Allen at HQ, he then went on to ANGAU HQ where he reported to Elliot-Smith, one of the few apparent constants in the ever-changing command. While at HQ he received the well-deserved personal thanks of Major General Morris for his efforts to date and was then wined and dined at Government House, where he spent one night in blissful comfort.

After these days of meetings and conferences, Bert sent out the following circular:

TO ALL STATIONS KOKODA L of C ANGAU PERSONNEL AND ALL NATIVES

For general information I have to advise that I have been appointed CO, L of C Kokoda and am now attached to HQ 7 Div, Advanced Base where I am now stationed.

Full details of all natives engaged, including Police and personal natives are urgently required and must be furnished at the end of September by 3 October to Lt French, who is engaged in gathering information. Also details of Europeans engaged as ANGAU personnel on each station. Also forward daily particulars W/O Bell who will in turn forward a summary to HQ.

No natives are allowed to go without escort from station to station and each European supervisor is responsible for his allotted team in regard to work, conduct and general health. Natives being returned must carry a pass to allow them to pass through various stations. A proper check of all natives is essential. NO interference by troops or unauthorized persons of natives engaged on L of C will be tolerated and this must be strictly adhered to. Full particulars of all natives taken off strength through sickness or desertion etc. at each station must be immediately supplied to W/O Bell.

It is essential for efficient working and control at all times that all orders issued be carried out without delay and in the right team spirit that should always prevail in this ANGAU unit. The success of this line depends entirely on the cooperation of all personnel and natives engaged.

A lot had happened back at the front while Bert had been ill and at HQ. Horii and his exhausted troops had captured Australia's last standing point at Iorabaiwa Ridge and could see the lights of Moresby and the glitter of the Coral Sea beyond the harbour. Yet, inexplicably to the Allies at the time, they suddenly stopped their advance. The reality was that when they had landed at Buna two months before, they had been given 11 days' rations and were expected to be well and truly in Moresby when those rations ran out. By this last week of September, the massively depleted Japanese troops were cut off by air, sea and cable. They were starving and demoralised. Potts's tactics had worked. To Horii's great consternation, because of the unexpected delay in reaching their target and events occurring on other fronts of the Japanese war effort, they had received orders from the Emperor to withdraw just when their objective was in sight. The order arrived at Japanese HQ that South Sea Corps were not to advance but that a portion was to secure the present lines, and the main strength was to regroup on the northern slope. By this it was understood that a small unit was to remain on the ridges, but the main strength was to withdraw to Kokoda. This was indeed a fortunate turn of events for Australia, but one for which its proud, determined troops could take a good deal of the credit.

The tide of this particular war, in this unknown part of the jungle, in this little known country, was about to turn.

8

ADVANCE TO THE REAR

Back at 7th Division HQ Bisiatabu, Bert was again under pressure to gather together as many carriers as possible – a very difficult task. The Australian offensive had begun in earnest on 26 September, and with two brigades of fresh, experienced AIF troops along with other ancillary battalions bearing down on them, the demoralised Japanese were scrambling back along the Trail. The order to withdraw had shocked and confused the enemy soldiers who had always been indoctrinated that a servant of the Emperor never retreats or surrenders – he dies first. There was no real word for retreat in their military language, only the equivalent of 'advance to the rear', and after some initial hesitation, this they did. Suddenly, wanting to live was very much on their minds, and dying for the Emperor was now coming a poor second. The heavy artillery had arrived and the fast-advancing Australian troops had to be kept supplied with the usual food, ammunition and medical supplies as well as the added weight of Vickers machine-guns.

Once again, the responsibility fell on Bert to make sure things happened. Now he had to feed and service a whole division with more or less the same, insufficient number of carriers. The troops were advancing rapidly but still needing breakfast, lunch, dinner and ammunition delivered to the front line. The diggers continually complained that they didn't get enough to eat, and many, young and naive as they were, had no idea of the logistics involved in keeping them supplied with the limited food and ammunition that they did get. If only they could have spoken to the Japanese, who did not have a Bert Kienzle or the equivalent to the ANGAU men, with the ability to control and organise the natives, they would have realised how lucky they were. Most of the boys of the 39th knew Bert and how valuable he was, but the soldiers of battalions that arrived at this later stage of the campaign had no time to consider such matters, as they were thrown straight into the thick of battle and could concentrate only on their survival from day to day.

Bert really needed around 5,000 carriers, but sickness and desertions had depleted immediately available numbers to less than 1,000. Natives who had been press-ganged into service by the Japanese started to drift into camp as the enemy retreated, and it was Bert's task to question them and gain as much intelligence about the enemy's status as possible. They told tales of horrific abuse by their captors, and of the Japanese being half-starved and riddled with sickness.

On 3 October, despite the urgency of his work at the base depot, Bert was suddenly summoned to be driven down to the air squadron at Ward's Strip, where he was to make a reconnaissance flight over the Kokoda–Wairope area in a dive-bomber to assist in locating targets marked for the day. As he bumped over the muddy, well-abused road to Moresby, he was surprised to pass an entourage of army vehicles heading in the other direction. In the midst of the cavalcade, in an open jeep, lounged MacArthur, attempting to look cool as a cucumber despite the bone-shaking status of the road surface, his corn-cob pipe clenched firmly between his teeth, his cap perched jauntily atop a large pair of dark sunglasses. This unexpected visit was all part of a media beat-up to paint the picture to the rest of the world that, thanks in the main to his Yankee determination, Moresby was now a safe place and the Japanese were on the run. Interestingly, all Australian journalists except for one lonely photographer from the Department of Information, conveniently and literally 'missed the bus' to this highly staged event. Out of place in their civvies, the troupe of accompanying politicians made sycophantic statements about the general, and posed with the somewhat bemused and cynical troops. Lieutenant Dalrymple Fayle wrote in his diary:

> The politicians spent their time getting amongst the troops promising them all sorts of impossible things and promising to write to their folks etc. They certainly admired the scenery and got frightfully sunburnt, especially behind the knees, but as far as we could see did nothing much but waste a lot of valuable time and use jeeps which were vitally needed for their real purpose.

Another story was told of a self-important politician in the group who approached a young soldier, shook his hand and said, 'How do you do. I am the Minister for the Army.' The digger innocently replied, 'Good on ya, mate – you padres do a great job.'

Curiously, Bert missed all this because of his orders to be elsewhere, yet when he got to Ward's Strip, the plane had taken off without him – he was told, because of a misunderstanding by ground control. As a result he spent the day at Squadron HQ trying to impart his knowledge by poring over maps. One wonders if Bert was purposely removed from MacArthur's presence in case, having such an intimate knowledge of what conditions were really like on the Trail, and with his rather unique and irreplaceable position in the army's chain of command, they thought it circumspect to keep him away from the Yank and the press? Who knows, and who knows what his real thoughts of MacArthur were? In his reports Bert was always very respectful and non-critical of his superiors.

Paul Ham expresses well what we all now know MacArthur to have been: in his book *Kokoda* he wrote: 'Macarthur was that rarity, a man who believed his thoughts and actions were integral to the fate of the world. Only Churchill and Hitler – for good and evil – seemed to share the same colossal self-definition and sense of personal destiny.'

After a wasted day, Bert was back at 7 Div HQ that night and next morning headed off early to check on his established dumps at '66' near Ubiri, on up the 2,000 or so steps of the 'Golden Stairs' to 'Ack-Ack' near the top of Imita Ridge, which was now being disbanded. These roughly formed stairs had been built by Australian engineers to try to make this horrendous climb easier, with limited effect. The raisers of each step were coarsely cut logs of varying size, and the clay base of the foot pads soon gouged out, making them hazardous for battle-weary feet. Sometimes it is better to zig-zag up such climbs than head straight, but the sappers had meant well.

Bert pushed on to Station '44' at the foot of Iorabaiwa, and then '88' between Iorabaiwa and Nauro. Australian troops had taken Nauro and were forging on to Menari. On his way he came across abandoned equipment and much evidence of the Japanese defences, plus many of their hastily dug graves. Near Nauro he observed his first Japanese prisoner, lying on a stretcher guarded by the Field Security Service. He was in an extremely weak condition, so Bert arranged for him to receive basic medical care and then be taken to the nearest interpreter for interrogation.

At Nauro, on 5 October, Bert writes in his report:

I interrogated rescued Rabaul natives who were in terrible state. They had all been half starved. One showed me wounds in the back where he had been prodded by Japs forcing him to carry when utterly exhausted. They gave some harrowing accounts of Jap brutalities. No medical attention when sick and death by bayonet. Their faces showed what they had been through. They were glad to be with us again. I immediately used this evidence as propaganda for our carriers who were quick to take in the fact that their treatment was totally different. This stiffened their morale noticeably and they were anxious to see this brutal invader driven out of their land. The only Orokaiva from Kokoda Village who was impressed by the Japs fell by the wayside exhausted and was rescued by us. He was able to give exact information of tracks taken by the enemy and confirmed Jap brutalities.

The Orokaiva people come in for quite a lot of negative comment from Bert and other ANGAU men during the Kokoda campaign. The problem started with the first group Bert took across the Trail with Templeton's Company; most of them deserted once they reached Kokoda. Then Bert received reports as the operation progressed of them aiding the enemy, particularly in the Kumusi River, Buna–Gona areas. In late August, WO Hylton Jarrett had been sent on a rather dangerous mission taking a different route down the mountains to the upper Kumusi region to observe enemy activity. He reported: 'The Orokaivas have joined forces with the Japs and some have been armed . . . suggest Major Elliot-Smith declare open season on these natives later on.' This was a little over the top even for those times, but indicative of his anger at this apparent treason. Bert wrote to Meryl at the time: 'The Orokaivas are in for a heavy time when we recapture that area, they are running with the Japs despite the cruelties inflicted, probably had no option.'

The last phrase shows that Bert once again tries to understand the thinking of the native people. In reality, they had no real reason to choose their current colonial masters over potential new ones, remembering that the history of their tribe's relationship with white man had not always been a good one. As the Japanese overran their part of the world very quickly, they probably did have 'no option'. One Orokaiva from Kokoda Village, Dide, later informed Bert that most of his fellow tribesmen were not assisting the Japanese at all. He told Bert that word of the rape of women by the enemy had spread quickly from the coast to Kokoda, and that most of his wantoks went bush. Despite all this, some coastal Orokaivas did receive harsh punishment after the war.

Of course, by this stage of the campaign, members of every tribe were deserting – they had had enough – they were exhausted, ill and scared. The current speed of the counterattack made maintaining the supply lines very difficult. It was decided to use air drops into Nauro, a relatively flat but swampy area in the Brown River Valley – not a good spot but the best option at the time. Bert supervised the retrieval and assembly of these air drops at Nauro while awaiting the arrival of Colonel Spry along with General Officer in Command of the 25th and 16th Brigades, Major General 'Tubby' Allen, who was most distressed to see the state of the supply situation. On 7 October he had sent a clear message to HQ:

> Implementation of airdropping programme cause of greatest concern. It would appear that air force cannot supply planes necessary to assure dropping of 50000 lbs daily . . . 50000 lbs covers maintenance only and does NOT repeat NOT provide for building up reserves . . . Unless dropping 50000 lbs daily plus additional to build up a reserve is assured, complete revision of plans will have to be made and large proportion of troops withdrawn to Imita Ridge posn. Any attempt then to occupy Kokoda will be jeopardised if supplies cannot be maintained by air.

On 11 October, the men moved forward to Menari where they joined Brigadier Eather for a further conference on the situation. The progress of the Allied advance was now such that Myola could soon once again be considered as a supply base, and Bert set off immediately to make his way to Myola 2 with the idea of finally building an airstrip there that would hopefully solve some of the current problems. On the track from Menari to Efogi, he saw many dead, skeletons and graves, and commented that the putrid stench of death was horrendous. By the corpses of the Japanese, he found several rising sun autograph flags *hinomaru yosegaki*. Emblazoned with messages of good luck and encouragement from their loved ones and comrades, these silk flags were carried by many of the soldiers. They served not just as souvenirs, but as a reminder to the soldier of his duty to honour his family and his Emperor. Their more practical use was as identification to aircraft to avoid friendly fire. Bert collected three of these flags, each stained with blood, and he kept them for the rest of his life. Perhaps they symbolised to him the first time it hit home that many of the 'yellow devils', as he had called them, were really just men like him with wives and family waiting for them at home.

At Efogi Creek, Bert came across the remains of a large white horse, which the natives said had belonged to a high-ranking Japanese officer. Bert later established that this was in fact General Horii's infamous white charger. What an amazing animal it must have been to have got this far over such terrible terrain, only to be brought down by the bullets of Allied airpower. It is believed this legendary beast was killed in an air strike that Potts had requested on Efogi the morning after the terrorising 'lantern parade', in which hundreds of Japanese soldiers ignited pieces of sigline wire, partly for lighting as they descended towards Efogi at night, and partly to scare the living daylights out of the Australians.

Also near Efogi, in one of those unfortunate accidents of war, two Orokolo natives had just been wounded when they lit their cooking fire over an unexploded enemy grenade. Fortuitously, an RMO was present and he was treating their quite severe injuries by the time Bert arrived on the scene. They were lucky to meet up with Doc Vernon the next day, and he gave them some morphine to ease the pain of being carried in Thomas splints all the way back to Menari.

Spending the night there, Bert joined Doc and young Sergeant Jack Simms of the Signals Platoon, who recalled some years later:

> At Efogi I shared a hut with Doc Vernon and Bert Kienzle and in the comfort of the hut during those days we had the luxury of a blanket a piece at night. I remember that conversation with Doc was difficult because he was so deaf. I also remember how he disappeared with his blanket to visit the carriers sleeping on the bare ground below us. After a

while he returned without his blanket and lay down on the floor to shiver through the night. Bert shouted – 'Where's your blanket?' – Doc replied 'Wrapped a carrier in it . . . poor devil, dying of pneumonia. All I can do to make him warm for his last few hours.

On 13 October, accompanied by Brigadier Eather and his party, Bert arrived back at Myola 1 to observe the damage done to his old camp and Advanced Dressing Station by the advancing Japanese troops. Much to the frustration of Major General Allen, stores had been dropped here the day before, when they were supposed to be targeted at Efogi. On this date, Myola was not where he needed them. This was a deliberate tactic of Blamey and his henchmen to force Allen to speed up the advance – the worst outcome of this stupidity being that often the supplies fell into the hands of the enemy. Bert organised their collection and at the same time set some workers the task of repairing the old shelters, most of which were just burnt-out shells, for a native labour camp. He was still convinced that Myola 2 would be the better place to re-establish the main supply station so he forged on towards it with Lieutenant Dawe of the Royal Australian Engineers. He measured up 800 metres of the best ground available and got some of the Koiaris with him, villagers from Nauro and Menari, to get busy building a camp. Although they did not come into contact with the enemy, they could hear the gunfire from Templeton's Crossing where the Japanese had finally slowed their retreat and were digging in on two fronts: one a ridge between Myola and Templeton's Crossing, and the other on the track from Templeton's to Kagi.

The pressure on Bert and his immediate superiors that was coming down from MacArthur, via Blamey, in the form of scathing telegraphs repeatedly criticising the slow progress back to Kokoda, plus their lack of appreciation of what was really happening at the coalface, is expressed well by Peter Brune in *A Bastard of a Place*:

From a supply perspective, Blamey and MacArthur's signals also demonstrate little if any understanding of the multitude of day-to-day obstacles that men like Bert Kienzle were facing and fixing. The fact is that Kienzle and his ANGAU personnel, the carriers and soldiers, were not only responsible for the gathering and moving of supplies, but for the very infrastructure that facilitated it. It was they who had to organise the clearing of sites, the building of camps, the allocation and deployment of the carrier line, the movement of casualties, and the very backbone of the transport system: the carriers. To Blamey and MacArthur's distant and ignorant eyes, the whole issue was merely concerned with dropping of supplies, adding them up, and then concluding that they had furnished the forward force with the ample implements of war.

After his meetings with the 'big brass', and because of the shortage of labour, Bert had reluctantly changed his system of organisation of the carriers. He now allotted a certain number to each battalion, station or dump; and an ANGAU officer, some of whom spoke Motu, was in charge of each group. From the beginning, there had been a shortage of young men to serve in ANGAU in these positions of authority over natives. Many of the pick of the crop of patrol officers and other suitable expatriates had joined up back in 1939 and 1940 to fight in Europe. Others who spoke some Motu and Pidgin were carrying out the important work of recruiting labour from villages along the south coast of Papua and other areas not occupied by the Japanese. Despite accusations that these 'fuzzy wuzzy angels' were virtually corralled, slave labour, the reality was that these European officers worked hard in each village convincing the young men that it was in their interests to help the Australian troops: that this was not just a 'war bilong white man'; that this enemy wanted their land and this was a tribal fight for territory. If Australia lost, so would they. Many understood this and joined up, if not willingly, at least with some understanding of the price of refusal. The lack of experienced men for all these jobs, and particularly to help

Bert control the native labour in the battle zone, certainly made his life more difficult and contributed significantly to the high rates of desertion.

Bert wrote in his report:

> I did not all together approve of this move of splitting my carrier line into small independent groups as I had only a limited number of experienced labour overseers who really could understand and handle the natives and most had to be taught. I took the risk that we would be in the warmer climate on the other side of the range within a fortnight and this would make all the difference to our strained carrier strength. Wet afternoons and nights did not ease the position of my carriers and they were feeling the effects of the cold mountain climate.

For this third week of October, he was back and forth between the two lakes and other stations, allocating carriers and supplies. At Myola 2, a Main Dressing Station (MDS) was being established and 100 natives were clearing the site for a landing ground. Bert was always proud of the fact that his native labour were three times as fast at this task as the Australian boys, this time mainly the men of Chaforce who were called so because their commander was Major Hugh Challen. This was a group of crack troops trained for far loftier duties than labouring so they weren't too impressed with this task allocation. Good progress was being made all the same, but Bert and the engineers still calculated that Marsden matting would be needed to make the landing ground long enough to be effective.

Marsden matting, sometimes spelled 'marsten' matting – both variations being derived from its engineering name of Mars.10 matting, or PSP (perforated steel planking) – was the brainchild of a Gerald Greulich. Called the 'air force's magic carpet', PSP is sheets of a quarter-inch-thick alloy of steel and nickel, rolled into 45 centimetres x 4.5 metre sections, perforated with holes so that it looks like 'a sheet of roofing iron hit by a cannon ball'. Each sheet weighs about 30 kilograms and incorporates a quick and simple interlocking system. The men who used it described it as 'a lot of holes tied together with steel', but they all appreciated its immense value for fast construction of bridges and airstrips. An airstrip 1,500 metres long and 45 metres wide required about 6,000 sheets, weighing 2,000 tons. Airstrips at Milne Bay, Nadzab and Port Moresby all employed the 'magic carpet' and pilots described the experience of landing on these strips as 'sounding like every rivet was popping out of the plane'. It would be ideal to solve the problem of the muddy sections of the area Bert had to choose for the Myola strip.

Bert was in regular contact now with Brigadiers Eather and Lloyd, with nightly conferences to give updates on the carrier positions and discuss strategies. Doc Vernon was ensconced at the Myola MDS and he recalls sharing a hut with Bert and sitting in the semi-darkness each evening waiting for him to return from these meetings so they could share a cup of coffee. Sometimes they would talk till midnight and they came to know each other even better during these times. They actually made a £10 bet one night as to when they would be back in Kokoda. Bert said – by the end of the month; Doc reckoned not until about 5 November. It turned out Bert was out by two days – our troops regained his old home on 2 November but Doc gladly handed over the cash anyway.

One evening Bert told him the emotional tale of one of his old boss-boys from the Yodda limping into camp. He and his family had made off into the hills, leaving their home and gardens to the invaders. Food was short and his little boy begged him for some of the bananas growing in their garden. He tried to sneak back but was caught and forced into slavery with the Japanese. He was very badly treated and saw many of his fellow countrymen bayoneted. In describing this experience to Bert in Motu, he said, 'Taubada, when I saw them killed I pissed with fright.' He also told Bert that many of the other men who had stayed behind at the goldfields had escaped to the hills when the Japanese arrived and had tried to rescue some of the Kienzles' possessions by taking them with them. Bert was hopeful that some of his smaller treasures may yet have survived the carnage. So glad to be back with his old *taubada*, he also told him of Alfred's old houseboy, a bit of a rogue called Hojavo, who sent a message that they were all waiting anxiously for *taubada baudana*'s return to the valley.

By this point of this ghastly fight, Bert was becoming more and more of a hero in the eyes of all the men, both black and white. His ability to organise and make things happen in this country where the enervating climate had resulted in the nickname over the years, 'the land of dohori' or 'the land of wait a while' never ceased to amaze those who worked with him. One veteran said after the war: 'That big fella Bert Kienzle was a miracle worker. He got the natives to work and kept them working though most of them were scared stiff and would have deserted as soon as his back was turned. We would have starved without him!'

The settlement at Myola 2 seemed to have appeared overnight, and one enterprising ANGAU officer erected a hand written sign, 'Kienzleville', at the entrance to the camp. Bert mentions to Meryl that he would have preferred them to call it 'Meryl-E', maybe to salve his conscience for calling the area Myola, not Meryl, in the first place!

As the wounded started to arrive at Myola 2 ADS from the horrors of Templeton's Crossing, so did the shocking tales of the evidence of cannibalism by the Japanese on dead Australian troops. Starving though the Australians now knew their enemy to be, this was beyond the comprehension of the men, and spurred them on with more intensified hatred and determination to rid this country of people that would do such things. After two days of repeated heavy attacks, they dislodged the enemy from their two positions near Templeton's. The Japanese then moved back to Eora Creek, site of the deserted Army Field Hospital, and set up a series of gun positions on the surrounding high ground.

Bert was working hard to convince his superiors to stop dropping supplies at Myola 1 and move to Myola 2, and also to plan to use the landing strip now nearly ready. On 19 October, a trial drop occurred at Myola 2, and with Bert's encouragement, 'Tubby' Allen sent the following heartfelt plea by telegram to Blamey:

In MDS Myola there are 150 patients. Of these, 35 serious battle casualties require evacuation asap. 10 of these require lying and 25 sitting accommodation if evacuated by plane. If evacuated by carriers whole 35 would be stretcher cases requiring 350 carriers. Field ambulances doing astonishing good work under extreme difficulties, but ADMS considers chances of recovery many cases gravely jeopardised if held forward or carried by stretcher to hospital over 6 or 7 stages. CRE reports landing strip 2100' ready in 2 days & I have received report from an officer experienced in flying his own plane that in his opinion light planes could land and take off at Myola 2. I feel that a pilot with experience of local conditions could be prevailed upon to make such a test landing. Further ambulance accommodation is an impending difficulty. Observed today that Lockheed Hudsons made complete circle within the basin of the lake, appearing not to be more than 300' from ground. This can be verified by pilots who made droppings. As air evacuation of serious cases would solve many difficulties, I do appeal for test landing.

Blamey never replied.

Allen and Captain Rupert Magarey of the 2/6th Field Ambulance kept the pressure on despite Blamey's indifference, and on 21 October a Stinson plane landed successfully at Myola. Colonel F. Kingsley Norris, who was then stationed there also, recalls three small planes landing at Myola and one of the pilots commenting 'Sure, this is a grand little strip', giving them all hope that their supply and transport of wounded problems were now over. One of the lucky few whose life was saved by a flight out of Myola was Colin Richardson of 3rd Battalion. Colin was badly wounded with a blast through his shoulder. Dr Geoff Mutton, brother-in-law of Meryl's good mate Eve, was the surgeon who treated him, at a point where medical supplies were virtually non-existent. Geoff had repaired the chest wound, only to roll him over and find that the exit wound on his back was far worse than the front. With only safety pins left to hold him together, Geoff did makeshift repairs but shook his head at his assistants, believing Colin could not survive. All the same, Colin was carefully carried to Myola by the boys and flown out on the last plane to take a load of wounded. As the Stinson accelerated down the strip, making a surprisingly smooth take-off, Colin lay on the floor of the aircraft, drifting in and out of consciousness. Staring through the open side of the plane at the receding dry lake bed followed by the passing clouds, he knew that if he survived this ordeal it would be thanks to Geoff and Bert. Colin lived to tell his tale.

Unfortunately, wet weather then prevented any more landings until 27 October, when a Stinson arrived with General Vasey on board and took General Allen out. Blamey and MacArthur still felt that progress back to Kokoda was not fast enough, and 'Tubby' was to be one more scapegoat and was to be replaced by Vasey. Yet the Australians had just had a major victory, at great cost, driving the Japanese back from Eora Creek. Their eventual triumph in this protracted battle was owed in the main to Major (later Lieutenant-Colonel) Ian Hutchison of the 2/3rd Battalion, a young but experienced commander who had taken over leadership from the wounded Colonel Stevenson. Hutchison led his men around enemy lines to a high spur further up the mountains than where the Japanese were ensconced with their guns. Charging down with nearly 600 men, Hutchison caught the enemy by surprise and scared the beshintos out of the exhausted Japanese, who literally ran for the lives. They virtually didn't stop running until they reached Oivi Ridge.

Losses at Eora were more than at the Isurava battle just two months before.

'Bloody' George Vasey, an affectionate title he attained because of his colourful vocabulary, was a larger-than-life character – down to earth, with a good sense of humour combined with a high intelligence. He quickly labelled this campaign a 'Q War' – dependent on the Quartermaster keeping up adequate supplies – and he soon established that his predecessor was on the right track and carried on with the tactics Allen had planned. He set off with Bert, ADMS Colonel Norris, Group Leader Colonel Spry and Assistant Quartermaster Lieutenant Colonel Canet on 30 October, past the supply station Bert had the boys set up there only a week or so earlier, which he labelled 'Dump 1', located on the north side of the first crossing of Eora Creek on the track from Myola. They continued on through Templeton's Crossing and Dump 2, another station Bert had just recently had established. After observing with horror the carnage in the Eora area, they pressed on to Alola, where they made camp for a new base for Advance HQ 7th Australian Division. They were now right up with the forward troops and some had not yet arrived. Supplies were running short and an attempted drop at Alola had limited success. The troops pushed on relentlessly and on 2 November had re-taken Kokoda without resistance – at last the circuit was complete.

When news of this success filtered back to Bert, he could not wait to get back to his valley. As he hurried on down through Isurava, he looked out and saw the many fires and through his binoculars saw the burnt-out houses at Kokoda Station and the Yodda. Early on the morning of 3 November accompanied by Colonel Spry and Lieutenant Colonel Canet, he set off from Deniki and arrived triumphantly at Kokoda at 8.35 a.m. to find all the houses destroyed, and to be greeted by locals complaining bitterly of the destruction of their gardens and villages. Later that day, at approximately 1.30 p.m. on the third day of November 1942, Bert stood proudly beside General Vasey as he raised the Australian flag on the site of the old administration building. George H. Johnston in his book *New Guinea Diary* described the scene:

Today Australian troops in ragged, mud-stained green uniforms, in charred steel helmets that had been used for cooking many a meal of bully beef on the Kokoda Trail, stood in ranks around the flagpole . . . There was no cheering. There was no band playing. There were merely the packed lines of these hundreds of weary Australians, haggard, half-starved, dishevelled, many wearing grimy, stained bandages, standing silently to attention in the rain.

The brand new nylon-weave flag had been airdropped by an American fighter pilot that morning for just this purpose, and once it was lowered, Bert would keep it in his careful possession throughout his life, a lasting memory of the day he was able to keep the promise he had made to his boys that they would be back in Kokoda by Christmas. Vasey particularly wanted Bert to have this flag. George had quickly realised that he and his ANGAU men were the key to the success of his 'Q War'. Without their organisational abilities, the troops would not have had the ammunition and supplies to fulfil their objective of retaking Kokoda.

Bert wrote of his return to his home:

It was a relief to see it again even though all the buildings were demolished. The native carriers came in later bedecked with flowers and shrubs and all smiles. They knew they had done well. Even here we could not rest for it was most urgent that supplies be landed on the landing ground as soon as possible. All available carriers which I could muster were put on during the afternoon weeding the landing ground which was overgrown. The Japs had not used it. I also selected a labour camp site next to the aerodrome. The local village people who I had known for years, came in to welcome our return. They told me pitiful tales of hardship and the losses of the villagers who were killed by Japanese. Some immediately joined up to come to the Coast as carriers for us. Our carrier lines started to swell from then. Morale was high. The white man had proved a superior fighter.

He was indeed greeted like a long-lost son, and after organising his men, Bert's next and most obvious priority was to get out to Yodda and check the damage to his home. What he found, although not surprising, fed his anger towards the invaders even more. He wrote with great sadness to his 'darling', the first letter he had had time to write for over two weeks:

Enclosed you will find a few personal belongings salvaged from our home after the japs had destroyed most of what they could. Everything was strewn about the place – piano wrecked, house smashed and riddled with machine gun bullets, mattresses smashed and generally a complete write off. My stamp collection trampled on and lost except for the few which were saved. Keep these and also the note. We will build a new home darling and also one for Mother & Dad. Dad's and Wallace's houses burnt right to the ground with everything in them. Otherwise for overgrowth and neglect it is the same old place – 'it will be again' is my motto. As long as the rubber wasn't slashed to pieces. Of course it is much neglected now but it can be cleaned up. The main thing for me is to know that you and the children are safe, also Mother & Dad.

Sure enough, old Hojavo, who had sent the heartfelt message to Bert some weeks ago, was there to greet him, and he informed Bert that more than 60 Japanese soldiers had been encamped at the homestead and that the houses had recently been strafed by American fighter planes. Also there to welcome him was one of his old boss-boys, Amburere, who had already set to cleaning up the rubber. Bert was most heartened with this and wrote to Meryl: 'There are some faithful among these natives and let anyone say anything against them and they will have me to contend with.' In addition to some stamps, he retrieved some photos, which he sent to Meryl when he wrote again the next day, repeating the details of the damage in case the first letter did not get to her. He reassures her that they will rebuild after the war because it is too beautiful and valuable a place to desert now.

All the livestock had been slaughtered by the Japanese and the vegetable gardens were a mess, but Bert managed to salvage some fruit and potatoes to take back to the most appreciative troops at Kokoda. Up on the plateau, he was lodged in a makeshift grass hut under the rubber trees, once again in the company of Doc, who was now very unwell with fever. After the required hand over of the £10 wager, they celebrated their return to their old home and Doc congratulated Bert on his promotion to captain, something Bert had been told about around the third week of October, although the official notification was yet to materialise. All the men who had been at Myola with him knew, and knew it was well deserved, so they were already calling him Captain, despite his protestations there was nothing in writing yet.

Telegrams of congratulations for recapturing this vital outpost began to arrive, even one from General MacArthur, which read: 'My hearty congratulations to all ranks concerned at capturing Kokoda. These fine troops must feel a pride and satisfaction at this splendid accomplishment which I fully share.' After all the criticism heaped on them in the past, these words were satisfying for the men at Kokoda. A reply was sent: 'Please thank Gen MacArthur for his congratulations which are much appreciated by all. With Kokoda behind the troops are rapidly preparing to chase the Japs further and destroy him.'

Finally also, some accolades were being given to the native carriers. The sixth of November was a red-letter day for some of Bert's 'angels'. At 4.30 p.m. he gathered them all together by the Kokoda airstrip, and as they stood proudly to attention with Bert interpreting, General Vasey thanked them profusely for their loyal service, saying: 'Without your help we would not have been able to have crossed the Owen Stanleys.' The boys, bedraggled and exhausted though they were, behaved magnificently, standing straight and tall throughout the ceremony, each with a bright croton leaf in his hair to add a touch of colour and festivity. Bert spoke briefly and congratulated his men, but also made the point that without the good leadership of his ANGAU assistants the natives would not have proved their worth. Bert would have issued dozens of awards if he could, but just five men were selected to receive medals for outstanding loyalty and service.

The first award, Medal No. 10, was accepted by Sergeant Bagita on behalf of Sergeant Sainopa, a policeman who performed courageous and loyal service at Kokoda with the 39th Battalion. Sainopa had been allocated by the ADC/OIC of Kokoda Station to B Company when they first arrived at Kokoda with Bert in July. He was a powerfully built man of coastal Northern District origin with a good knowledge of the area, and he gave outstanding assistance to this small garrison of men throughout the overwhelming enemy assaults at Awala, Wairope, Gorari and Oive. What he was best remembered for by the diggers of B Company was when way back in July he led them, unflinching, in that 'dark of night' peculiar to the jungle, through enemy lines and along the hazardous Oivi Creek. As they cursed and clattered with their noisy hobnail boots and splashed and splayed on the slimy rocks, Sainopa would put his finger to his lips for them to hush – there were enemy about. 'How do you know?' they whispered. 'I can smell them,' he replied. On they crept, down row after row of rubber trees and through dense tropical scrub, safely to Deniki to join the rest of their exhausted men. Bert would later say of Sainopa that he was a member of that band of PNG nationals who fought and acquitted themselves in a valiant and proud manner throughout the Kokoda Trail/Owen Stanley Campaign.

Gasu, from Kiwai Island, who with others carried stretcher cases under fire at Isurava for the 21st Brigade, was issued Medal No. 11. A Boga Boga native called Kaiduma was awarded Medal No. 12 for giving loyal service to the 25th Brigade, and a Tufi tribesman called Gainde received Medal No. 13 for showing outstanding devotion throughout the campaign. The fifth medal, No. 14, was reserved for an absent native called Bo-o from Delebia, who gave outstanding service to 16th Brigade. He received his medal two days later when he arrived at Kokoda. The other carriers were issued with gifts of tobacco, jack-knives with much valued lanyards, and a *rami* each, and were then treated to an evening feast with many European rations included. Bert had thoughtfully arranged all this back on 22 October when he sent a message to HQ 7th Division Advance Base saying: 'Native Carriers Kokoda L of C Special order for feast for natives when Kokoda taken. 1500 ramies (red calico) 300 lbs tobacco and Double Issue of rations for one day. Also if possible, 1 days rest.'

All of this was a great boost to morale, which was still much needed, for the battle was far from over. The Japanese were still swarming all around the north coast of Papua New Guinea and there was still a huge job ahead for everyone. To further encourage the local people and to demonstrate the army's gratitude, the following memo was sent on 20 November by Major J. H. Jones for distribution to all overseers:

MEDALS – AWARDS TO NATIVES

In view of the many natives engaged in connection with Army operation or associated with rescue work, it has been decided to award medals to natives who have performed brave or gallant acts or rendered services of an outstanding nature. For this purpose officers of the Field Staff will report any instance of this nature worthy of consideration. Well authenticated facts are necessary and citations should be concise and condensed.

The Administrator will make the recommendation for these awards and, where possible, will make the presentation.

The service of native carriers are indispensable to Army operations and the arduous task of carrying supplies and, at times, wounded personnel over hazardous mountain tracks has fallen almost entirely upon the natives. On the course of this, there have been numerous cases of not only conspicuous devotion to duty but of actual courage.

Bert could have listed at least half a dozen other Papuans who should have received medals, one of whom was his loyal mate Kordunga. Back in September, when they had been pinned down in Menari by a Japanese woodpecker machine-gun that was firing down from Brigade Hill, Kordunga said to Bert, '*Oi naria* (you wait here), *taubada*'. He disappeared off into the bush with nothing but a bush knife for a weapon. After a time, the woodpecker went silent and the barrage stopped. Potts sent out a patrol to see what was happening and they met up with Kordunga walking back down the track towards them threading human ears on his belt . . . Japanese ears. By the end of the war, his belt was full of them.

The euphoria of these celebrations at Kokoda was dramatically destroyed when, as the festivities reached their conclusion, a Kittyhawk fighter plane flew low over the plateau, passed over the crowds on the airstrip and, as they watched with trepidation, proceeded to perform a victory roll. As he completed the risky aerobatics, the American pilot, 2nd Lieutenant Nelson B. Brownell of the 49th Fighter Group, lost control and crashed north-west of the strip not far from Saga Village and less than 2 kilometres from the site of the celebrations. The pilot was killed instantly and his plane destroyed. Bert sent several natives out to recover the body, and three hours later they returned with it wrapped in a parachute. It would be many years after the war before Bert and others would manage to salvage the wreckage of the aircraft.

Having been brought back to reality with a real crash, it was on with work again for all the troops the next day. The Kokoda aerodrome was again in a bad state and, as before the war, was of little use in wet weather. Labour was quickly organised lengthening, grading and trying to repair the drainage of the strip. Other carriers were given the task of moving supplies forward to the front line, now at Oivi–Gorari. From 4 to 6 November, up to six DC3 planes a day landed in convoy at Kokoda and disgorged a plethora of supplies never seen before by these battle-weary personnel: jeeps, new weapons and ammunition, fresh meat and vegies, a variety of tinned goods not enjoyed for months, even chocolates, bread, jam and butter. The only disappointment was that a plane with the much needed quinine for the assault on the swampy coast did not arrive. Subsequent investigations revealed that the disoriented pilot dropped the medicine at Amboga Crossing, 50 kilometres north-east of Kokoda and at the time occupied by the Japanese. Then wet weather set in and the next plane was not able to land until 10 November. It brought in Captain Lambden of ANGAU, who was sent in to encourage the local people to reopen their gardens and try to get village life back to normal. This became the mop-up job that befell many ANGAU personnel from here on in. Blamey and others were in a big hurry to see plantation production, particularly of rubber, back on line for the war effort as soon as possible.

Kokoda had become what the Allies had hoped it would be back in July, and what the enemy made a big mistake in not making it become from then on – a vital air base for delivery of supplies and evacuation of wounded. As Bert would say in a letter to author Peter Brune many years later, supplies of food, ammunition and medicines should have been flown into Kokoda way back before 1 July in preparation for the arrival of Templeton and his B Company 39 Battalion – instead of by the slow boat to Buna. Most of these stores ended up in enemy hands. Air force support that now began to occur would have made a huge difference to the whole nature of the Kokoda Campaign if it had been made available earlier in the year.

Soldiers lucky enough to be carried to Kokoda got back to Moresby way ahead of those still languishing at Myola, some of whom were there until two days before Christmas. Despite all Bert's efforts, only around 40 wounded were ever flown out of Myola, although planes did land and depart quite regularly with light loads. On 23 November, the Trimotor Ford VH-UBI flown by the very experienced pilot Tommy O'Dea hit a soft patch on landing, flipping on its nose – what is called a 'ground loop' – and giving Tommy a nasty gash on his head that warranted him being carried down to Kokoda and evacuated from there. This crash was probably the main reason for the final loss of confidence in the airfield. O'Dea had had the same problem at the Yodda almost exactly a year before, when Yodda workers had to push the UBI out of a bog at the end of the strip. The Myola mishap was actually the outcome of someone moving the markers to make the airstrip longer without establishing that the extra length created was mainly mud.

If only they had had the Marsden matting as requested by Bert. On another day a single-engine Stinson crashed on landing. The pilot, along with others who had experienced difficulties, reported that the strip was too short, with too steep a climb at take-off needed to clear the lip of the lake. In a postscript to the sad tale of the wasted opportunity of Myola, on 31 December, the minister for air wrote to Prime Minister Curtin: 'The Air Board recommends that approval be given for the purchase of 20 air ambulances for the work of evacuation of wounded in New Guinea, a special type of aircraft necessary in view of the mountainous nature of the terrain'. When this was passed on to MacArthur he said 'not necessary . . . normal aircraft are suitable'. If this was the case, why were more than 1,000 wounded carried painfully out all the way back along the Kokoda Trail if 'normal aircraft' could have airlifted them? Norris wrote in a damning report at the time: 'In spite of every effort, air evacuation was neglected. Why this was never adequately undertaken – why, after three years of war no adequate ambulance planes were available – why certain casualties had to remain in a forward medical post after being wounded – these and many other questions remain unanswered.' This situation certainly remains the biggest frustration of all of Bert's efforts during 1942.

§

On 11 November, while searching for a suitable new dump site en route to Gorari, at the village of Sengi 2, Bert came across the site where the bodies of seven wounded diggers of the 2/14th and 2/16th, along with their selfless medical orderly, Thomas Fletcher, had been found after their execution by the Japanese. Back in September, this small band of men, many badly wounded, had endured an exhausting and terrifying trek behind enemy lines, heading in the opposite direction to their retreating Australian mates. On reaching the small but friendly village of Sengi, their CO Captain Buckler decided these poor damaged souls, including one Corporal John Metson, who had literally crawled from Eora Creek, his ankle having been shattered by a machine-gun bullet, should remain in the village. Fletcher selflessly volunteered to stay with them, and Buckley and the rest of the relatively able-bodied men headed towards the Kumusi and over the range from there to Moresby. They quickly arranged a mercy airdrop into Sengi but to no avail – the Japanese had discovered these trapped and injured fighters and executed them all, including Fletcher.

As Bert was passing through this village, haunted as it was with the ghosts of heroes, in what has since been called the first decisive strategic land victory in the Pacific War, the 25th Brigade had ousted the enemy from Gorari. The clever outflanking and encircling movement had been planned by a determined Vasey in conference with Bert and Colonel Spry. There were not too many creeks in this valley that Bert had not investigated for 'colour' in his search for gold. He was able to explain the terrain to Vasey, allowing him to formulate his vital, ultimately successful plan of attack. The Japanese had doggedly tried to blast their way out using one of their mountain guns, but they had to abandon this valuable piece of equipment as they made their escape back to the Kumusi River. This ferocious battle became known to the Japanese as the 'Death Valley Massacre'.

It now became a daily race for Bert to establish camps and arrange air drop spots as close as possible to the front, which was shifting faster than he could keep up. By the 14th, planes were dropping supplies at Wairope and Bert, being the first ANGAU man to arrive, found about 300 Rabaul natives stranded on an island in the Kumusi River. Like their wantoks, who Bert had come across in previous weeks, they were in a bad way, emaciated and sick, with many of them bloated from eating spoiled rice left behind by their enslavers. There was much evidence of Japanese activity at the Kumusi as it had been a key staging point in their thrust forward. Rubber boats were found abandoned on the river's edges along with about 500 carcasses of horses, most of which had been shot by their handlers. Other horses were found wandering in the bush, still alive but in terrible condition, with sword wounds across their backs inflicted so they would be of no use to the advancing Australian troops. At some point during this hurried advance, Bert came into the possession of a Japanese samurai sword, which he kept for the rest of his life. The steel blade was stained with blood, and although this most likely belonged to one of these poor unfortunate horses, Bert could not help but think of the horrific Tol Plantation massacre where these men from the Nankai Shitai used their swords to behead many Australian soldiers.

Bridges across the Kumusi River had been demolished and the Rabaul natives reported that the Wairope bridge had been rebuilt at least four times by the enemy each time it was destroyed by Allied aircraft fire. The local natives were all very friendly and pleased to see Bert and his men. They brought fresh food to them gladly, and advised they had not seen any enemy for some weeks as they, the villagers, had been in their hideouts in the bush and nearby hills. News filtered through from captured prisoners of war that General Horii had drowned near the mouth of the Kumusi while trying to make his escape on a roughly built raft. The story was later told that Horii's feeble craft broke up in the rough seas, and the general, who could not swim, fell overboard shouting a final *banzai* as he slipped beneath the waves.

The Orokaiva people now had a chance to redeem themselves. On 9 November, Bert had sent a message to WO Davies re Recruiting Campaign Orokaiva District: '. . . proceed quickest to recruit all available fit Orokaiva men in all districts in our control and beyond. They are to be engaged for one year at 10/- per month for general work and carrying for the army.' He sent his old mate Hojavo off to help Davies with this task.

At Sangara Mission on the 18th, Bert saw first-hand the devastation, with the church and all buildings razed to the ground, and heard with horror the terrible tale of the death by bayonet of the resident missionaries who were betrayed to the enemy by people of nearby Perambata village. He left a message for Elliot-Smith that read:

> Dear Sydney, An urgent request operationally for as many natives as you can possibly rake in in the shortest time. A landing strip is to be made near Popondetta on the Sangara side in the large kunai patch west by morning 22 Nov. All natives impressed should bring knives and axes if available. Our natives are being used to pick up at various planned dropping areas and to carry forward. Send Marsh if you can with natives to supervise . . .

From there, he proceeded to the Higaturu Government Coffee Plantation, where the residence had been burnt to the ground but some outbuildings remained standing. Here, Major Elliot-Smith caught up with him and together they moved on to Popondetta to work together on the landing strip that had been requested by Vasey to supply for the push to the coast. Both Davies and Marsh had been successful in recruiting the Orokaivas, and others, and progress was fast on the first of what would later be one of many airstrips in the Popondetta area. A plane was actually able to land on the strip after only three days preparation – the boys had done well. David Marsh, now a lieutenant, told Bert a little of what he had learnt about events at the Yodda; in particular, that his boys Goga, Mori, Osuna and Imisi had all made for villages in the hills and taken some more of the family's belongings. Unfortunately, their village homes and all the contents had subsequently been burnt by the enemy, so Bert's hopes of recovering some more gear were quickly dashed.

Bert was briefly based at Soputa, where he was busy constructing another landing strip, plus building an MDS and Division HQ, including staff accommodation. Wounded were

arriving in distressing quantities from the fronts at Sanananda
and Gona, and the native labourers were busy carrying out their
many and now varied duties of moving supplies and wounded
plus building roads, aerodromes and housing. Bert had put in
a request for 3,000 more workers for all this work, but actual
numbers fell well short.

One day during this period, a native police boy proudly
walked into Bert's camp with a Japanese prisoner in tow. He
had come across three of the enemy on the Jimburu track all
with empty rifles. Two had escaped but one he managed to
capture and deliver to Bert, who arranged for him to be taken
to HQ. The arrival of jeeps supplied by the US Army had eased
the load and distances that gear had to be hand-carried, and
it was indeed a relief for Bert as well, to be able to get around
on four wheels instead of on foot all the time. A quick trip
by jeep one day may actually have saved his life. He wrote to
Meryl on 29 November:

> I missed being blown to pieces 2 days ago, when our HQ
> was bombed & strafed for the first time in this show. Four
> of my natives were killed and fourteen wounded. That day
> someone asked me to take a run & see Sydney Elliot-Smith
> and the new landing strip, so I went and pleased I was there.
> We were some distance away. I returned about 5pm to be
> greeted with the awful news. One of my personal lads was
> killed, bullet through the back and in stomach. The swine
> also bombed 2 hospitals and killed a number of patients. Two
> of the doctors, very fine fellows, were killed – Vickery &
> Macdonald. They are putting up a most stubborn resistance
> for that small coastal strip and it is annoying to be paying
> such a high price.

Two Japanese Zeros had flown over the MDS the day before
but not fired at all. On 27 November, however, a dive-bomber
formation came over, making quite a few runs and dropping
several bombs, killing the two young medicos and narrowly
missing Colonel Kingsley Norris. They deliberately strafed both

the Australian and American hospitals, which were situated close by with the 7th Aust Div HQ between them. In Bert's report of the incident to HQ, he goes into further detail, naming his 'personal lad' as a young police recruit, RPC Embopa, and noting that several of the other natives killed were Rabaul boys who had survived the brutality of the Japanese only to be killed by them from the air. He notes that these are the first direct casualties in this campaign on the Kokoda L of C as a result of enemy bombing and strafing, and that all the natives behaved splendidly under cool ANGAU supervision, with very few deserting.

Much of this information in Bert's letters and reports appears in his diaries and notebooks along with many other gems, like one page of a little notebook where, amidst the never-ending lists of personnel – ANGAU officers and natives, their names, ranks and locations – he notes the following apparently useful and important piece of information.

'Jungle Juice'
4 tins peaches
10 lbs sugar
3 gals water
4 dessertspoons dry yeast
Mix yeast in cup of warm water. Add to rest of ingredients.
Strain after 4 days & 'see sparks'!

Another popular recipe for this recreational beverage was – 'milk of a green coconut, a tablespoon of sugar and six raisins': when the raisins floated after a few days the brew was ready to consume but it was recommended there be no naked flames in the vicinity at drinking time.

The first week of December saw Bert among it all at Popondetta. Eichelberger, Commanding General of the US Corps, was there trying to regroup and reorganise his demoralised troops. Major Grahamslaw, now Chief DO of the Mambare District, had arrived from liaison work with the American Forces and had been ordered to concentrate on native administration, in particular vigorous patrolling of areas now cleared of the enemy. Both Sydney Elliot-Smith and Doc Vernon were also at HQ. Bert had been put in control of all the labour in the Northern District – more than 3,000 natives all up, with only a handful of European officers to help. Many of his best ANGAU men had been evacuated sick, and of concern to all was that the ever-attentive Doc was still no better himself. Indeed, all of them were suffering from the muggy and malaria-ridden coastal climate. Bert wrote Meryl:

> The climate here is enervating, fever is bad and the troops and carriers are suffering from the strain of the long and arduous campaign. I'll be glad when it is over. Such a lot of valuable lives wasted. War is a wicked thing. It will be a long time before these men recover. Have seen so many go out on stretchers. Don't want to go out that way but I suppose that's the only way I'll get leave. They keep a willing horse going until it drops.

This coastal warfare was very different from the jungle fighting of the Kokoda Trail; probably even worse in some ways. Instead of the steamy but at least shady jungle, the battlefields were muddy, stinking swamps riddled with disease-carrying insects and vermin, or scorching, shadeless kunai grasslands. Roads were virtually non-existent or such quagmires they were impassable except in tanks, which did not arrive on the scene until mid-December. Hiding from the enemy could only be done by sinking into the sucking-mud mires, or digging trenches in the creek banks – something at which the Japanese became expert, making attack from the air by US planes ineffective. To add to the men's extreme distress was the belief that this fight was completely unnecessary and that they were really only fighting and dying to salve the egos of MacArthur and Blamey. They knew that the enemy were starving and had no way of replenishing their supplies. All they needed to do was sit it out and the Japanese would either die from lack of food or surrender, yet more men were killed in the battle for this meagre strip of coastline than were lost in the whole Owen Stanley Campaign.

Bert's workload was enormous; in addition to control of all labour and ANGAU staff allocations and movements, he was handling leave applications, commission applications and recommendations for promotion along with continually dealing with interrogations of recaptured natives. There was a real skill in handling this process, as Papuans are notorious for telling the white man what he thinks he wants to hear, rather than the truth. Bert's knowledge of the language and his ability to pick fact from fiction was vital in these cross-examinations.

In addition, Bert was responsible for investigating and reporting on all native deaths. One such death that caused quite a stir occurred on 5 December when WO Schache shot and killed Pte Sorhe of the 1st PIB after an altercation that was witnessed by three native women. Bert went to Popondetta to investigate the case and, along with Major Grahamslaw, attended a court of inquiry into the matter on 9 December. Doc Vernon's medical report of the incident noted that Sorhe had been shot five times – in the leg, thigh, groin, armpit and lung – the last two wounds being what killed him before he could be operated on. Bert was quite angry about this case and most concerned about the impact it would have on the attitude and morale of other Papuan personnel. A much more trivial case Bert had to investigate was the report from one of his loyal policemen, Sergeant Jinga, that a certain RPC Tohi had 'brought a woman onto the station and slept with her away from the barracks after 9 p.m.'. Tohi pleaded guilty and was fined 20 shillings in default of one month's gaol. He was also recommended to be transferred to another station.

The quick trip away to Popondetta for the Scache investigation once again probably saved Bert's life. In his absence, nine Japanese bombers and 15 fighters raided the landing ground near the MDS and HQ where he was based, and dropped bombs about 700 metres from the runway. One native was killed and the rest fled, all but about 60 being rounded back up in the afternoon. Bert gathered them all together and gave them a pep talk about standing firm and keeping to the instructions given to them by their ANGAU bosses. The next day, the Japanese enraged Eichelberger and the US Army when they bombed the American Field Hospital at Buna, despite the large red crosses clearly marking the top of the tents.

It was around about this time that Bert received word that his tin trunk of personal items left behind in the rushed exit from Kokoda and being flown to him at Popondetta, had been destroyed when the aircraft burst into flames and crash-landed. All his letters from Meryl, his photos, personal papers and reports plus his precious typewriter were lost. He handled this news pretty philosophically, really; by now all he wanted was to survive and these other things paled into insignificance. What did really anger him was news that because the official notification of his promotion to captain still had not come through, his associated pay increase had not been effected. He was not made aware of this for some time because his paybook had been lost by the army bureaucracy. When it did arrive and he saw the oversight, he sent a rather curt telegram to HQ insisting the error be rectified.

Despite all his own problems, Bert still took the time to think of Christmas for his boys, and on 14 December ordered from HQ:

> 3500 ramies coloured red, black, blue
> 3500 7" knives if available
> 300 lbs tobacco.
> If practical, an issue of tea, jam and butter in addition to daily ration scale.

Bert would not be there to see if these Christmas gifts were ever given.

Another frustration that started to irritate Bert as he began to feel more unwell and mentally and physically exhausted was the difficulty in identifying all his native carriers. In August he had requested that a system be introduced where the details of each native on the Kokoda L of C – their name, home village, next of kin, etc. – be placed on a card that was to be held at their base station. He asked for 2,000 of these cards to be printed with the numbers 1–2,000, along with metal discs with the same numbers. The natives would be issued with the discs for identification purposes, similar to 'dog-tags' or 'meat tickets' as the diggers called them. He also intended they could be presented at the end of the war to ensure everyone was fairly paid off. He wrote at the time: 'I do want to see that promises of payment to natives are properly carried out as it is essential for the efficient conduct of our work that faith is kept.' This system was never introduced and Bert wrote on 13 December to ANGAU HQ when replying to a query as to why identification of injured and killed natives was taking so long:

> Regret no detailed records have been possible owing to unsettled conditions during active operations in forward areas and bad communications between stations. My services have been fully occupied meeting demands of Div Comm and various services, necessitating my active outside direction and assistance at all times. Either a Contract of Service or a printed card for each native should have been made available, as suggested by me earlier in the campaign. It would facilitate proper records being kept. The only list of names I have ever received was compiled end Sept and forwarded 2nd Nov.

From this point, Bert's health deteriorated rapidly. Throughout the campaign, as a line-up of other leaders had fallen or been pushed by the wayside, Bert had remained steadfast and irreplaceable, but the physical and mental stress had taken its toll. His diary contains a series of short notes:

15 Dec	Not feeling too well.
16 Dec	Down with fever and diarrhoea.
17 Dec	Evacuated to MDS about 2100 hrs. Dysentery & Fever. Feel terrible and washed out. Air raid.

18 Dec	Moved to Medical Ward. Feel very ill & tired out. Air raid.
19 Dec	Still in MDS. Malaria test negative. Pains still severe but easier in afternoon.
20 Dec	Feeling weak but slowly noticing less blood & pus in motions.
21 Dec	Evacuated to Popondetta Main about 1000 hrs. On arrival advised no planes owing pressure of Zeroes. Feeling weak and all in, take 36 Sulphagera in addition to 60 previous day.
22 Dec	Leave by first plane for Moresby 'Hells Bells' – magnificent flight & view of range. Valley clouded. Myola clear – what thoughts crowd back! Arrive safely at Wards 'drome. A tremendous change has taken place here. What a relief to be in hospital, clean sheets, sisters. Feel better already!

As Bert had feared but predicted, the only way he would eventually get out of there was on a stretcher.

9

CLEANING UP

The 14 months that Meryl was in Sydney waiting patiently for her Herbert to come home safely were sometimes lonely but always busy. With two young children to care for and both her parents and in-laws in the city with her, her days were full. It was the lonesome nights in bed that she most despised. Bert and Meryl's was a sensuous and very physical relationship as well as a real friendship. Until the day he died, Bert could not keep his hands off his little Meryl – she could not walk past him without being grabbed for a kiss or cuddle. Their letters to each other expressed longings of many kinds: they even developed a code for expressing those private thoughts in writing. Many times, Bert wrote that he dreamed of long hours in bed with his sweetheart and that that is where they would spend their time when they were reunited.

Meryl's days were filled with running after Carl, who was a lively boy, always into mischief and becoming quite a little 'tiger'. Meryl's reports to Bert of his development evoked responses like, 'I hope Carl grows up to be a hefty, solid, straightforward young Australian', just like his father, with 'an eye for the beautiful girls'. At one stage, Bert cautioned, 'Don't let him put it over you, my darling.' Unlike his father, he was showing quite an interest in things mechanical, and drew pictures of cars and tractors to send to his Dad. Mary was a quiet, more serious child, hanging close to her mother's side and somewhat overwhelmed by her brother's boisterousness. Her father's letters dream that she, too, will grow up to be 'just like her lovely mother'.

Much as Meryl loved receiving letters from her dear husband, they were also full of requests that she sometimes found hard to fulfil. His hints that she should write more often, holding up as examples the likes of Myola Elliot-Smith, and another young soldier's wife who wrote to him every day without fail, brought much sighing and rolling of her mischievous eyes. Each letter requested things like chocolates, cakes and lollies, magazines and newspapers, shaving soap and tooth powder – and always, photos, photos, please – of her and Carl and Mary. Often when she would put these parcels together they would take weeks to get to Bert, or never arrive at all. His letters, and hers to him, would come in lots of three or four, some three weeks old.

Living at Penrith with her Aunty Dinah Jones, with two young children and their grandparents coming and going was not easy, although Dinah was always most welcoming and helpful. By July, having spent more than six months in this arrangement, Meryl set out to find her own home and had to very quickly learn about business, banking and loans. With family help and Bert's good reputation plus his regular army pay and a monthly stipend from Yodda Goldfields behind her, she organised a loan through the Commonwealth Bank to purchase a house at 68 Wellbank Street, Concord in Sydney. Her success at arranging all this brought copious praise from Bert of how proud he was of his little wife, and in a move that was quite unusual for a man of his generation, he eventually transferred all their funds, including fixed deposits, into a joint account. Mind you, every letter would then include a comment about being very careful with that money, not to spend too much on the house, as 'a man does not need a lot of possessions to be happy'. He liked to know exactly what was in their bank account at every opportunity and had requested Meryl to update all his insurances and be sure to pay the premiums on time, always concerned that she would be okay if something should happen to him. Several times he reminded her, and his parents, to make lists of all their belongings of value that had been left at the Yodda, so that after the war they could claim for the damages. He particularly bemoaned the loss of his stamp collection, something he believed might have been quite valuable.

Meryl's own parents, Nan and Pop Holliday, were in need of accommodation, and her sister Audrey was unwell and demanding of care and attention. They all moved into the three-bedroom house at Concord with Meryl, so Carl and Mary were relegated to sleeping on the verandah. Ailsa and Laura were both still nursing at Sydney Hospital, Laura having had to leave her husband Harry behind in Port Moresby where he had been working for the health department since 1938. They would relieve Meryl whenever possible, keeping an eye on their parents. Audrey remained locked in her room most of the time chain-smoking cigarettes and taking copious quantities of Bex powders. No doubt today she would have been diagnosed with depression but in the 1940s 'a Bex and a good lie down' were the standard cure for such ills. It created an interesting environment for Bert's children, and Wallace in one of his letters to Elsa after the war comments that, in his opinion, Carl and Mary had been overexposed to female company for too long and that Carl particularly needed some 'toughening up'. The reality was that both Pop Holliday and Alfred Kienzle, who Carl called 'Gwongingi' (a mispronunciation of grandfather or a variation of a Papuan word, no one really knew where it came from), were both pretty tough old codgers and would not have given him much quarter.

As Meryl made the move east from Penrith to Concord, she was really going against the flow. Thousands of Sydneysiders were at the same time heading west to the Blue Mountains, Bowral and Bathurst. The rush became a stampede when Japanese submarines arrived in the harbour and shelled some of the eastern suburbs. Alfred and Hally even considered moving to Melbourne, following the lead of General MacArthur, and feeling it would be safer, but in the end decided to remain in their tiny bedsitter apartment at 7 Elizabeth St. Alfred and Hally now always used the surname Kingsley, and Meryl opted to go by that name during the war, registering the children at school when they started as Carl and Mary Kingsley to try to protect them from some of the bullying and bigotry that had resurfaced against people with German names.

Until the reports by ABC correspondent, Chester Wilmot, were broadcast, Australians had been ignorant about the war in New Guinea. But as reports of the fighting began to appear on the front pages of the newspapers all this changed. Indeed for a while the Australian public was exceptionally well informed. But after Blamey relieved Rowell, Chester Wilmot was disacredited, access by journalists to senior offices was cut off and the press was effectively gagged. Most people just carried on with their lives believing what they were told or wanted to hear. Attendance at sporting events continued, although in an effort to get across to the public that there was a war on and some sacrifices should be made, Prime Minister Curtin banned mid-week sport! The Minister for War Organisation John Dedman began an austerity drive that became known as 'Dedmanism'. Women's fashion was severely restricted. Things like silk stockings, fur coats, evening gowns and swimsuits – symbols of frivolity – were banned from sale.

As the months progressed and Bert heard reports of the activities of absent Australian soldiers' wives and girlfriends, his letters became more heartfelt in his love for Meryl, reassuring her that his passion has not been diminished by absence. He told her of men under his command who had poured out their hearts to him about unfaithful wives and broken marriages. Meryl repeatedly assured him of her fidelity and that with her hectic life of family responsibilities, the opportunities for socialising and fraternisation, particularly with the infamous American GIs, were non-existent. This deep fear that tore at many Australian troops was exploited by the Japanese who airdropped leaflets behind enemy lines, some with drawings of an American soldier having sex with a beautiful woman and the caption: 'Take your sweet time at the front, Australian. I got my hands full right now with your sweet tootsie at home'. The troops treated this propaganda with the disdain it deserved, using the flyers to wrap their tobacco.

Bert made sure he reported to Meryl on any friends or relatives he met up with on the Trail. At one stage her cousin Jeff Jones was given leave to spend a day with him in late September. He wrote of this visit:

> Just imagine who has just walked into my camp – Jeff Jones your young cousin – he looks well and his CO (my cobber) let him off for the day. Gave him some lunch and my cookboy made some jam rolls of sorts which were like peaches and cream to him and the others. Didn't we have a chinwag about my darling wife and her relatives.

Bert caught up with Jeff again in late November, down near the north coast, and of course Jeff then made a point of visiting Meryl soon after his safe return to Australia. He was more than just impressed with the 'jam rolls'! He reported to Meryl that he was absolutely amazed to find Bert, clean-shaven and clean clothed, living in a roughly built but relatively warm and comfortable hut. Amidst the destruction and squalor of a jungle war, he was a beacon of civilisation – but this was Bert. His fastidiousness and desire for order and organisation meant he went to great pains to maintain standards when at all possible. His one Kapakapa 'houseboy' come cookboy' and general batman knew what Bert required and did his very best to meet his needs. Bert would not have survived as he did near the front, longer than any other white man without a break, without some attempt to adhere to his strong values on cleanliness and appearance. No matter how bad the situation, Bert nearly always seemed to manage to remain clean and clean-shaven – he believed this was all part of retaining the respect of the boys and of instilling confidence in all around him. His policy had always been that just because you go bush there is no need to go 'bushy' and apart from at 'wash-wash' (*diku diku*) time, Bert would never be seen without a shirt on. He often commented that white men without shirts on in a black man's country stood out like witchetty grubs in black soil.

Meryl in turn passed on to Bert anything and everything she heard that might interest him – even the gossip of the exploits of the actor Errol Flynn. This infamous cinema star had arrived in the Territories in the early 1930s, trading in copra among other things. He ended up living in New Ireland on his schooner *Maski* with a local girl with whom he had at least one child. Flynn had apparently since been accused of the rape of two young girls, and Bert's comment on this bit of gossip was 'as if he didn't get his own way many times before'! There was much excitement when Alfred came across an article in the newspapers about the job Herbert was doing and later a photo taken by Damien Parer of some of his carriers, but no photo of him. He avoided publicity at all costs, part of his nature and for his own fears about security, but something that no doubt contributed to the slow recognition for his efforts during the campaign.

The most distressing letters that Meryl received were those describing the carnage at her home in Papua. The images of her precious piano smashed beyond repair, mattresses with their innards ripped out, refrigerators buckled and destroyed and her personal belongings strewn all over for all to see brought tears of sorrow and anger to her eyes. Bert would later inform her that the initial ransacking had been by Australian troops, followed by occupation and destruction by Japanese finishing off with strafing of the homestead by Allied aircraft. The bullet-riddled roofs then leaked and the resultant water damage really finished the job and left a terrible stench to greet Bert when he arrived. His letters repeatedly reassured her that they would rebuild after the war, but Meryl found it hard to get her head around that thought from way down in Sydney. He wrote:

When this is over we will build a house on a spot selected by you. Somehow it will be different if we open up the roads etc. How many years will it be before we can settle down. It will not be easy having to start all over again . . . if I am lucky enough to get leave, I will just come home without sending you any radio etc. Somehow can't see it happening until after Christmas now.

Meryl also had the unpleasant task of passing on to Alfred and Hally the news that once again they had lost their home and all their possessions as a result of war. Although he always kept his emotions bottled inside, the injustice of it all did not go without its effect on Alfred and his health began to deteriorate significantly. Wallace wrote of his father in a letter to Elsa the following year: 'Life did not treat him too kindly but with all the hardships he has had to put up with he gave us a shining example of "grin and bear it" as I for one never heard him moan either about his loss during the last show or this one.'

Meryl became very frustrated as she heard of and saw many of Herbert's colleagues getting leave, and she read his letters as he despaired if his turn would ever come. She knew he was working long hours seven days a week and she felt it unfair that he was not being given any respite at all, although in her heart she acknowledged he was probably indispensable. His November letters were particularly poignant and introspective, for example when he wrote:

Wonder if we will meet this year again, my darling – don't worry my sweetheart – remember we must win through in the end & you are everything in this world to me. When it is all over I only hope it will be a better world . . . don't know what they will do with me but dare say will have to continue here organising country, natives, production etc. However, I would love to go south on leave to be with you even if it is only for a fortnight. Surely someone else can carry on in my absence. Seems absurd the way they like to cling to a fellow. All very flattering in a way and no doubt feel I have earned it. They rely on a chap a lot. Better that way than to be somebody's doormat. When all this is over will be able to have a good laugh. You will have to sing and nurse me when I come home. Mary & Carl will have to help too. When I come home you will have to promise to be with me every minute of the day and night!

One gets hardened to the sights, smells, acts of mankind in a war. A lot of these men will be different and I maintain should have a say in matters shaping the world after the war. A number of fellows up here who had such a lot to say before this show started are not bad at deserting. When a job has to be done, a man does it to the best of his ability and then can have an easy conscience. If he gets killed in the attempt to fight & work for his country that is just hard luck. Everything else is just so much baloney, when one sees the stark realities of life & death, chiefly death in this game . . . I wish I could spend a few weeks with you & the children. SES promised that I would be going as soon as they can spare me. Suppose as soon as this is over they will want me to open up all the rubber plantations in the district. That will suit me only I want to see you first. Haven't got used to being ordered about and not my own boss. The army just orders.

On 14 December, in what was to be his last letter from the front, and after the loss of his precious tin trunk and all its sentimental contents, Meryl's heart ached when she read his words:

When a man joins the Army he lives in two worlds or has two different lives. The daily one is devoted to his duties for the Army and for his country of which he, if in the frontline, necessarily takes a fatalistic view, and if it comes and he loses his life – well, that is part of the unhappy job. He comes back to his senses whenever he gets mail or gloats over his sweetheart's photo. This makes him realize there's another world where killing and maiming are not the one aim in life. That is the life every sane man wishes to see again ... my life revolves around you, dearest ... Do have a quiet but happy Christmas. Sorry about the presents my darling.

The only 'presents' Meryl had been able to receive from Bert were some of their possessions rescued from the Yodda plus some Japanese postcards and occupation money he sent down 'for the kiddies' when the enemy was retreating and being captured. This money, printed in Japan for use in the Philippines and Australia once the Japanese had occupied those countries as part of their conquering of the Pacific, brought home to Meryl more than anything how serious and committed the Japanese were to taking Australia. It is a pity the majority of the rest of the Australian public didn't really want to acknowledge this reality.

It was with a combination of worry and relief that Meryl learnt soon after receiving that last letter that Bert had been medically evacuated to the 2/9th Australian General Hospital in Moresby. At least she knew he would be safe for Christmas but it was to be the middle of January before he was back in her arms again. During Bert's period of illness, the Australians had made great progress in pushing the enemy off the north coast of Papua, reclaiming most of the coastline from Gona in the west to Buna and Cape Endaiadere in the east. In his communiqués back home, this triumph was attributed by MacArthur to the Allies and lauded by his superiors back in the US of A but the reality was it was first and foremost an Australian victory.

Although Australia is and should be eternally grateful for America's huge part in defeating the Japanese as an Allied enemy, the truth is they contributed very little to the success of the Papuan Campaign, apart from in the final battles for Buna and Sanananda. They started off making the same mistake as Australia by sending raw, untrained and uninformed troops to the northern beaches. Jack Wilkinson would tell the story to Bert after the war of meeting General Eichelberger one day at the American HQ at Sinemi. Eichelberger was blowing up about the Americans being pinned down. He asked Jack, 'Why can't our boys do as well as your boys. Our boys start to attack then stop and get pinned down. They haven't got enough to keep going. Your boys go ahead and take a place and hold it. What is the matter with ours?' Jack told him what most of the Australians knew. The first lot of Americans had landed unprepared and were soon riddled with malaria. Their training was mainly lectures – Jack's comment: 'Too much motoring and ice cream in their training.' They were not seasoned troops, yet they still thought every one of their bullets would find its mark. The Australians had been fighting for two years and were toughened up. Jack did not like to take credit for it, but he noted that from that point the general used Australians as assault troops and Americans as holding troops.

Then there was the fact that they were never, ever on the Kokoda Trail but made claims in newspapers back home that they 'saved the day in the Owen Stanleys and were instrumental in the Japanese retreat'. This, combined with their criticising of the efforts of our diggers there, is still a sore point with the surviving men of the campaign. It is also the reason why some insist the Kokoda Trail is the Kokoda Track because of a strong belief that it was given the name Trail by the US command – not necessarily so, but having borne the scorn of MacArthur, one can understand the animosity and the desire to distance all things American from this defining battle of Australia's war. Even Wallace showed a little rancour when he commented in a letter to Elsa in mid-1943: 'Australia has a lot to thank the American equipment for but as I have said to those Yanks who try to ram it down our throats, they sent it out here to fight their own war as well as ours.' Bert, on the other hand, was loath to criticise his US colleagues. They were good to him and made his life easier with their generosity during the time they worked together in the Popondetta area. He often enjoyed a drink with them at the 'Tropical Paradise' 'tavern', a decorated Papuan hut that some enterprising Allied soldiers had constructed and set up as the local 'watering hole'.

Bert was relieved to hear news of the progress on the other side of the ranges as he lay in bed in Port Moresby, and also to hear from Sydney Elliot-Smith and Captain Baldwin, when they called in to visit him on Boxing Day, that WO Rae had taken over his duties and seemed to be coping quite well. Although Bert was feeling considerably better and enjoying the slightly improved food – especially the 'cooked fowl and potatoes' on Christmas Day – his haemorrhoids had flared up again and required an operation, which was performed on 28 December. He then needed two weeks convalescence before they felt he was fit to make the journey to Sydney. On 13 January he received a set of leave instructions, the bureaucratic balderdash of which brought a wry smile to his face.

You have been granted 31 days recreational leave at Concord in the State of NSW. Attached find leave pass.

For movement to Australia, take with you:
Messing Gear, Helmet Steel, Water Bottle, Emergency Ration, Mosquito Net and Blanket, Items of personal Kit and Clothing.

Return to RQMS before departure:
Kit surplus to leave requirements, Pistol, Compass, Binoculars, Rifle, Bayonet, Holster, Pouches Amm., Ammunition and Blankets. Obtain receipts.

Neatly bundle and label all packages deposited with the RQMS.

Considering he was never actually issued with arms and had to get special permission to provide his own protection in the form of his own Webley revolver, he found this amusing. A series of other instructions followed on movements from and within Australia, and the final paragraph read: 'Get back as soon as you can. There are others waiting.'

§

Bert had always said in his letters that when he eventually got leave, he would not tell Meryl he was coming but would just turn up on her doorstep. With his illness and evacuation to Moresby she felt sure he would be home soon, but this did not detract from the pleasure and joy when he knocked on her door at the Concord house on the afternoon of 19 January, having been delivered to this home he had never seen before in an army staff car. He had first been flown from Moresby to Townsville, then travelled by rail to Sydney, changing trains at the Interstate Railway Station South Brisbane and arriving at Central Station Sydney about 10.30 a.m. (those bloody trains again!), a long and tiring journey despite the relative comfort of a first-class berth. His appearance brought back memories of the dark days when he had blackwater fever, pale and thin with dark circles under his eyes, but his embrace with what Meryl called his 'gold panner's elbows' was strong and his distinctively timbred voice was still the one she had dreamed of during the many lonely nights. Carl threw himself into his Daddy's arms, demanding to be perched on his shoulder and Mary clung possessively to his long serge-trousered leg. As Meryl had also promised in her letters, she nursed her husband back to health, feeding him up on his favourite meals and catering to his every need and desire. The whole family came to share her joy at his safe return, and even Hally showed visible signs of emotion at the safe return of at least one of her stepsons. Wallace remained in the Middle East and she still despaired at the lack of regular news from him.

Bert was originally granted one month's leave exclusive of travel time, which meant he would have to leave Sydney on 19 February. When he was asked to attend the Department of Information and Fox Movietone in connection with his activities in New Guinea, he was first given an extra seven days but he applied to have this extended when they all heard the great news that Wallace would be arriving back in Australia by ship on 27 February. His request was granted so that he did not have to be back in Papua until 7 March. It was more than three years since Wallace had seen his brother and father, so it was wonderful to catch up. They shared war stories and Bert brought him up to date on events at his home in Papua. He convinced him that his service would be invaluable in the ongoing defence requirements up there and Wallace quickly applied for a transfer into ANGAU.

Even before he had left the Territory, plans were being made for what Bert would be doing on his return now that the Battle for Papua was over. The Japanese had virtually been cleared out of this Territory, and on 22 January, Lieutenant General E. F. Herring CBE DSO MC ED, GOC New Guinea Force published an Order of the Day, stating:

> The campaign we have engaged in for the recapture of the Buna–Gona area is now virtually at a close. I desire to express to all Australians and Americans alike who have taken part in this long and tedious campaign my heartfelt congratulations and appreciation for all you have done . . . We have won a striking victory but a long and hard road lies ahead. All I ask is that you maintain the standard you have set. I know you will.

John Robertson in his history, *Australia at War 1939–1945*, summarises the six-month campaign as follows:

> Never again in the Pacific war were Australian ground troops to be involved in so fiercely contested a campaign The Japanese committed about 20,000 men, the Allies 33,000 – the American 32nd Division, the Australian 7th Division and another four Australian brigades. About 13,000 Japanese and 3095 Allied soldiers died. The rate of one death for each eleven soldiers in battle made this one of the Allies' costliest victories in the Pacific. The Australians sustained 6500 battle casualties, including 2165 deaths, the Americans 2000, including 930 deaths. Sixty-two percent of the Australian losses were sustained in the beachhead battles.

Soon after arriving in Australia, Bert received two more letters, one from the AMF finally confirming his promotion to captain – pay increase only to be effective from 16 January 1943 – and one a forwarded letter from Colonel Kingsley Norris.

> I hope by now that you are with your family and having at last a well earned spell. We are still in the same place – for how long we do not know – the rains have come and all the place is a quagmire. I am glad to hear that you will again be our Fairy Godfather & make our existence possible by your splendid organisation which has been so keenly appreciated . . . Now just forget the place for a while and have a good rest and accept for all you have done our thanks & best wishes.

Norris and other ANGAU staff had just that day received a telegram from HQ that included the advice that after return from the mainland Bert would remain at HQ Soputa for administrative duties.

In early February, Bert accepted a request to be interviewed by the press to report on the Kokoda Campaign and on 13 February an article appeared in the *Sun* headlined 'Natives Plucky Under Bombs' – once again Bert goes out of his way to give the credit due to his 'fuzzy wuzzy angels'. The article began:

> Natives who once ran as though seven devils were after them when a bomb exploded, stood up to the strain of being under fire during the Papuan campaign and then proudly showed their wounds to their tribesmen. Fuzzy wuzzies who were cookboys, lorry drivers, stewards and engine drivers before the war shaped up well in battle conditions as carriers.

Bert is quoted as saying:

> We had to use a little propaganda on the boys. When the Rabaul boys who had been in the hands of the Japs were

captured emaciated and ill-treated, I lined them up before my boys and showed them what the enemy did to them. That went well. I told them we must not rest until the Japs had been driven right out of Papua.

Another Sydney paper headed its storyline: 'The Man Who Blazed the Kokoda Trail ... Captain Kienzle in Sydney' and quotes Bert as saying:

The natives did a job which will ever remain an epic in the Pacific War. They moved army provisions, blankets and all manner of stores over parts which once seemed impassable. The New Guinea natives now realize whose side they should be on for they are convinced that Australia is fighting to preserve their territory from devastation by the Japanese.

As Meryl and her children farewelled her husband once again at Central Station on 5 March, he hoped at least that on his return to his beloved Papua, his life would be a little more civilised and safer although he accepted there was still a lot to do and there were no guarantees as to when he would be back with his family once again. He certainly made sure that Meryl had a permanent reminder of his visit. A little less than nine months after his departure, Diane Meryl (Kingsley) Kienzle was born on 4 November 1943.

§

Back at ANGAU HQ Soputa, Bert was straight into work, and in addition to his newly defined position of OC ANGAU Labour Mambare District he was working with the US Army 41st Infantry Division, which was now under the command of Major General Horace H. Fuller. The many airstrips in the Popondetta–Oro Bay area had become an important base for the battle for the western Pacific region, which was developing into a US project more than an Australian one. The Japanese were still resisting strongly in New Guinea and on the islands of Bougainville, New Britain and New Ireland. All the US commanders and troops were instructed by Major Eugene S. Tarr, AGD, Adjutant General to cooperate fully with Captain Kienzle on all matters pertaining to inspection, pick-up and transfer of natives in the area. Bert later received a personal note of thanks from Major General Fuller that read:

I desire to commend you for the excellent manner in which you have performed your duties during the last 5 months. Throughout this period of time you have been in close contact with the 41st Infantry Division in your assignment as Administrator for the natives of the area. Your loyal, coopera- tive and willing assistance at all times in the assignments, movement and allotment of natives has been outstanding and of extreme value to the Division in the performance of the tasks allotted it. In addition to commending you officially, I wish to add my personal appreciation for all that you have done to assist this division in carrying out the duties which have been assigned.

Along with many other ANGAU officers, Bert was also involved with the rehabilitation of Papua, its village life and its plantation life. Many of the people had been badly affected by the decimation of their homes and gardens, and starvation and malnutrition were an ongoing threat. Bert saw to handling of compensation claims and to distribution of emergency rations and of vegetable seeds and seedlings to rejuvenate gardens. 'Gal' Loudon, now a major with ANGAU and assistant quartermaster general, had the responsibility of reopening plantations in the district as soon as possible and, in early March, again placed Lieutenant Graham in charge of all the rubber estates in the Kokoda area, most of which belonged to the Kienzle family. They had six leases going when war struck, a total of 1,450 acres. As before, Bert would rather have been there doing this job himself, but accepted this was not where he was most needed by the war effort and appreciated that Loudon instructed Graham to keep in touch with him at all times. Bert arranged for WO Booker to be transferred to Kokoda to act as Graham's assistant, and he set about trying to arrange up to 100 recruits for the plantations at Kokoda.

One issue that was starting to cause Bert a few problems was the new relationship developing between natives and expatriates. Brigadier Cleland, now DA and QMG of ANGAU and therefore Loudon's boss, had also communicated to Bert his concerns in this area. The American servicemen were far more familiar with the local inhabitants than Australians had been taught to be – understandable when there were quite a few African-American GIs. In the case of the Australians, including many of the ANGAU staff, they had fought, suffered and died along side their coloured comrades and the old colonial ways now seemed out of place. But from Bert's point of view, although he understood and acknowledged the trend, now was not the time to loosen discipline. There was still a huge job to be done and maintaining control was vital. He was moved to issue routine orders at the end of March re-establishing how natives should be treated in all matters. This directive went to US and Australian staff and troops and covered everything from issue of paybooks and ID discs (now finally available for some native labour) to medical evacuation and relations with, movement of, trading with and discipline of natives.

Not long after his return to Papua, Bert received by telegram the distressing news that his father had passed away after a series of heart attacks on 21 April. Alfred had been actively applying to the military authorities for permission to return to the Yodda and get on with rebuilding, but fate was not to allow him to get back to his much-loved home in the valley. It was fortuitous that Laura was there to nurse him for his last days, and Wallace was still on leave in Australia and so was able to handle all the necessary funeral arrangements and location of Alfred's last will and testament. Wallace wrote to Elsa in America:

> No doubt you are interested in the contents of the will which in commonplace language is as follows: during Mum's life all

income from various sources goes to her. On her death, 750 pounds cash goes to Herbert and the residue is equally divided between the four of us or children as the case may be. Most of the income is what comes from home so the sooner we win this war, the better for all concerned. However, Mum will have quite sufficient to live on so there is nothing to worry about.

Wallace thought that this clear explanation and the family's knowledge of what had happened at the Yodda during this war would have put an end to discussion, but both Elsa and Laura would belabour the whole issue of Alfred's will for several more years. This eventually caused a huge rift between Bert and his sisters, with Wallace trying to be the peacemaker until he also lost patience.

Back at the Yodda, Lieutenant Graham continued to arrange for the necessary repairs and renovations to be made to the Kienzle plantations so that tapping could start again soon. In addition to the positions of deputy adjutant and quartermaster general, Brigadier Doug Cleland had been appointed chairman of the Australian New Guinea Production Control Board (ANGPCB) responsible directly to the minister for external territories in Canberra. The Curtin Government in consultation with Blamey had allowed plantation owners to start returning to Papua in January 1943, but even two years later only 64 of the 93 operational rubber and copra plantations were back under the control of their owners. The problem with all this for Bert was that if he was back at the Yodda he would have got straight back to mining the gold, the proceeds of which would pay for the rejuvenation and continued planting of rubber. This was what they were doing when war broke out. However, there was no one aside from himself and Wallace capable of reopening and operating the goldfields. The PCB was not paying the expenses involved in restarting the plantations, nor was it as efficient as Bert and his family, who had always been very careful with their expenditure. For example, they had a system that they continued for their whole time at the Yodda where all workers had gardens and so could supplement their rations of European foods with their natural diet. This saved money, but Lieutenant Graham did not re-instigate this system and hence the bills Bert started to receive for labour and associated costs were way above his budgets.

Also frustrating for Bert was the lack of action he was receiving on his claims for compensation for damages by both the Allies and the enemy to his houses and possessions. About the only thing he seemed to get paid for was the vegetables he provided to the PIB when they first crossed the Trail in March 1942. It would appear Bert had been advised by someone in the bureaucracy that the one place where there were available funds was for provision to troops during the campaign. He therefore put in a claim for 105 tons of sweet potatoes valued at £490. However, he did not receive this until May 1944 and in the meantime, correspondence flew back and forth between his solicitor in Sydney, J. N. Gammell, and the ANGPCB.

He was able to fill Wallace in on all these problems when he called in to see Bert in July on his way to Bougainville, where he was to be stationed with ANGAU, much closer to the front than Popondetta as the Japanese still occupied half of that island. They spent 10 days together and Wallace again put in a request to be stationed in the Mambare/Northern District closer to home but this was not to be. He must have done a good job despite preferring to be stationed elsewhere, because in August he was promoted to captain. Soon after he wrote to his sister of their big brother:

Herbert has made a really marvellous name for himself up here and is spoken of in the highest regard by all high ranking officers. Any day now his promotion to Major should be through and not before time: if he had been in the American Army he would have received the DSC. Actually some of our Colonels that I have spoken to cannot understand why he wasn't decorated.

Bert was never actually promoted to major; nor did he receive anything like the accolades he deserved. Major Noel Symington was quoted as saying after the war:

> I do not consider that sufficient recognition was made to this gallant officer by the army commander or his country. They gave him an MBE or something: a bloody insult.

Bert had actually been mentioned in dispatches in the *Commonwealth of Australia Gazette* No. 114 dated 27 May 1943, but none of this really worried him too much except that he would probably have liked to have received the extra pay of a major to help cover the mounting bills from the ANGPCB.

§

From the early stages of 1942, news and reports were filtering back to the Australian Government of atrocities committed by invading Japanese troops in New Guinea and its islands, most notably the Tol Plantation massacre of Australian prisoners on New Britain, followed by abuses at Milne Bay and on the Kokoda Trail. In December 1942, Australia applied to join the United Nations War Crimes Commission, which had been established initially to examine the charges against individual criminals for extradition by the ally laying the charges. In June 1943, the government issued a commission to Sir William Webb, Chief Justice of Queensland, to take evidence from witnesses of war crimes in Australia's theatres of operation. Much to Webb's consternation, he was not permitted to carry out this Atrocities War Commission in Port Moresby because it was still considered to be an operational area, and hence not safe. Bert, along with Tom Grahamslaw, was brought to Mareeba in North Queensland on 23 October to give evidence before the commission, where he was questioned on several matters in which he had been involved in the initial discoveries or inquiries.

He and Tom took turns acting as interpreters of native witness reports: in Bert's case, he spoke for two of the men, Aikere and Jajata. With regard to the evidence of cannibalism of Australian soldiers by Japanese, he was questioned at length about whether it was possible that the native carriers may have been the culprits, rather than the enemy. Bert stated that to his knowledge, the Orokaivas, who were the main Papuan tribe known for cannibalism in the past, and some of whom were carrying for the enemy, had not been known to commit acts of cannibalism since before the turn of the century. It was said that a Mambare chief consumed white human flesh around 1905, but Bert believed that the boys under his control would not revert to such barbarism. He could not guarantee this of the enemy's carriers, as the Japanese used rather than worked with the native people. He also commented that if white man should leave the country altogether, the natives would probably revert to their cannibalistic ways before too long, but concluded by saying he did not believe the evidence of cannibalism that he saw had been committed by Papuans.

In the investigations into ill-treatment of natives, he gave evidence of the boys he had come across, many with bayonet wounds in their buttocks, who had obviously been stabbed when they became too tired to continue carrying. They were also emaciated, with badly damaged feet and some with their toes worn to the bone. He repeated the tale he had been told by an Orokaiva called Dide who had witnessed 11 Biagi natives being bayoneted to death near Kokoda. Many of his examples were then corroborated by Doc Vernon, who had the job of treating the poor damaged fellows.

Bert was also questioned about the bombing of the Australian and American Field Hospitals at Soputa in November, and stated he firmly believed that the enemy pilots could not have mistaken the buildings for anything other than hospitals and that they deliberately strafed these unlawful targets.

Of further interest to Bert, part of the commission's brief was to investigate the case of the now infamous betrayal and murder of two missionaries, Misses Hayman and Parkinson, killed near Popondetta. Also detailed was the not so well-known story of nine other people bayoneted to death by the Japanese at Buna. This group included three women, two of whom were European missionaries, a child and five men. It is suspected that an Australian officer who had been with the group was also killed. All of these deaths were attributed to betrayal by Orokaivas but this commission was only concerned with treatment of the captives after they were handed over to the enemy. The matter of the treason of the natives had already been handled by a court in Popondetta in September.

Captain W. R. Humphries, who had been Senior Resident Magistrate in Port Moresby before the war, and had at some stage during his 31 years in Papua served as OIC of every district except Daru, was the presiding magistrate in this controversial court case. Assisted by the investigations of Major Grahamslaw, Humphries carried out four separate trials and over 100 witnesses were called. The outcome of these trials was that a total of 34 Papuans were found guilty of treason and sentenced to be hanged. Twenty-two of the hangings occurred at Higaturu Station about 12 kilometres from Popondetta over two consecutive days, five on the first and 17 on the second. The spectacle was witnessed by several men, including Bert's fellow ANGAU officer Captain Russell Smith. Although Bert acknowledged that some sort of example needed to be made of the guilty men, like many others, he felt the decision to hang them was pretty rough justice. The leader of the traitors, Emboge, long an adversary of the white man, was defiant to the end despite admitting to watching the beheading and mutilation of the two missionaries after handing them over to the enemy. Emboge, being an expert at 'running with the wolves and hunting with the hounds', once he realised the Japanese were the losing side, had been a great help to David Marsh in recruiting workers for the Popondetta airstrip construction. Unfortunately, this good deed was not enough to change his punishment. Humphries pronounced the sentences, having court-martialled and tried the men fairly and properly, and established that they had no defence and could not justify what they had done. In his *Recollections of Angau*, Tom Grahamslaw wrote:

> The day before the hangings relatives and friends of the condemned men trooped through Higaturu wailing and beating drums. These groups included women who had gashed their foreheads and cheeks until blood welled. As a group reached the flagpole near the office, their wailing would suddenly cease and they would pound the earth in unison with their feet. These expressions of grief accentuated the feeling of depression which permeated station personnel, European and Native alike. On the morning of the executions the hillsides surrounding the gallows were packed with thousands of natives and there was a hushed silence as we appeared.

The hangman was a reluctant soldier who was ordered to do the job, and it is believed the Australian Government was not consulted or immediately informed about the decision. In fact, most of the details of the whole event were hushed up until well after the war. Russell Smith would later say that he believed it was 'the best kept and darkest secret in modern Australian history'.

§

The Atrocities Commission completed, it was Sir William's policy to have every witness verify the accuracy of the transcript of their evidence by signing it in his presence. Bert was not able to check his evidence before the commission was due to depart for Rockhampton, so he was required to wait in Australia to catch up with the commissioner either in Brisbane or Sydney at a later date. Bert, of course, opted to sign the transcript in Sydney, so was granted leave to visit his family there awaiting Sir William's return from Queensland. The timing could not have been better. It meant he was there for the birth of his third child and second daughter, Diane Meryl, born on 4 November.

In Bert's absence from the field, Captain Russell Albert Smith handled his work, taking on the position of DADNL (Deputy Assistant Director, Native Labour) – Buna, Dobodura, Oro Bay areas. A year before, as warrant officer, Smith had led the 2nd Battalion 126 US Infantry Regiment across the Owen Stanleys via the Kapakapa Trail, making them the only Americans to cross the ranges on foot. At the time, the Americans described Smith as 'a tireless worker, extremely capable in handling natives and enjoying the respect of all personnel'. He had been a journalist with the *Papuan Courier* before the war, and Bert said of him that he was one of the best linguists he had ever met. Bert could relax knowing Smith would do an excellent job. He still took time while at Concord to keep communicating with his solicitors with regard to the control of his plantations and they did manage to convince the PCB to allow payment of amounts owing to be deferred until either the plantations were in full production, or he or Wallace was granted leave from the army to return to the properties and reopen the goldmining operation.

Wallace, after a stint in hospital with a bad bout of malaria in September, was now firmly ensconced at Bougainville, and had been placed in charge of nine other officers and 387 carriers in the operational areas of the Numa Numa Trail across the island. ANGAU was experiencing continual problems with the quality and control of native labour in this theatre of operations so there was little chance that Wallace would be released from his duties to return to the Yodda.

Sir William Webb arrived in Sydney on 14 November and Bert was able to sign his transcripts on the 15th and make his way immediately back to PNG. The outcome of investigations of Sir William and his panel of four assisting judges was a report presented to the government on 15 March 1944 entitled 'Report on Japanese Atrocities and Breaches of Rules of Warfare'. Later in that year, Webb travelled to England to present his reports on this and the other two similar commissions over which he presided to the UN War Commission.

§

Bert returned to his duties in the Northern District, continuing to coordinate all aspects of ANGAU's responsibilities in the area that related to native labour and the native peoples' lives in general. With Oro Bay now a US naval deepwater port connected by road to the Allied airbase at Dobodura, and Buna a port mainly used by Australian shipping, this area had become the major base for Allied seaborne operations on the north coast of New Guinea and the Solomon Islands. Labour requirements were massive, resulting in a major disruption to village life in the area.

On 23 December, Captain Herbert Thomson Kienzle was most heartened to hear that he had been awarded the MBE. An extract from the *Commonwealth of Australia Gazette* No. 271 read:

> To be a MEMBER of the Most Excellent Order of the British Empire. MBE. Military Division. His Majesty the King has been graciously pleased to approve of the Award for Distinguished Services in the South-West Pacific Area, to the undermentioned.

> During the campaign in the Own Stanley Ranges, Lieutenant HT KIENZLE was at the HQ 7 Aust Div as OC Native Labour and has remained on Div HQ ever since in that appointment. In the march over the ranges, most arduous conditions were encountered. The rough and mountainous nature of the country made the work of the natives difficult and exhausting and only the skill, patience and perseverance of this officer were responsible for them continuing their tasks. He constantly cared for them and looked after them, and his efforts and ability were largely responsible for reducing the number of desertions to an absolute minimum. In conditions that were always arduous and trying, Lieutenant Kienzle always retained control of the situation. In his handling of the natives upon whom the division relied for transport of

its stores and for the evacuation of wounded, he contributed in no small degree to the success of the division. Lieutenant Kienzle is accordingly recommended for the MBE.

Military records at this stage still noted Bert as lieutenant, temporary captain but at least he was finally receiving some recognition for his efforts. Telegrams began to flood in from the likes of Majors Baldwin and Lambden, Colonel Norris, Brigadier Cleland and Lieutenant General Herring, and eventually there was even a personal letter from General Blamey, Commander in Chief Australian Military Forces, which read:

> Dear Captain Kienzle, I wish to congratulate you on your appointment to be a member of the Military Division of the Most Excellent Order of the British Empire MBE, bestowed upon you by His Majesty the King. Your unfailing loyalty and keen sense of duty is well deserving of the high honour conferred upon you. You have set a fine example to those serving you and been a source of great encouragement to all. It is a great pleasure to congratulate you on the recognition of your services.

It was satisfying to now see the military beginning to acknowledge what a huge role Bert had played in the success of the Kokoda Campaign, but the true importance of that role was probably best put in the words of Dr John Bain of ANGAU, who commented some time after the war: 'I have often reflected on how different things might have been had Kokoda not had Bert Kienzle.' Many years later, Alan Powell, author of a book about ANGAU, *The Third Force*, was to go even further when he wrote: 'No man on the track did more to ensure the Australian victory than Lieutenant Bert Kienzle.'

10

TRIUMPHS AND TRAGEDIES

It was to be late June 1944 before Bert was able to return to the Yodda, and this only occurred because of a series of other events in ANGAU. Major General B. M. Morris DSO was still GOC ANGAU, a position he held throughout the war period. Dudley McCarthy, the war historian, described Morris as 'an unassuming and cautious man with a strong sense of duty and sound common sense'. In late 1942, Brigadier Cleland was appointed chief of staff ANGAU. Initially, he and Morris seemed to be on different wavelengths, but Cleland, who had the full support of Blamey, used his diplomatic skills to overcome this tension while at the same time maintaining the respect of the planters. He was, however, finding it very difficult to cope with both this job and that of chairman of the ANGPCB, particularly as Morris was away a lot travelling the country on his much favoured inspection tours. To assist Cleland, Colonel W. E. Graham took up the appointment of deputy chairman PCB and carried out most of the board duties. The resultant reshuffle of staff meant that Bert was moved back to the Yodda Valley and made OIC Kokoda Group Plantations, still in the employment of ANGAU.

Cleland continued to do his best to demilitarise Morris's administration and to placate the planters as they returned to their estates and adjusted to army control. Many felt that they were going to be left out of the loop when it came to post-war planning for the future of Papua and New Guinea. Some facetiously called the Territory 'Angauland', and commented that it looked like becoming an exercise in socialism for the Australian Government. Cleland tried to bridge the gap, but to add to his woes, in August 1944 Morris's Beaufort aircraft in which he toured the Territory overshot the runway at Cape Gloucester, leaving Morris with two broken legs. His evacuation to Australia for treatment left Cleland with more than he could handle, and Graham's presence was a godsend. The latter succeeded Cleland in both his posts of DA and QMG ANGAU, and chairman of the PCB, in March 1945.

This transfer of Bert back to his home came almost too late. He had become very frustrated and a little disillusioned with his job at 7th Div HQ. He felt there were now others quite capable of doing his duties and there was obviously no room for advancement where he was. By this time, the Japanese had been driven off the whole of New Guinea and its islands. Not long after his return from Australia in March, some of his 'brass' colleagues suggested that the best course of action for him would be to offer to serve overseas with the AIF, into which he had been officially transferred in January 1943. They felt that he would warrant the rank of colonel if he were to do this. Bert wrote and offered his services to the AIF. Considering his achievements, and the fact that he was still not quite 39 years of age, he received a rather interesting, bureaucratically condescending reply to his application from the military secretary on 7 April 1944:

I am directed by the Commander-in-Chief to inform you that, as it is not proposed to second the AIF officers, who, by reason of age or medical classification, could not be posted to an AIF unit or formation for service overseas, it is regretted that your commendable offer for service with the AIF cannot be accepted. It has been proved by experience that the conditions of modern warfare are such, particularly in tropical areas, that officers above the upper age limit for the various ranks find it most difficult to perform their duties under the conditions of present-day active service and at the same time carry out those duties efficiently. The incidence of casualties and sickness in such cases has already been excessive. You will readily appreciate that unless an officer can be accepted for AIF service anywhere, it is undesirable to gazette him to the force. Although you will not be gazetted to the AIF it has been decided that you may continue to wear the title 'Australia' and the grey background to your colour-patch, if you so desire, a token that you have volunteered for service anywhere. Your readiness to offer your service is, however, a criterion which gives the Commander-in-Chief confidence that you will fulfil your duties with unabated efficiency, and he desires you to know that your endeavour to serve the interests of your country anywhere is fully appreciated.

Although the comments about tropical warfare amused Bert, it was probably a good thing his application was refused, and it is also doubtful with his hip damage that he would have passed the physical examination anyway. Soon after receipt of this letter, he was back in hospital with a bad attack of malaria, this after also being bedridden with fever in January. The AIF division he would have joined was ultimately sent to Borneo and was involved in the horror of the Sandakan death march.

So, with no choice but to remain in PNG, Bert set about in earnest getting the plantations up and running again. Without Wallace there, and while still under the control of ANGAU, he could not get the gold going, so the financial situation continued to be of concern, as was finding and keeping good workers, most of whom were employed elsewhere or just enjoying some time out back in their villages. One light at the end of the tunnel was the fact that the more mature areas of rubber, those on Mamba Estate, were starting to produce quite well. The forced spelling when they probably normally would have been tapped had given them extra maturity that began reaping rewards. Also, the newly built factory had not been damaged too badly and was able to be completed and put into operation fairly quickly. Along with labour, roads, road transport and housing were his biggest challenges. He had managed to acquire one jeep but found it most frustrating knowing there were lots of unused army vehicles down around Popondetta that at this stage, despite his requests, he was not allowed to procure. Even though there was an acute shortage of rubber brought on by the war, with price control the price of rubber remained fixed at Aus 12s 6d a pound. The argument used for maintaining this price was that synthetic rubber was now being used more and more in the United States, making up for the increase in demand by the war effort. To increase the price of natural rubber, especially to the levels suggested of 'dollar rubber' – 1 US dollar a pound – would, advisers believed, be economic suicide for countries like Malaya and Papua New Guinea. In Australia, although some processors were changing to synthetic rubber, it was proving to be harder to work and slower to process, thus involving more labour hours. It was also not suitable for making quality tyres. Despite this, because the sale price of their products was also fixed by the government, the likes of Dunlop Rubber had to go along with the 36c/lb London set price of natural rubber, which was not of much help to Bert and other planters who were experiencing increasing transport and labour costs.

Having thoroughly assessed the situation at the Yodda, Bert wrote to 'The Superintendent of Claims, War Damage Commission, Martin Place Sydney' detailing his estimates of war damages and finishing his letter with the statement:

> The temporary loss of this income during the period of hostilities, coupled with the additional loss through war damage, has depleted available capital resources of the owners to a minimum. It would be very helpful in the question of finance if representations could be made though the correct channels to the War Damage Commission, who have accepted our claims and particulars can be furnished, to pay the assessments

now, thereby assisting the development and rehabilitation of the properties.

The result of his letter was a total payment from the War Damage Commission for War Damage to Property of £500 16 shillings. This, on top of the money received for sweet potatoes in May meant he collected a total of just under £1,000 compensation for all the damage to his properties, and the goods he supplied to the armed forces.

In August 1944, just a little less than one year after his last visit to Sydney, the pain in Bert's hip from the damage he had done in 1942 was becoming a real problem. Osteoarthritis had set in. He was sent south for treatment in the Military Hospital in Sydney, being transferred to outpatients by late September. He obviously wasted little time, and nine months later on 31 May 1945, his second son, John Alfred Stanfield Kienzle was born. Once again, Dr John Mutton delivered this latest addition to the Kienzle clan, and this time his wife Eve, Meryl's best mate, shared the trials of pregnancy, herself giving birth to a daughter Helen only five weeks later.

§

Returning to Papua in early October, life continued with a certain amount of routine for Bert throughout the rest of 1944 and early 1945. During this period, there was much debate in the Australian parliament and in both the local and mainland press about the future of Papua and New Guinea. Many of the Labor politicians in power at the time began to demonstrate a trait that would continue for more than 30 years – a real ignorance and lack of understanding of life in the Territory and of both the European and native people who inhabited it. Despite warnings that no decisions should be made on the future administration of the Territory of Papua and the Mandated Territory of New Guinea without close consultation with its residents, rhetoric coming out of parliament indicated an intention to impose regulations on the 'slave-driving exploiters' many ill-informed politicians believed the Europeans in New Guinea to be.

Much of the source of this misnomer was a misunderstanding of the indentured labour system that had been in place in the Territories before the war. Exaggerated reports of natives being dragged from their villages, forced to work for slave-level wages, and kept away from the families for up to seven years were tabled by fanatical socialist MPs. Articles appeared in both Australian and Papuan newspapers by experts attempting to clarify how this system worked and how successful it had been, especially in Papua, where Sir William MacGregor had framed the Native Labour Ordinance as far back as 1892. On commencing as administrator in 1906, Sir Hubert Murray set about ensuring that the policing of this Act was properly performed and the result was a system that far from exploited the natives. It actively protected them. Most planters felt that indenture was necessary if industry was to survive because the Papuans had not yet learnt the responsibility of employment arrangements and the need for continuity of work.

The indenture system ensured that labourers were given an adequate wage, good and plentiful food, housing far more comfortable and hygienic than they were used to back in their villages, and a safe return to their homes when their contracts ended. The term of indenture was limited to three years, although a one-year contract was more usual. No native was permitted to work under indenture for more than four years without returning to his village for a time therein and remaining there long enough to re-establish his rights and status in the community. No pressure was to be brought to bear to induce natives to join up, and all contracts had to be signed in front of a magistrate, who would confirm that the native wanted to be employed and had not been coerced. The Department of Native Affairs sent representatives out to all employment locations on a regular basis to ensure all terms of contracts were being met. Recruits were expected to work 50 hours a week and only at the work specified on their contract for which the magistrate had established they were suitable.

There were punishments in place for any overseer who struck a native – three strikes, and he would no longer be allowed to employ native labour.

How this system could be a 'monstrous injustice', as one politician claimed, was beyond the understanding of Territorians. To add insult to injury, these same 'pollies' made accusations that most of the European residents shot through to Australia as soon as hostilities began with Japan. Apart from the Daru Derby participants, who were mainly bureaucrats, this was not true, and they were told so in no uncertain terms by journalist Judy Tudor, who wrote to the editor of a Sydney newspaper:

> In answer to Mr Bryson (Lab. Vic), the men of New Guinea and Papua have a war record second to none. In 1939 and early 1940, every able-bodied man who could, left the territories to join the AIF, Navy or RAAF. Many of them paid their own fares to Australia to do this: others enlisted in NG contingents in the territories. They served in Africa, Syria, Greece, Crete, over Europe and in every ocean. Many will never return. Those who remained were mostly over-aged men from WWI. Almost to a man they joined the NG Volunteer rifles when the Japanese invaded the Territory, they stood to fight in the truest tradition of the ANZAC. Other members of the NGVR on the mainland were for months employed as scouts. Located in enemy occupied territories as far afield as Aitape and the Sepik River, they risked their lives hourly to keep Allied HQ posted on Japanese movements. These men were the spearhead of the Allied advance in the area: they led patrols wherever it was humanly possible and their peculiar knowledge of the country was invaluable to our cause.

Three Liberal politicians at the time, Messrs Anthony, White and Abbott, also stood up against Bryson and accused him of lying, which only awarded them a reprimand from the speaker.

Meryl kept Bert informed of all this by sending him the newspaper cuttings and it certainly did not help his state of mind with regard to the Australian Government of the day and its understanding of what had occurred and should now occur in Papua. In February 1945, Bert wrote to R. W. Robson, editor of the *Pacific Islands Monthly* and later author of *Queen Emma*, expressing his concern at the lack of understanding by Australian parliamentarians of the whole situation in the territories.

> All your warnings and those of the press have not made any difference to the one-sided policy adopted by Canberra and, according to the latest advice, to be enforced shortly in this Territory. There are many subjects to express an opinion on and I am anxious as an old Territorian of 18 years standing and one 'who remained to fight for his country and the Commonwealth' organised, encouraged and led the now famous 'fuzzy wuzzy angels' over the Owen Stanley and Buna campaigns, to see that the truth is known to the public. These natives would NOT have given such loyal and outstanding service in the early days of the campaign, when the enemy was in strength and our forces were few, without the few men (mostly residents of Papua in AMF) who kept them together. It is not widely known that the men who actually were in charge of the natives were ex-planters, miners and commercial men. Later men of the Administration acquitted themselves in an outstanding manner also. This war was fought by all sections of the community and as part of the British Empire which gave its contribution, the European community of able-bodied men in Papua and New Guinea were loyal and dependable. I have always felt that a large measure of the loyalty of the natives especially in Papua was due to the fact that under Sir Hubert Murray's administration (a wise policy that has been put in the background by Canberra) the European residents in Papua pre-war had a more sympathetic understanding of the natives. This did not mean 'buying' their friendship or understanding with policy speeches or votes. It was the personal courage and good conduct of most of the Europeans. Not enough credit is given to Murray's policy . . . Hasten with self-government and other new ideas of improvement slowly and wisely. Also take

into consideration the economic factors which will arise soon when peace comes . . . the statements made by some members of parliament are damaging, untruthful and slanderous and should be exposed as soon as possible for what they are. Perhaps one day I will reveal the truth about the 'Kokoda Trail' as I was the only one in the show who experienced it from start to finish.

Another letter that Bert wrote to Robson in August prompted the editor to reply:

I note that you, like myself, hold some pretty strong views on the subject of native labour policy . . . There are few better qualified than your good self to express an opinion on the subject, but I think it would be wise for you to hold your hand and your pen until you are finished with ANGAU. Some of those brass-hats take a very dim view of men who write for the newspapers and criticise their policies – although God knows that they need criticism. As soon as you are clear of the Army, however, I shall be very happy to collaborate with you in every possible way in revealing the truth about what has happened there and about the general situation.

One outcome of all this for Bert was a deep-seated dislike of Labor governments, and a determination that he would rather not vote at all than ever vote Labor for the rest of his life.

In March 1945, Bert was saddened to hear of the death of Major General George Vasey. Hailed in the newspapers at the time as 'Australia's most picturesque general' and considered one of the AIFs most popular commanders, Vasey was killed in an air accident near Cairns. Bert had always liked 'Bloody' George and had never forgotten his generosity and under-standing in agreeing to present service awards to some of the 'fuzzy wuzzies' at both Kokoda and Buna in November 1942.

The news of the safe arrival in May of his new son John giving him now 'an heir and a spare' filled him with joy. Not so good was the news from Wallace, now a major and still stationed at Bougainville, that he had had two stints in the Lae hospital, one with very painful kidney stones and soon after, a leg fracture – the result of a fracas in the mess with some mates.

The best news of all, of course, was the announcement in August that the war was finally over. Wallace in his usual forthright manner made the comments to Elsa in one of his letters at the time:

> Well, Elsa, the war in Europe has at last come to its finality and the carnage over there should act as a big deterrent for many years to come. All those places you know so well should now be almost flattened – it is a terrible thing to gloat over the destruction but I am afraid the Germans 'cast their bread on the waters' and it returned in the form of 'bread baskets' of destruction!!

Along with all around him, Bert celebrated the end of hostilities, but he was a little concerned with some of the content of the radio broadcast to the Papuans on 30 September 1945. The broadcast, given in Motu, was written by Captain Tom Grahamslaw, who was by then Regional Commander of the Southern Region. It began:

> The war has ended. The Japanese have been beaten and the British, Australian and American soldiers are in Japan. These soldiers are taking away from the Japanese all their guns, warships, fighting aeroplanes and bombs and will destroy them. They are also taking all the Japanese machinery which has been used to make things for the war . . .
>
> The men of Papua did very good work helping carry food, guns and bombs, making roads, bridges, and aerodromes, carrying away the dead and the wounded and other war work. The RPC and the PIB killed many Japanese and received many medals for their bravery. Village people received medals for their good work. The soldiers have talked about the work of the Papua and New Guinea natives and in the British Empire

and Americas the name of the people of Papua and New Guinea is held high. The parents and wives and children of fighting men are grateful to the native people for the help they have given to our fighting men. The native people are grateful to the fighting men for saving them from the Japanese. That is as it should be . . .

The Army Govt and the new Civil Govt have decided that no more men will be signed on to the Army for work on plantations and that as soon as possible men signed on now to work on plantations will be paid off and returned to their villages. As many men as can be spared will be paid soon . . .

The men of Papua & New Guinea helped to win the war and now they are wanted to help win the peace too. Tell all your friends of this talk of the Govt and ask them to help too by working on the plantations, or with other Europeans or with the Govt or the Missions or in the village. There is a lot to be done and work for everybody to do and we must all work together just like a cricket team.

Putting aside the fact that most villagers would not have known what a cricket team was, Grahamslaw was doing his best to prevent a mass exodus of labour back to their villages, just as he had done back in November 1942 when Vasey had made the medal presentation to natives at Buna. At that time, the general made the statement that Allied soldiers and carriers would now be able to go home. This would have been disastrous for the labour requirements that still existed, so in his interpretation into Motu Grahamslaw changed it and said, 'The allied soldiers can now go home but we ANGAU Europeans and labourers still have a job to do and must stay at our posts.' Despite Tom's efforts to soften this latest blow, Bert was very concerned about the impact this broadcast would have on his already depleted labour force.

With the reinstatement of civil administration in October, Bert began the process of application for demobilisation. This involved providing the information to the army, which prioritised applications on a point system. The length of service in months was multiplied by two, giving Bert a 'score' of 84. The age at enlistment was also multiplied by two, giving 74. Then Dependency Status, which in Bert's situation equalled months of service, 42, was added, giving a total score of 200. Apparently this score meant he could be discharged any time after 21 November 1945! Bert headed out on 7 December and it was oh so good to be back safe and sound with his now much expanded family in peace-time Sydney, almost exactly four years after he first left them on the bombing of Pearl Harbor.

Meryl and her Herbert were very honoured to be invited to spend Christmas day at a celebratory breakfast and lunch on board the HMAT *Duntroon*, which had recently returned with troops from Singapore. Commander of the troop ship, I. L. Lloyd, put on an amazing spread considering war short-ages that would have still been in place. Breakfast included Fried Whiting au Citron, Crumbed Lamb's Brains a l'Orly and Savoury Omelette. The lunch menu covered a choice of smoked NZ Blue Cod au Beurre, Beef Steak and Kidney Pie with a dessert of Steamed Romsey Roll, Golden Syrup and Rice Custard. What a treat, and some small compensation for the deprivations of the last three years.

§

Having reached the rank of major and been mentioned in dispatches for 'gallantry with commendable service', Wallace had begun the demobilisation process in September and, strangely, considering his total length of service, his 'priority points' amounted to 186 so that although he headed south on the HMAS *Taroma* and arrived in Sydney on 15 December, he was not finally discharged until 7 March 1946, Bert beating him out by three months. At the time, Bert received a letter from Brigadier A. R. Baxter-Cox, Military Secretary, conveying the gratitude of the commander-in-chief for services rendered. It went on to say:

On termination of war-time services, all officers must be either transferred to the Reserve of Officers, be placed on the Retired list or be Retired: you will be advised in due course of the form of your disposal . . . The CIC [Commander in Chief] hopes that you will retain an interest in the affairs of the Army in whatever form it may take in post-war years.

By the same post, he received a note from the Repatriation Commission with 'Temporary Authority for Medical Treatment', for osteoarthritis of the right hip joint. He subsequently checked into the Prince of Wales Repatriation General Hospital and began the first of a series of operations that he was to endure over the next 40 years. His recovery from this operation was slow. Bert returned to Papua in early May, but soon after his arrival he was very saddened to hear of the death of his great friend Doc Vernon, who passed away at the age of only 63, the years of pushing himself to the limit finally taking their toll. Doc had been writing to Bert about once a month, bringing him up to date on where he was and checking on progress with production and war damage claims for Komo Planting Syndicate, in which he still had a share. In one letter in January, he gave his opinion of Colonel Kingsley Norris's report on the Kokoda Campaign, expressing particular amusement at the use of the name 'Old Kokodonians' for the likes of Bert and himself. He commented that there probably weren't really enough of them to form an OK association, but maybe once a year dinner would be nice. He proceeded to get a real bee in his bonnet about this idea and each month wrote further on his plans for an annual dinner in Moresby on 2 November, the anniversary of the retaking of Kokoda, as well as get-togethers in other centres like Kokoda and Buna. He even listed his strict prerequisites for membership of the OKA – no two-day fly-ins welcome!

After some encouragement from Bert, Doc had written up his diary of what he called the 'Range Campaign', sending Bert the first carbon copy, and when Bert told him that he had enjoyed the read, Doc wrote back: 'Glad you like the diary, in your case to type it out was a labour of love and I knew you would appreciate.'

Doc was also considering setting up his sister and her husband on a 250-acre lease he had surveyed next to the Komo, which he called White Streams. He was weighing up whether they would be better to settle there, or stay at his property at Samarai called Round Hill. As fate would have it, after finally receiving his discharge in March, and before making a planned visit to Kokoda, he fell ill and was taken by boat from Round Hill to the hospital at Samarai, where he passed away on 16 May. Bert was unable to attend the memorial service that was held at the London Missionary Society Church at Hood Point in Papua and officiated by Rev. H. J. E Short, whose eulogy summed up Doc's life:

> Handicapped by deafness from injury in the first world war, Dr Vernon came to Papua to settle on a plantation. He responded to every call of sick natives to such extent that his commercial interests were neglected. His contribution to medical needs on the Kokoda Trail is an epic that should be recorded. His exceptionally tall, gaunt, loose-clad figure with the majestic mien of a venturer, periodically wandered into the jungle. He wanted to study the flora of the land, but the need of sick natives took precedence of that. Whenever he reappeared – unobtrusively always – white and brown folk were anxious to hold him. He loved Hood Point and served graciously there, but none could come to rest. With his whimsical smile he would stride on, doing good. Circumstances precluded him being an active Churchman, but his way was Christian in the deepest sense. He hid his wounds and sickness and one thinks of his dying as the drawing of a stainless blade from a battered sheath.

In letters back and forth to Vernon's niece Marcia after his death, they agreed that Doc had 'burnt himself out'. When taken to hospital he had a bad dose of tropical ulcers and was suffering from a raging fever, but the cause of death was ultimately noted as heart failure. Doc had made a point of telling Marcia's mother should anything happen to him, he wanted Bert to have his beloved dogs, three little fox terriers. When Marcia wrote to arrange to honour this promise, Bert told her to keep the dogs there at Round Hill as it was their home and he knew she and her father Heck were fond of the animals too.

Bert keenly felt the loss of this mate, who had been his closest, most valued companion during the hell that was the Kokoda Trail. Theirs was a mutual admiration society, their letters demonstrating the huge respect they held for each other's skills. In one letter in November 1945, Doc congratulates Bert on his handling of the Papuan people, both back on the plantations, and during the campaign, noting:

> Your knack of retaining labour on the estate is entirely due to your own personality, proof of this if wanted lying in the similar tribute to your character while trying to keep the Range Force together. As a matter of fact, your influence then was a model for other ANGAU men to follow, which few did, having their own ways of treating natives much inferior to yours.

§

Wallace had headed straight home after his discharge, glad to be out of the army and keen to get back to work on the plantations to make up for his absence of more than six years. He continued his run of bad luck in getting air transport to the Yodda – not that any planes crashed this time, but he waited three days in Moresby for a direct flight, then opted to fly to Lae and wait for a plane to Dobodura. After waiting some days for this flight, it had to be followed by the long hell haul along the road from Popondetta to Kokoda, which involved 'shanks pony' over the new, roughly constructed Wairope bridge across the Kumusi (according to him these swinging suspension bridges were 'best crossed at a horse canter') and picking up a different vehicle on the other side. To really salt the wound, when he went to start this vehicle, someone had pinched the fan belt! Questioning the locals, he established it had been 'borrowed' from the vehicle by a patrol officer from Kokoda when one on his vehicle broke. Wallace used his trouser belt to make the temporary repairs but when, half an hour into his journey, he got a flat tyre, and found that his spare had also been removed, Wallace was fit to be tied! When he eventually reached Kokoda, he paid a visit to this hapless young patrol officer that the latter would never forget! It was also the start of a long and frosty relationship between Wallace and members of the civil administration.

Demonstrating his ongoing irritation, at the end of this journey Wallace wrote a letter to Elsa that rambled most unflatteringly about the state of the civil government in Papua, commenting that the sooner all transport was put into the hands of private enterprise the better. He took stock of the situation on the plantations, and then wrote another long letter to Elsa attempting to explain the state of affairs to her. He pointed out that their problems could not be solved merely by an injection of capital or even by an increase in the price of rubber. He continued:

> In any undertaking in this country it is necessary to rely on the local labour sources who, through the infinite charitableness of the Army throwing copious quantities of largesse to the multitudes, largesse that came out of the coffers of their country, have a surfeit of money and no real inclination to work.

He noted that the grant of a significant wage increase was making not one iota of difference – he had sent for labour just the previous week and got no takers. One solution he considered was getting the trade stores up and running quickly, encouraging the natives to spend fast and thus need to work to earn again. He quickly got two stores going on the plantation, then complained of now having to be a 'counter jumper' in among all his other jobs. Typical of his wry sense of humour, he told Elsa:

The modern fuzzy-wuzzy is going through the pre-revolutionary era of the French as regards bodily hygiene, whereby it was considered extremely damaging to health to destroy the body juices by washing, much better to preserve them and add a lustre to their odour by copious applications of scent. We sell large quantities of brilliantine and perfumes, the stronger the stink the better the saleability.

The other problem, aside from transport and roads, was supplies. All shipping was under government control, which created its own headaches. His description of what was involved in getting stores to the Yodda gives a good picture of the challenges.

Cargo is offloaded from a boat at Oro Bay, 90 miles from here. Handled by natives without supervision on to trucks driven to Soputa, 20 miles, then ferried across a river. Trucked from here by a European to his place and offloaded. Trucked to Wairope and distance of 45 miles, carried cross a wire suspension bridge and then jeeped under our control the last 25 miles. In all about seven handlings, the loss occurring during transit being enough to offset the prewar cost of freight, let alone the ensuing paper war! We have one jeep. There are about nine jeeps that have been lying idle at Oro Bay awaiting some action by the Commonwealth Disposals Commission for the past six months. We have asked for two of them plus a lot of other stuff that is rotting there but nothing has happened.

Much has been said against the NG exploiter, Australian nomenclature for the Planter. Personally I think that I am an exploiter but no more than any other employer of labour, black white or brindle. The only other thing that I would like to point out is that I have yet to meet the planter from

NG who has made a fortune, so I have my doubts whether we exploit enough.

With Bert's return, the two brothers agreed that the only solution was for Wallace to embark on a recruitment drive similar to the one Bert had done before he first arrived at the Yodda. He did this for the whole month of September, with limited success. In his absence, Bert concentrated on getting things ready for the expected return of Meryl and the family in December. After discussion with his sweetheart while on leave the previous year, he had chosen a new site to build the houses and workshops, and what a beautiful site it was! Perched on a cliff overlooking a sharp bend in the magnificent Mambare River, to the south-west it had views of the Kokoda Gap and to the north-west, of Mount Victoria and Mount Huxley, which was locally called The Thumb, for obvious reasons. The new house was considerably closer to Kokoda than the old Yodda homestead because, as the Yodda airstrip had fallen into disrepair, they would be dependent on air transport into Kokoda from now on. The new station site was located within the boundaries of their Mamba Estate lease, and thus, among the oldest and most productive rubber. Bert and Wallace carefully designed the layout of all the required buildings, including a new factory, located more centrally with ready access to the large amounts of water needed in the processing of raw rubber. Bert's long convalescence had put him well behind in his planning to have everything ready for the family's return, and the acute shortage of workers also meant commencement of construction of the new family home was delayed until well after he got back to 'Mamba' – the name that now started to replace 'Yodda'.

Pop Holliday had earlier in the year begun the process of application to return to Papua, hoping to get work assisting in the rebuilding of Sangara. Meryl and the children were ready and keen to come home as soon as school finished for the Christmas holidays. Meryl's impatience had been obvious back in July when a letter from Mary arrived telling Daddy that 'Mummy said she is fed up with kids and she said come and mind your own children.' Although the house was nearly finished, with its shingled roof and tarred paper walls, there was no running water, so showers were the old bucket type and the toilet was a dreaded long-drop. Bert had to advise them they would be living fairly rough but this did not deter them – both Mary and Carl had by now been put into boarding school and they could not wait to get out and go home.

Meryl knew that this had to be one of the most difficult decisions of her life – to send her children away for their education – but she had no real choice. There was no money for a governess, if you could even get one to come to such a remote place, and she had no desire to take on correspondence for two children while still having two pre-schoolers to care for. Also, it was accepted among the planters in PNG that in order to do the best thing by your family, to support your husband in the difficult life he had chosen, you must send your children away. Not to do so would be frowned upon.

In early December, Bert headed back down to Sydney to help Meryl make the move home. There was no way she was willing to cope on her own with four young children on the long flight from Sydney to Kokoda. They arrived in the second week in December and settled into life in their basic but comfortable home. After all he had been through, Bert could not believe his good fortune. Life was not easy financially, but this paled into insignificance against having his beautiful family and his much loved younger brother Wallace safely back in the valley. Christmas was a great occasion, with all Bert's family and his loyal workers, most of whom had returned to work when Bert sent word he needed them, included in the celebrations. Out of respect and appreciation for his Papuan friends, it was now that Bert started a tradition that he would carry on until the day he left the country. No family members could have their presents, unless they were from Santa Claus of course, until his long-serving Papuan employees had received theirs.

For young Carl, who had left his jungle home when only four years old, this was a whole new world of adventure. The problem was that over the last five years, he had lived the city life surrounded mainly by protective women and elderly men. He had not developed some of the common sense that country children seem to cultivate by osmosis from those who surround them as they grow. He was a happy, boisterous and adventurous nine-year-old boy, into everything and like many boys his age, fascinated with fire.

One afternoon in the middle of January as Meryl sat with Mary in the sitting area of their 'bush house' home, she was startled by blood-curdling screams, then the horrific sight of Carl appearing at the top of the rough wooden stairs, half his body covered in flames, the intense heat causing the timber steps in his wake to smoulder. Meryl shot out of her seat and yelled to her houseboy for a blanket. Using her own body to smother the flames, she shouted at Mary, who stood in stunned horror, to go to her room and to the houseboy once he had fetched the blankets to find *taubada baudana* quickly. Bert was some distance away tallying latex production figures before the rubber was taken to the factory when he heard the frantic yells of some of his boys who said his house was on fire. Meryl forced herself to remain calm and remember her nursing training. She put Carl into a cold basin of water, then into bed where she kept him warm, treating his wounds as best she knew. He had sustained burns to more than 30 per cent of his body and the pain must have been horrendous. Yet he complained little and remained stoic as his mother dressed his wounds and administered what painkillers she had. Bert came as quickly as his legs and damaged hip could carry him, and quickly realised that his most important job was now to get his boy to hospital. It was late afternoon and the light was fading. All radio calls to both Lae and Port Moresby were met with the reply that it was too late for aircraft to depart for Kokoda. The weather had closed in and it was not even an option to line the airstrip with fires to guide an aircraft in after dark. There was no choice but to wait until morning. All Bert could do was send for the medical orderly from Kokoda to come and assist Meryl.

As the night wore on, with both Meryl and Bert by his side, and heavily dosed with morphine, Carl seemed to settle and they were hopeful that he might get through this, but in the early hours of the morning he took a turn for the worse, unable to keep down any fluids, his temperature raging, his heart racing, his little body racked with convulsive shivers. Meryl held him tight, doing all she could to prevent the shock that obviously was now setting in, from worsening. It was to be to no avail. At 7.50 a.m. on 17 January 1947 their darling boy was gone.

The next 48 hours were a blur for the whole family. Losing a child is the most horrific experience any parent can know, but to also have to prepare that child for burial, build his coffin and bury him before the heat of the tropics did its damage, is beyond the comprehension of most people. Bert insisted on making the little coffin himself but he asked the medical orderly to prepare the body. Wallace selected a site to bury his nephew and set some workers to digging the grave. Meryl went into a state of silent shock. Her three other children were kept away from her by her Papuan house staff. Diane and John had no real idea of what had happened but poor Mary had briefly seen Carl in flames, then had quickly been sent to her room and kept there while the drama unfolded. She was confused and hurt by the fact that her parents didn't seem to want her around just at the moment. She wanted to help but couldn't. From that day and for many years to come Mary developed a nervous tic under her eye that would return to haunt her whenever she became stressed.

Carl was buried in the newly created cemetery about halfway between Kokoda and the homestead in a patch by the road on top of a rise, among the rows and rows of young rubber of Amada Plantation. Rev. Taylor performed the burial service and Carl's body was interred at 3.45 p.m. Bert wrote to Elsa of the day 'our first burial in this Valley where we were setting up a home with all the attendant difficulties and hopes'.

The Kokoda War Cemetery.
Bert wrote: 'Where I would like to RIP when the time comes'

Carriers from Rigo area in celebratory dress, November 1942

The view over the Mambare River from the house Bert built for Meryl in 1946

Mamba House, called 'The Big House' built in 1958

The Trimotor Ford bogged at the Yodda airstrip in 1941

Above: The house Bert built for Meryl in 1946

Left: Sergeant Hitolo Jinga – a loyal worker for Bert before, during and after the war

The Kienzle men at the Yodda – (*left to right*) Bert, Alfred, Wallace

The first few pages of Bert's copy of Raymond Paull's book, *Retreat from Kokoda*, inscribed by Japanese veterans with their names and casualty statistics

Bert with some of his 'boys' in 1959 at the opening of the
Carriers' Memorial, Kokoda plateau

Meryl and Bert with Carl at the Yodda, 1937

Bert with Japanese veterans on the lawn of Mamba House, 1970s

Bert and Meryl survey the magnificent view from their home overlooking
the Mambare River and the Kokoda Gap

A typical Christmas Day at Mamba in the 1960s and 1970s

Bert (*left*) with 39th Battalion veteran, Alf Salmon,
in front of the Fuzzy Wuzzy Memorial 1972

Bert in his office at Tweed Heads in 1982

Carl's headstone simply reads: 'In memory of Carl, Loved son of Herbert & Meryl Kienzle, Born 18th May 1937, Died 17th January 1947'. It remains in the same spot to this day.

§

Meryl had now realised the worst fear of every European mother living in Papua, the death of a child. How devastating to have gone through the war without her husband by her side but with Carl as her little 'man of the house', then to lose him so soon and so horribly. As the days passed and the reality of her loss set in, so did anger – anger at where she lived and how it had killed her child. As far as they could work out, Carl had been playing with one of the many candles they had been using for lighting when the generator had been playing up. This small lighting plant, which they had only owned for a few months, was located under the house and normally provided them with power for most of the day. A dish of petrol had been left out that had been used for rinsing parts when the generator was being repaired. Apparently, Carl had lit a candle and dripped some fuel from the dish along the ground, wanting to see what happened when he lit it. Of course, the fire shot along the ground to the dish and the whole thing went up in flames. He had burns to his hands, chest, abdomen, thighs and face. Why was this dish of fuel left out? Why were the matches and candles left where a child could reach them? All these questions circled in Meryl's mind, but most of all her anger was directed at Papua, this country where you couldn't even get transport to a hospital when it was a matter of life and death. The deep love she knew her husband had for this country, and that had begun to grow in her too, died with Carl that day.

For a week, Meryl and Bert remained in stunned grief. Bert was unable to face returning to work or even to correspond with family and friends, all of whom were sending telegrams of condolence.

But as time progressed after the funeral, Bert seemed to snap out of his inertia and he decided that what he and Meryl needed was as many family around them as possible. He communicated with them all and they responded. Laura arrived in early February and Ailsa soon afterwards. The other children, thoroughly confused by the loss of Carl and the change in their parents, began to get their attention again as Bert and Meryl started to count the blessings that they still had. Their philosophical and optimistic approaches to life gradually returned, although probably never in full. Meryl would describe this loss of a child in a most poignant and evocative manner in later years. She would say it was like somebody had ripped out a piece of your heart: as the years go by the pain of the removal of that piece eases, but the emptiness that it leaves behind never goes away.

§

Wallace did his best to help Bert and Meryl through this tragedy but sympathy and emotion did not come easily to him. He had a strong streak of the tough German inherited from his father, and had experienced an existence that had left him hardened to the unfairness of life. His only way to show he cared was by working even harder and taking as much load off his brother as possible. Although he didn't really display it, he was quite pleased when Ailsa arrived back on the scene. He had enjoyed their correspondence during the war even though he had become a bit slack about keeping it going since returning to Papua. Laura and Ailsa did their best to help Meryl with the children and with her grief. Life began to return to some sort of normalcy, except for little eight-year-old Mary. Despite the deep sense of loss and real loneliness she was feeling after the death of her best mate and big brother, and the resultant change in her parents and her life, in early February she was bundled off back to boarding school at Meriden School where she had started in kindergarten four years before.

Laura spent nearly a month with Meryl, then headed back to join her husband Dr Harry, now based at Samarai, a beautiful spot once called the 'Paradise of the Pacific' before the ravages of war destroyed much of its magnificence. She and Harry had first moved to Papua in 1938 when he took up a posting at a small bush hospital at Misima, and when war broke out he was one of only four medical officers serving in Papua. Although they had been married for more than 10 years, they had not been able to have children. Laura devoted her time to helping the local children and had fostered a Papuan boy and girl for a short time. She was seriously considering adopting a native child, and the only things that prevented her taking the final step were concern about the impact it would have on that child's life and the opinion and reaction of other members of the European expatriate community.

Wallace and Ailsa began spending more and more time together, so no one was surprised when they announced their engagement followed by their marriage soon afterwards on Wallace's birthday, 18 June 1947, Wallace now being 33 years old and Ailsa nearly 38. Finances were so tight for the groom that he made the wedding ring himself, out of a two-shilling piece. Ailsa treasured that ring all her life and insisted it be buried with her. She often joked that they probably weren't really married, as in the excitement and nerves of the big day, during the vows she made her promise to 'Walfred' instead of Wallace Alfred, Kienzle. The two brothers had married two sisters and the Kienzle and Holliday families were now inextricably intertwined.

In America, Elsa had been making plans for some time for a big trip to Australia to see Hally and then on to Papua to visit Laura at Samarai, and of course the rest of the family at Mamba. After much to-ing and fro-ing making arrangements, it all came together in time for Wallace and Ailsa's wedding. Bert and Wallace welcomed with great excitement their sister who they had not seen for so many years – in Bert's case, more than 20. At last Elsa was able to see first-hand what life was like in this jungle home her brothers had created; to appreciate the difficulties they were having rebuilding after the ravages of war; and to understand the devastation of losing a child to the vagaries of an existence in such a remote, undeveloped land.

11

NEW BEGINNINGS

The last three years of the 1940s were difficult and draining for the Kienzle family. Post-war Papua was a challenging place to survive and there were several occasions when both Bert and Wallace debated packing up and leaving it all behind. In 1945, the Australian Government had passed the PNG Provisional Act allowing Papua and New Guinea to be administered as a single territory. The new administrator was Jack Keith Murray – no relation to Hubert or Leonard. In 1947, he expressed his noble if somewhat naive sentiments:

> New spirit, new ideas, new demands and new standards have spread through the native community. I do not propose to attempt, even if I could hope to succeed, to stifle that spirit so that European employers can return to the standards of a vanished world. On the contrary, that spirit will provide the energies for new production and activities under administrative guidance. The period of change is not an easy one for any of the parties concerned and employees cannot be exempted from the need for adjustment.

The Kienzle brothers were more than willing to embrace necessary changes but warned continually that the administration should hasten slowly for the sake of the Territory's economic and long-term stability.

Bert's hip continued to cause him huge amounts of pain and highly restricted his movements. He had walked with a stick since the end of the war and in 1949 he endured another round of operations that were intended to fix his problem once and for all, but did not. He returned from this trip to Sydney by the ship *Bulolo*, as he needed two walking sticks to get about, which made air travel difficult. It was to be some time before he could cut back to the one walking stick.

Soon after Carl's death John became quite ill and needed Laura's nursing skills to cure him. At the same time, Meryl developed painful ulcers on her legs, brought on no doubt by her weakened state after the tragedy. Over the next couple of years, she suffered a series of miscarriages, losing twins and one other child. Wallace and Ailsa also suffered bouts of illness, including a dash to Australia for an appendectomy for Ailsa and one for Wallace to have most of his teeth removed after a painful abscess convinced him he was better off without them. Bert had reached the same conclusion some years previously when living at the Yodda – no place for a toothache. Wallace and Ailsa's greatest sadness, however, was their inability to conceive a child. Although it was most likely Ailsa's age and other factors working against them, Wallace blamed himself, and wrote to Elsa: 'I am obviously not quite the man everyone thought I was.'

The plantation side of things was now running fairly smoothly, but it was still not making a lot of money and there was certainly no motivation to carry out any further plantings. With Wallace's encouragement, Bert set about reopening some of the gold leases. Yodda Goldfields had ceased trading on the stock exchange in October 1948 and Bert's involvement with that company ended. At the end of 1947, Wallace had been contracted to go to Bougainville to help a new company that was prospecting for gold there, to teach them where to look for good pay dirt. From there, he went to Wau to observe a big gold operation in that area and see what he could learn about any more modern methods of mining. He was happy when in 1949 Bert succeeded in renewing one of his old gold mining leases, giving him Miner's Right No. 264 for one year at a fee of 10 shillings. Wallace went back out to the Yodda, glad to get away from the rubber, which was never really his scene, and happier in an industry where at least he felt he knew from day to day just how the bank balance was standing. Although he was camping in one of the old war-damaged huts out there, he was not really roughing it too much. Each day Ailsa would send their houseboy out with a basket of lovingly prepared food covering three meals and two 'smokos'!

In early 1948, Bert was contacted by Raymond Paull, an employee of the Australian Broadcasting Commission who had taken on the formidable job of preparing a narrative account of the fighting retreat across the Owen Stanleys by the 39th Battalion and 21st Brigade in July and August 1942. Paull had served at Brigadier Potts's Brigade HQ at Darwin after the latter was transferred from Papua and subsequently was sent off to PNG as an ABC/BBC correspondent. He had been with the ABC news before the war and returned after the war to take on the uphill battle of developing the 'News for the Inland and the Islands'. Bert promptly replied to Raymond answering all his questions, keen to see the events of 1942 recorded before they were forgotten. He pointed out that very few proper records were kept during the campaign because of a shortage of staff and the failure of the army to arrange a correspondent to be with each battalion or company. Well-known reporters Osmar White and Damien Parer did not arrive until late August, and even then, were restricted in the information they could release.

Parer's iconic Oscar-winning production *Kokoda Front Line* was first shown to the Australian public in late September 1942, and Bert commented that it 'brought home to the smug and complacent in Australia just what type of war we were waging to try to save Australia'. As always, he mentioned the importance of his mates, Doc Vernon and the Papuans, writing:

Without the part and effort played by staff, natives carriers & stretcher bearers the campaign could not have been waged, of this fact I am certain. Of course, this includes the splendid part played by the medical corps and particularly Dr Vernon and his care of the sick natives. Dr Vernon was a personal friend of mine of many years and during the campaign that friendship was added to the feelings that soldiers only know of when going through times of stress.

Paull went on to write *Retreat from Kokoda*, not published until 1958, but probably the most definitive account of the campaign, indeed the only specific one at the time, until the plethora of publications that began appearing from the 1990s onwards.

In 1948 and 1949, the price of rubber remained at levels that made profitability borderline and then only with the best management. For eight months in 1949, the market for rubber was virtually non-existent and the Kienzles were not able to sell their product at all. The Australian Government eventually stepped in and made an offer to clear the stockpile that had accumulated from all the plantations in Papua New Guinea. The trade store business had become less profitable, with other stores opening up in the area, particularly at Kokoda itself. The two brothers often despaired for their future and were always looking into alternatives to diversify their interests. Wallace became quite keen about becoming involved in tea production, and when an expert was brought out from India to investigate its viability in Papua New Guinea, he made sure he met him and obtained a copy of his report. Disappointingly, although not surprisingly to Wallace, the gentleman concluded that tea would never be a proposition in Papua while the current native labour policy was in place. The government, in its enthusiasm and desire to quash all accusations of exploiting of the native people by businesses in the Territory, had introduced new laws on employment of natives. They had gone ahead and abandoned the indenture system, throwing the Papuan economy into disarray, but what irked the Kienzles most was the requirement to provide extensive food rations to employees, even though on their estates all resident workers were allowed to cultivate gardens that provided them with all the foodstuffs on which they had survived quite comfortably before white man arrived on the scene. Wallace wrote to Elsa:

> The increase in wages, is, I think, a fair thing but what amazes me is the fact that they wish to alter the natives' diet based on the highly technical basis of vitamin content etc notwithstanding the fact that until the advent of white man the native population everywhere managed to exist and multiply with natural regularity, and appeared singularly free from diseases that have only made their appearances with association with the whites . . . the native now has to be fed a ration which is imported foodstuffs of a calorific content about four times that enjoyed by people in Britain. The same calorific content could quite easily be obtained by use of their own foods but our hierarchs in diet counsel that we will be better with the addition of European foodstuffs.

In Port Moresby and other town centres, the lack of preparation for, and generally bad handling of, the transition from war to peace was causing all sorts of social and economic problems. Of greatest bewilderment to observers was the apparent government policy of almost 'scorched earth' when it came to army equipment left behind that could have been used as a basis for rebuilding. Some auctions of equipment were held in Lae and other centres along the north coast and the Kienzles managed to obtain several vehicles and some heavy equipment at these. Labour plus transport and communications remained their biggest concerns.

Fortunes took a slight turn for the better, at least at the family level, towards the beginning of the new decade, with Meryl carrying a baby to full term. Like most of Meryl's pregnancies, this one was not exactly planned and, at 42 years old she did not have an easy time of it. This was a particularly large baby and her blood pressure and glucose levels reached the stage where she was advised to travel to Moresby and await the birth of her child in hospital for the last month of her term. Confined to bed for the duration, it was comforting to have Ailsa come and spend some time with her close to her delivery. During one such visit, Meryl commented to Ailsa that the pregnant woman in the bed next to her looked like a football. Ailsa's reply was: 'You should talk – you look like a soccer ball.' Of course this sisterly joke was radioed back home to Mamba, so that when a baby boy was finally delivered on 6 February 1950 the telegram was sent: 'The soccer ball has arrived.' The new baby was christened Wallace Harold Wilson Kienzle but was always called Soccer or Soc.

By this time both John and Diane had a governess to teach them through Blackfriars Correspondence School, but Mary was going off to Meriden each year and spending quite a bit of time with guardians because of the high costs of getting her home for holidays. Meryl continued to have quite a few health problems after Soc's birth, so she was most appreciative of the help of the governess and house staff.

§

As is often the case in rural industries, the misfortune of others was about to become the good fortune of some. With the onset of war with Korea, the demand for rubber instantly soared, and from prices being in the doldrums for so many years, they quickly climbed to reach those dream levels of 'a pound a pound'. It even became economical to airfreight the rubber out of Kokoda, avoiding the long haul to Popondetta and Oro Bay. Air services had started to improve considerably with Qantas Empire Airways Ltd gradually building up their business from 1945 onwards. They had been a little slow to start servicing Kokoda, and for nearly three years after the war the wartime track reverted to its old purpose as a mail trail. Letters were carried by native policemen back and forth to Moresby and heavier parcels had to take the circuitous route to Buna and on to the capital by sea. By August 1949, Qantas had introduced a weekly flight from Moresby to Kokoda and on to Popondetta, and the Trail was finally officially shut down as a mail route in October 1949.

There were other adjustments to make in this post-war 'colony' as the divide between black and white narrowed after what the two races had been through together during the war. Papuans were looking to learn more skills and not just be the 'navvies' for the white business owners. More women were looking to continue working as they had had to do during the war, and as their husbands and fathers got used the idea that this was acceptable. Although the administration had great intentions of improving access to education, this responsibility continued to fall to the missions for some years yet. The law forbidding native men to wear shirts was repealed, though many still opted to wear their *ramis/laplaps* and the women, skirts and *meri* blouses. There was still significant segregation, particularly in the towns, with very little social interaction between Europeans and Papuans, but the employer–employee relationship was certainly evolving. Mick Healy, Wallace's old mate from his Fly River expedition days, explained it quite succinctly when he spelled out to Rachel Cleland, the brigadier's wife, how to handle her house staff.

> There are three basic things to remember. Firstly, no one needs to work for you – all have their land in their villages and only come to work for you if it suits them. Secondly, your success with staff will depend on the personal relationship you can build up between yourself and each one as an individual. Thirdly, in his eyes, he works with you not for you.

The Kienzle brothers were by now employing other Europeans, all of whom had to obtain a permit to enter and work in the country, even those who had stayed on after the war. New arrivals were carefully investigated – no troublemakers, political activists or religious fanatics welcome. The eyes of the world were on this Australian 'colony'. Meryl had even had to apply for a permit to return in 1946, and she was not officially allowed to work without permission. This system continued for many years, although it was not closely policed in family businesses like the Kienzles where everyone 'mucked in' to keep the enterprises profitable and make their contribution.

§

In late December 1950 and early January 1951, the Kienzles noticed a huge increase in the numbers of *gurias* they were experiencing – *guria* is the New Guinea word for the small earth tremors that are quite common on this geologically young island. Stories began to reach them of increased activity at Mt Lamington, a 1,680-metre volcano near Higaturu Station, about 30 kilometres as the crow flies from Mamba and only 10 kilometres from Sangara Rubber Plantation's homestead. Local administrators had been sent to observe the volcano and returned with the consensus that it was not a threat, as it was 'letting off steam gradually'. Unfortunately, vulcanologists were not properly consulted. The local minister from a mission near the base of the angry mountain is said to have climbed to its summit and prayed that if it had to blow it would blow in the opposite direction from his little church. On the morning of Sunday 21 January, messengers were sent carrying notes to all parishes in the district assuring them that all was well, but at 10.30 a.m. in a huge Peléan eruption out the side of its northern face, 'Berepo', as the local people called the mountain, blew. It threw devastating steam and smoke over a radius of 12 kilometres and dust that carried as far as Port Moresby, 50 kilometres away. The noise could be heard up to 270 kilometres away. The ensuing pyroclastic flows, which are hot, sulphuric, gas-rich avalanches of ash and pumice, left a 100-square-kilometre zone of devastation.

At Mamba, as the family sat around after a peaceful Sunday morning breakfast, the house shook quite violently and the rumble could be felt and heard quite intensely. The houseboys screamed and ran for cover and, as the sky turned black and blocked out the sun, they panicked even more, believing the end of the world had come. By the time the hot black ash began to fall crackling onto the roof, Bert had managed to make radio contact with stations closer to the scene of the disaster and confirmed what he suspected – the mountain had indeed blown and the damage was horrific. Wallace quickly set off with some reluctant helpers to see what he could do to assist and to check on the state of their store rooms at the Kumusi and Sangara. As he came closer to the scene, he saw first-hand the shocking devastation. The rivers and creeks flowed black with ash, and in among the debris, the charred bodies of victims floated grotesquely. Wallace stopped and collected what bodies he could, stacking them by the side of the road. He had grabbed supplies like blankets and basic food items from the trade stores at Mamba, and he handed these out to the stunned survivors, many of whom were badly burned. More than 6,000 people were now homeless.

The self-preserving local minister's mission on the opposite side of the mountain may have been safe, but the Anglican mission at Sangara and the government station at Higaturu, which in 1946 had taken over as the new HQ for the Northern Division after the destruction of Buna, were completely destroyed. Thirty-seven Europeans were killed, including District Commissioner Cecil Cowley, who had contributed to the decision that evacuation was not necessary, and Rev. Dennis Taylor of Higaturu with his wife and four children. Over 3,000 natives perished, many of their deaths caused by inhalation of the deadly *nues ardentes* – the mixture of smoke, incandescent dust and gas that usually accompanies Peléan eruptions and causes instant suffocation. Such a catastrophe so soon after the war was devastating for this battered district of Papua. This was the worst natural disaster ever to have occurred in an Australian-administered territory.

Medical personnel, including Dr Harry White who came up from Samarai, mission staff, government and plantation workers quickly rallied to set up emergency hospitals and a disaster relief headquarters near Popondetta – it was like the war all over again. Qantas and other private air companies gave their entire local resources to ferrying of wounded, medical supplies and food to and from Lae and Port Moresby. The RAAF sent two DC3s loaded with rice, tinned meat, wheatmeal and sugar. They landed at Popondetta and at the smaller airstrip at Wairope, where 4,000 evacuees were established in a camp. As everyone's food gardens were destroyed, they would need rations for many months to come.

Casualties from the eruption continued for many days after the actual event. Innocent natives dipped their hot feet into creeks expecting to cool down, only to discover that they flowed with boiling water. The delayed effects of burns and inhalation continued to take their toll. After-shocks carried on for many months, with minor eruptions and rumbling occurring until as late as 1953. The rivers and creeks took years to recover. All would be well when the dry season was on, but with each rainstorm, the filth and debris would once again clog the waterways. Trees for several metres up the banks had been killed by the steaming waters, their trunks and branches left an ashen grey; eerie ghostlike posts scattered along the river edges. Within a year, due in part to the generosity of the newly established newspaper, the *South Pacific Post*, which launched an appeal and raised more than £20,000 to aid the survivors, all the homeless had been re-established in villages or camps. The dead not buried near their villages were interred with the Europeans in a newly consecrated cemetery at Popondetta.

Mamba's buildings not being damaged, Wallace was able to rescue most of the stores from their bases at Sangara and Kumusi, the majority of which he gave to the relief effort. Fortunately, the price of rubber was good and transport was now mainly by air, because road access to shipping at Oro Bay was completely cut off. Wallace remained positive and wrote to Elsa in May 1951: 'We're better off than most.' He told her that the volcano was by no means asleep: 'It has built up a very large dome of rock and ash in the original crater and if she blows again could be as bad as the last time.' Higaturu looked like a moonscape and the mountain itself now appeared somewhat larger than it used to be and was continuing to eject large pieces of molten rock that set fire to everything in their path. When it finally settled down, as Wallace had noted there was a 560-metre-high lava dome in the centre of the crater.

Medical assistant Albert Speer, who worked to aid the wounded even as a second eruption was imminent, wrote in his diary at the time:

> Taylor described the eruption . . . as the rolling effect of a flood tide rather than a blast effect . . . The bodies too, that were lying on their backs had their chest bones broken, the chest cage was crushed with what was apparently a great weight. The corpses were as if they were covered with grey cement. Some in the fringe houses that were still standing were actually seated at their tables as though cement had been poured on them. It was grotesque . . . it was similar to what you read of Pompeii.

Back at Mamba, the days were like nights and it was too dark to work or play outside. To keep the family entertained, including Mary and her visiting school friend Janet Cridland, Bert showed the movie *The Barkleys of Broadway* several times – forwards and then backwards. Bert had a projector set up in the office and this form of entertainment, showing movies with their own cinema-size projector, would remain a Mamba tradition until the advent of videos in the late 1970s.

When life eventually began to return to normal after this catastrophe, one positive outcome was that volcanic ash dissolving into the soil boosted agricultural production in the whole area, including at Mamba. Finally the Kienzle brothers were starting to make some real money and Bert began to feel that all the years of hardship and hard work were at last starting to pay off. The only disappointment was that the price, productivity and production costs of gold meant it was becoming unviable, and the decision was made to cease mining. This was a sad day for Bert, as he still believed that with the right equipment one day good money could be made out of the Yodda gold. Wallace would comment some years later:

> We know where the gold is and where it isn't around here. There's hardly a foot of country we haven't tested from here right up to the mountains on the other side of the valley. Some creeks show good samples, others nothing, yet they are all in the same country. We got to the bottom of every creek, diverted the water and scraped every crevice. A lot of hard work but we got the gold.

As a souvenir of this enterprise that had given him his real start in the Yodda, Bert kept the best specimen he had found not far from his first camp, a half-inch slug of pure gold rounded like a medal. All that remained on site at Yodda as a remnant of those years of struggle was the old steam boiler that Bert had put together those many years ago.

Politically, significant changes were occurring. The Papua and New Guinea Act had been passed in Australian Parliament in February 1949 and Port Moresby had been officially declared the capital of the now united territories. The new Menzies Government created a Department of Territories and appointed Paul Hasluck as the first minister. Hasluck was a man of energy, talent and vision, and he strongly believed that if Australia was serious about preparing the Territory of Papua and New Guinea for self-government and ultimately independence, education of the predominantly illiterate masses was a basic requirement. He developed policies on education, political development and economic growth. With Administrator Murray and Brigadier Doug Cleland, who had come back to the Territory as assistant administrator in 1950 after a brief return to his law practice in Perth, Hasluck began to implement these policies that would ultimately create a Territory that even indigenous historians would later admit was well ahead of other similar 'colonies'. In 1952, Cleland took over from Murray as administrator, a position he would hold for 15 notable years.

12

ANGUS AND AEROPLANES

With the rubber booming but the gold no longer operating, Bert and Wallace were still keen to diversify, as they both were realistic enough to accept that when the Korean War ended, the glory days of rubber would probably end too. At Hawkesbury Agricultural College, and when visiting his cousins, the Schoeffels, now at Echuca, Wallace had developed a real interest in beef production and had always been responsible for the care of the few cattle they had at Yodda. He began convincing Bert that this would be a successful addition to their enterprise. Other Europeans, particularly some of the missions, had also brought cattle into the Territory for their own purposes but there were no commercial herds in Papua at the time. Wallace planned to bring more cattle in as quickly as possible and initially put them to graze under the rubber trees, but he was aware he would need to establish proper pastures if this was to become a successful commercial enterprise.

He set out clearing new areas of jungle to plant to pastures and paid a quick visit to a research station on the Atherton Tablelands in Queensland to select suitable grasses and buy seeds. He returned with seeds and cuttings of brachiaria and kikuyu plus guinea, molasses, guatemala and elephant grasses to establish the first true pastures in the Territory. Wallace had trouble getting permission from the PNG Agriculture department to import these seeds, yet ironically, only a short time later, they would come to Mamba for cuttings for their Highlands Research Station. He also carried home an earful of dire warnings from Australian cattlemen that if he opted for British breeds of cattle he was doomed to failure because of parasite problems and footrot. Wallace was unperturbed, as he knew that the soils at Mamba were well drained and that he had the labour to ensure regular preventative treatment for parasites. His detractors also cautioned that the long coats of the Aberdeen Angus he had selected would cause all sorts of health problems, but as it turned out, the cattle adapted to the climate very quickly and remained short-haired throughout the year. The altitude at Mamba, and the more noticeable seasonal change there than on the coast, all helped in this adaptation.

In 1952, the first load of 20 Aberdeen Angus heifers and one bull arrived by air from the property of W. S. and P. F. Gill of 'Diglum', Calliope in Queensland. The interior of the DC3 aircraft had to be specially modified with individual crates for each beast and a coating of sawdust on the floor. Although the animals weren't tranquillised, they seemed to handle the journey quite well. On arrival at Kokoda airstrip, a ramp, race and holding yard had to be hastily constructed leading from the plane so that it could quickly be unloaded and return to Moresby for the next consignment. In later years, when Mamba had its own cattle truck, it would just be backed up to the aircraft and the cattle quietly guided straight onto it for transport to their various paddocks. Over the next two years, several more loads of Angus were flown in, and then in 1955–1956, after seeing the success their friend Lisle Johnston was having with the breed at Sogeri, some Red Poll Shorthorn were introduced to add hybrid vigour to the herd.

The cattle did not do so well on the grass that grew under the rubber trees but once the pastures were established they thrived. It was, however, a very labour-intensive operation in this place where life was a continual struggle to stop the jungle re-encroaching on any cleared land. Lines of machete-wielding workers continually hand-cut the voracious weeds. The natives had to be taught cattle husbandry fast, not an easy task with a people who had little experience with domesticated herd animals. Paddocks had to be regularly rotated and cattle routinely yarded for parasite control, but the biggest challenge of all was control of the screw worm fly. This prolific maggot, peculiar to the wet tropics, can have horrific consequences on a beast if left unchecked.

Successful beef cattle production therefore became dependent on perpetual vigilance and the cowboys would wander through the herds almost every day, especially at calving time, checking each beast and treating them on site if possible or yarding them when necessary. The cattle as a result became fairly quiet and used to regular walks to the yards for the many treatments required for them.

In 1959, Chas Lock, long-established Australian Agriculture Company Dalgety's Stud Stock Officer, visited Mamba and Sogeri, and was impressed with how well the British breeds were doing, but felt goals of a carrying capacity of one beast to the acre were probably a bit optimistic. Mamba did eventually achieve this rate, but other areas where soils were not so rich were not as successful. Lock concluded that the beef industry had an exciting future in Papua New Guinea, provided it was not stifled by red tape and government interference and negativity. Bureaucracy was becoming a real problem for businesses in Papua, with the fastest growing portion of the population in Port Moresby being the public service. The animosity between private and public sectors was now even more obvious than it was pre-war. Some cynics even circulated what they called the 'Official Public Service Prayer', which went: 'O Lord, grant that this day we make no decisions, neither run into any kind of responsibility but that all our doings may be ordered to establish new departments forever and ever. Amen.'

By 1954, even though the Korean War was over, rubber prices remained at profitable levels, and Bert was confident enough to start extending plantings of rubber. This time he imported the seed of high-yielding varieties from Malaya, and he planted an average of 100 acres a year for the rest of the decade. Labour laws had been relaxed removing the necessity for part payments to workers in the form of rations, many of which – things like wheatmeal, dried peas and dripping – were just thrown out.

By 1958, Mamba Estates produced half the total Northern District rubber yield of more than 500 tons of RSS rubber, and had more than 400 head of Aberdeen Angus and Red Poll Shorthorns.

§

If cattle were Wallace's extra-curricular interest, Bert's was aeroplanes. Administrator Hubert Murray had initially discouraged air travel as a means of transport for government officials because he felt they would lose contact with the villagers by not regularly walking through their districts, but he eventually accepted that it would be vital to the future development of the Territory. From his first flight in the 1930s, through his dependency on air supply at the Yodda and on to their vital part during and after the war, Bert was fascinated by, and eternally grateful for, aeroplanes, whereas to Wallace and Meryl, they were just a necessary evil. Reliability of air transport was a big problem in the post-war years, and getting their rubber produce out in the 1950s, with road transport so cumbersome, was a continual source of stress.

In the early 1950s, two pilots, Cliff Jackson and Frank Goosens, began a small air service operating a Waco-Fox Moth and an Avro Anson. In 1954, they set up a company called Papuan Air Transport, having purchased another Anson and taken on a third shareholder, Hank van Santen, who became chief pilot. In December of that year, one of the Ansons crashed, followed less than a week later by the other Anson, which, piloted by Goosens, was downed by high winds in the Myola 2 area. This left the company devoid of its main assets and it was necessary to charter other aircraft to bridge the gap, at considerable cost. More capital was needed to survive, and

Jackson decided to approach Bert, who was a regular customer of the airline with his rubber. He knew Bert was doing well at the time and that aviation was a keen interest of his. Initially, Bert put up some funds and was a shareholder when the company finally received its charter licence in October 1955. The company, now known as Patair, grew using mainly Anson aircraft until 1958, when, after rejecting a takeover offer from Mandated Airlines, they decided to purchase their first DC3. This reliable workhorse of an aircraft carried from 21–32 passengers and around 2.5 tonnes of cargo. The 'Gooney Bird', as it had affectionately become known, played a major part in World War II, and there were plenty of them available after the war for purchase by private operators. The Department of Civil Aviation (DCA), was reluctant to issue the necessary permission to operate this larger aircraft and before they could get their airline licence, the directors of Patair had to approach the minister for transport and ultimately the prime minister, and then carry out a court action against the director-general. They had gone ahead and purchased the DC3, giving it the registration VH-PAT, and were using it to run scheduled services, without the licence but with DCA permission. Even after they won their court case, restrictions still applied, and to add to their challenges the company was being faced with severe competition from Goilala Air Service and Carsair Air Service, both of whom set out to undercut Patair's rates.

Bert was asked to become a director of the company, which he did in July 1959. His first move was to join the push for purchase of a Piaggio aircraft. This Italian-built, wooden frame plane was ideal for a small operator like Patair. With its high wings allowing good access to side-door loading, the Piaggio had excellent vision, and with its short, rugged undercarriage, was well suited for landing on the grass and dirt airstrips of PNG. Bert knew it was popular in South Africa and his further research convinced him it would be ideal for Patair, which was the first to bring this type of aircraft into the Territory. By 1960, the company was operating two Piaggios, which the pilots affectionately called 'Pigs', and one DC3, having by now abandoned the Ansons.

§

For Meryl, the 1950s were all about home, health and family. With Herbert and Wallace so busy, she and Ailsa filled in their days running their households. Meryl was by now an expert at ordering in bulk, making her own bread – or at least she had trained the houseboys to do so – and at making the most of the different local vegetables that were available: taro, sweet potato, yams and pumpkin leaves. They continued to try to add variety to everyone's diet by giving the villagers citrus tree and English potato seeds to be grown in the villages at higher altitudes in the mountains around Mamba. Leisure time was spent cooking and sewing, and playing the ever-popular Scrabble, and card games of gin rummy, whist and solo.

Meryl had a large brass bell she would get the houseboys to ring if anyone was late for meals. If it rang between the designated meal times, Ailsa – or 'Flo' as Meryl affectionately called her – knew that her sister was ready for a game of something or to catch up on the latest news and gossip. She would hop on her trusty pushbike and pedal across from her house to Meryl's.

The European women continued to assist in running the trade stores and to use their nursing skills to help in the plantation 'hospital'. With Wallace's help, they had devised a special brew for treatment of malaria, which was a paludrine tablet added to a tablespoon of cod-liver oil followed by a bite of a *sipora* (Motu for lime). This was a very effective cure but, black or white, it was guaranteed to make your head spin and your eyes roll.

Wallace and Ailsa had constructed a large home, made almost entirely of cedar, harvested and milled on Mamba, upstream on the cliff overlooking the Mambare, only about 100 metres from Meryl's still fairly basic residence. Although John and Diane had started their education with a governess, they would both be sent off to boarding school at about eight years of age. In Sydney, the house at Concord had been sold and replaced by one at Wakeford Road, Strathfield and a couple of years later, Burlington Road, Homebush.

The year 1953 saw Meryl and Ailsa's mother pass away, followed in 1956 by Hally. Then in 1957 Pop Holliday and Audrey also died, but the greatest shock in that sad year was the sudden death of Bert's sister Laura from a heart attack, leaving her husband Dr Harry distraught and alone in Port Moresby with his adopted Papuan son. Having been childless for many years and fostering one or two orphans in Samarai, Laura had eventually adopted a baby boy called Sam, son of Samara Munjier from Gora Village in the Northern Province. Sam's mother, Ijibiri, who gave birth to him at Ela Beach Hospital, had suffered some sort of mental breakdown after his birth, and was not able to cope. Laura took on his care and eventually officially adopted him. At only four years of age, he was now a huge responsibility for Harry, whose job as Assistant Director Health (ADH) in Port Moresby was very demanding. Laura was buried in the cemetery at Mamba alongside Carl.

Around this time, Ailsa also began fostering local children whose mothers had died in childbirth or had other problems. One little girl called Namavi was with them for quite some time and even took a trip to Australia with Ailsa, causing quite a stir in a conservative, 'White Australia Policy' nation. Ailsa learnt a lot about Australian bigotry during that trip, and would often take Namavi to the shops in Sydney just to watch the reaction of people as they excitedly looked into the pram to be met by the dark skin and eyes and rich black fuzzy hair of little Namavi. The reactions ranged from disgust to embarrassment to outright curiosity. Many jumped to conclusions about Namavi's parenthood and therefore Ailsa's morals; others wanted to know the whole story. On one of these trips, Ailsa decided she wanted to buy a goat to take back to Mamba for its milk. She called into the airline office one day, with Namavi in tow, to ask them what was involved in taking a baby goat back to New Guinea. When she explained to the girl behind the counter that she had a 'kid' to take back to New Guinea and she assumed it would have to go into the hold, the hostess looked in shock from Ailsa to Namavi and said 'No, madam, your baby can travel in the passenger cabin with you!'

In 1956, at the tender age of five, young Soc was sent off to boarding school at Trinity Grammar in Sydney, joining John, who had now been there about three years. Of course, he was miserable and begged to be allowed to come home. By mid-1957 he was home, testing the patience of Mrs Jane O'Dea, wife of pilot Tommy. Janie was employed to teach both Soc and Diane, who was unhappy at Meriden in Sydney and demanded to do her Intermediate year at Mamba by correspondence. The special 'school house' erected near the family home was once again put to use. By this time Mary, now aged nearly 19, was living at Burlington Road under the guardianship of Betty Mouritsen who had been Bert's nurse at Sydney Hospital during one of the series of operations he underwent for his hips.

§

For Bert, memories of the war were never far away, and many events occurred and people visited to keep it alive in his mind. In October 1953, he and Meryl were invited by Administrator Cleland to attend the opening of Bomana Cemetery in Port Moresby. By that year, the British War Graves Commission had done its best to locate the remains and collect the records of all those killed in the Territory. They set up three war cemeteries, Port Moresby, Lae and Rabaul, in which were buried a total of 7,989 soldiers, sailors and airmen from the 1942–1945 conflict. In 1942, with the retaking of Kokoda, a cemetery had been established there below the plateau on the site where the school is now located. The few enemy graves located on the plateau had been moved down to the opposite side of the creek. These were removed after the war by Japanese, who came to collect their dead. In February 1946, all the Australians graves at Kokoda, 362 of them, were reinterred first at Soputa, then at Bomana, 22 kilometres outside Moresby. Bert was sad to see this happen. On the back of a photo of the Kokoda War Cemetery taken in 1944 he wrote: 'This is where I want to rest in peace when the time comes.'

This relocation was followed by exhumation of graves at other sites until all bodies in Papua were moved to this new cemetery, with simple wooden crosses to mark each grave. These crosses would soon be replaced with marble pillars, earning the graveyard the title 'The Marble Orchard'.

The governor-general of Australia at the time, Sir William Slim, who had served at Gallipoli and won both a Military Cross and DSO in World War I was the VIP guest speaker for the occasion, and alongside him were generals, admirals, air vice-marshals and various ministers and numerous other distinguished guests, a big occasion for a still somewhat depressed post-war Moresby. Lady Rachel Cleland was present at the ceremony, and described the cemetery in her book *Pathways to Independence*:

> You enter Bomana Cemetery at the bottom of a gentle slope and see rows and rows – four thousand five hundred white headstones, set in beautifully kept lawn with colourful shrubs and landscaped trees. On a rise behind the headstones is the Cross of Sacrifice and a steep hill beyond is crowned with a Greek rotunda, bearing the names of the missing inside its columns, while a brass marker table shows the direction and the distance of the battlefields. Standing there, you look straight at the foothills of the Sogeri plateau where, twenty miles away, blue and beautiful, is Imitia Ridge, where the Australian 25th Brigade turned back the Japanese.

As acting lieutenant general in World War II, Slim was given command of 1 Burma Corps and was credited with transforming a defeated force into a proud army. 'Uncle Bill', as he was affectionately known, pointed out in his speech something that many in Australia were not aware of, or were beginning to forget.

It was Australian soldiers, airmen and sailors who broke the spell of Japanese invincibility on land, and inflicted on their arrogant enemy its first defeat. Let Australians never forget this. It is, like Anzac, part of their most noble tradition – and these men made it.

The ripples of this first victory in the land war against Japan spread beyond these New Guinea shores. Far away a haggard army, battered and bitter with defeat, clung to the fringes of Burma. To it, this victory brought a gleam of hope. If the Australians could do it, so God willing could they. I was one of them, and for that other army I would now pay our special tribute of admiration and gratitude for the men who fought here.

Along with many others, Bert placed a wreath on the cross, his in memory of the carriers, and afterwards he and Meryl attended the dinner held on the lawns of Government House. This was the first time they had met Lady Cleland, and they would catch up with her quite often in the ensuing years and come to know her quite well. Not long after this Bomana ceremony, she flew out to Kokoda with the brigadier on an official visit to see the ADO at the time, Bunny Yeomans, and his wife Jessie. Mrs Yeomans was a qualified teacher and had taken it upon herself to set up a school underneath her home to teach the children of people working on the Kokoda Station, along with any other interested young ones from surrounding villages. This she had done with no government assistance, and it was the Kienzles who came to her aid with funds for materials and books. Bert was a great believer that the vital key to progress of the Papuan people was education, and so once the government school was built at Kokoda, conscious that it was too far for the children of Mamba workers to travel and, as always, with the interests of his people paramount, a year or so later, he built a school on Mamba. The school was situated on a prime site on the banks of the Mambare, adjacent to one of the many great swimming holes in the river. Bert and Wallace completely funded this school from its construction, and through its resourcing, to paying of a government-trained teacher. It proved so popular with the employees and their families that they soon had to extend it to two classrooms, and it kept operating until the late 1960s.

After the poignant memories that flooded his mind at the opening of Bomana, Bert began to plan the fulfilment of another dream that he and Doc Vernon had shared in the last days of the Kokoda Trail campaign. They had talked at length one day about how Australia and Australians would ever be able to show their gratitude to the 'fuzzy wuzzy angels' when the war was over. First and foremost they wanted them to be awarded medals, which had happened to a certain extent but not nearly enough for Bert's satisfaction. Secondly, Doc said he would like to build a top-class hospital at Kokoda. He did not live to fulfil this dream. Their final idea was that there should be a monument at Kokoda specifically dedicated to these heroes, without whom the outcome of the battle, indeed maybe even the war, could have been vastly different. Bert now felt that in order for this dream to ever come true, he would have to do it himself, for his own satisfaction and to honour the memory of his old mate Doc.

The AIF had sponsored the erection of a simple cairn on the plateau at Kokoda soon after the war. But by 1957 Bert felt it was time for the local people to get their own overdue recognition, so he first sought permission from Administrator Cleland, then approached the Australian War Memorial (AWM) in Canberra for advice and assistance on how to go about the project. They put him onto well-known sculptor Ray Ewers, who had already done a lot of work for the AWM and had himself served on the Trail. Ewers was pleased to assist with the design and construction of the memorial and plans went back and forth between him and Bert until they settled on the monument that stands on the Kokoda plateau today. Built of cement and faced with the richly coloured rocks from the creeks around Kokoda, the monument is in the form of a stone base surmounted by two stone pillars, linked near the top by a bronze bar with a circular bronze plaque on each side of the monument. The bronze bar symbolises the unity of the two races – Australian and Papuan – to one purpose, the defeat of a common enemy. It reads 'Owen Stanley Campaign 1942'. The two circular plaques were designed to signify the medals that Bert felt the carriers should have all received – so these were like 'medals for all'. One of the plaques depicts carriers straining under the weight of a stretcher supporting a wounded soldier, and the other shows carriers moving up the Trail with military supplies. The inscription on a long brass plaque on the rectangular base of the monument reads: 'In memory of the native carriers of the Kokoda Trail'.

As the monument was completed in mid-1959, it was decided to have its official unveiling on 2 November, 17 years after the retaking of Kokoda. A big event was organised and paid for by the Kienzle family, and this included flying in 30 carriers from their homes throughout the country to join those living around Kokoda. The police band was flown in from Moresby to make its first appearance in the district. Ray Ewers was brought back up from Australia and various other dignitaries arrived on DC3 charters from Port Moresby, including Administrator Cleland, who was to perform the ceremony, accompanied by his wife Rachel and Secretary C. R. Lambert, representing the Department of Territories.

What a proud day it was for Bert and his boys. A brilliant sun shone on the Kokoda plateau, now planted with colourful shrubs surrounding a rich green manicured lawn, and hibiscus and croton lined paths. The river stones of the monument had been polished to reflect their dark lustre and the carriers were mostly dressed in electric blue new *ramis* issued to them by Bert on their arrival. They stood proudly to attention beside their Australian comrades as Brigadier Cleland gave his moving tribute to these now immortalised 'fuzzy wuzzy angels':

No stirring call of martial music, no plaudits of a cheering populace lifted the hearts of these men as they moved to their duty and their partnership with the Australian troops. The sobering awareness of unchecked successes and allied reverses was in the mind of every Australian soldier and filtered through to the carriers who marched at their elbows. Nobody had any illusions about the task ahead, and the Papuans as they took up their burdens, to serve the needs of the Australian troops, faced with bewilderment the fact that their peaceful isolated land had been plunged suddenly into an alien invasion which if unchecked could reach every Papuan home. Moreover this was a quarrel not of their making, the great issues of the war were beyond their comprehension. They were men called from quiet hamlets into an arena of international conflict waged under conditions of appalling hardships, and where the urgencies of the military situation demanded the last ounce of endurance and strength from every man. Often, like the troops, they were short of food, sickness struck at them, torrential rains forced them to struggle ankle deep in mud and on the higher levels of the range they often huddled sleepless without shelter through bitterly cold damp nights.

And just who were these carriers? They were Kiwais, Goaribaris, Kikoris, Koiaris, Biagis, Orokaivas, Mambares and Warias, men from the Bamu region, from Orokolo, the Mekeo, Rigo, Abau, Baniara, Tufi, the Milne Bay District and other areas of Papua. Their loyal support of the Australian troops established a tradition of service and sacrifice which showed the true measure of the Papuan people.

May this monument, standing below the ramparts of the Owen Stanleys, be a symbol to all of the people of the Territory and those who visit here from beyond the seas, of the vital part played by the Papuan carriers in the crucial campaign of the Kokoda Trail.

Bert, reluctant as always to speak publicly or draw too much attention to himself, briefly addressed the crowd of over 2,000 natives now gathered on the plateau, interpreting Cleland's words into Motu and adding his own heartfelt thanks. Some of the natives flown in from other districts apparently did not quite trust the reasons given for this gathering, as one of their spokesmen approached Bert and said, 'Hey, if you are thinking of having another war, count us out! We've already done our bit!' They were most relieved when they realised that it really was just a celebration in their honour. The blessing was given by Bishop (later Sir) Philip Strong and after the ceremony refreshments were provided at the ADC's house, on the edge of the plateau overlooking the site of the old war cemetery.

§

On Mamba itself, the 1950s saw much construction activity also. In early 1958, Bert decided to build his wife and family the plantation home of their dreams. As they wanted it on the same site as their current house, this one had to be pulled down and temporary accommodation built nearby for the family to live in while their new home was built. Since construction of Wallace and Ailsa's home, Mamba Estate had its own sawmill, and so began the task of logging and sawing all the necessary timber for what was to become a splendid dwelling, the largest private residence and most impressive plantation home in the Territory for many years. The 1000-square-metre, two-storey edifice was designed by Meryl and built by Jack Reid, a builder who came out from Moresby and lived at Mamba for the duration of the project. The final product was basically a large u-shaped structure with an imposing staircase that was edged by rock balustrades leading up to the main entrance. The words 'Mamba House'. were set in wrought iron either side of the main entrance, but it soon became known as the 'Big House' The roof was painted Meryl's favourite deep blue and the timber walls white – an imposing sight from both land and air. Upstairs was a large lounge–dining room, pantry and kitchen. The main bedroom, with spectacular views up the Mambare River, had an en suite, as did the little bedroom next to it, which was Diane's – the privilege of her own bathroom having been won by doing well in her Intermediate exams.

Another big bathroom was shared by two more bedrooms, one being John and Soc's room and the other for Mary on the rare occasions she was home. Then there was what came to be the famous 'Blue Room' – a guest room with en suite, also with a fantastic view, where guests were always most honoured to stay and in whose beds many famous names in PNG's chequered history would rest over the years.

Downstairs was designed for coolness, comfort and entertainment. Under the kitchen was a storage room and a dressing room with a shower for the house staff. A large open-plan floor allowed plenty of space for guests, and up one end was the office, with visual access so Meryl and Bert could see and communicate with each other during the day. The wall of this office served as a picture screen for the weekly, Saturday-night movies that would be brought out from Moresby by plane and to which all plantation management staff and everyone from other plantations and the government station were invited. A full-size, genuine slate billiard table soon arrived, plus a new piano for Meryl. A bar with a clock saying 'No drinking allowed before 6 o'clock', with every number on the dial being a 6, fitted well with every Territorian's reputation for enjoying a prompt pre-dinner 'planter's punch'!

The family moved in with much pleasure and celebration in August 1958, inviting guests for a housewarming, including Bishop Strong, who they asked to bless the library as a private chapel and to consecrate the family cemetery, which now held two graves, Carl's and Laura's. This family cemetery was then able to be officially gazetted later that year.

§

In July 1959, Mary turned 21 and her coming-of-age present was a trip with her father to Fiji, Hawaii and the USA. For Bert, this would be his first return to his birthplace since leaving there under such unpleasant circumstances in 1917. For Mary, it would be the first time she learnt of her Samoan ancestry.

They flew to Suva, where Bert's cousin Wallace Caldwell was in the Royal Fiji Police Force.

Mary and Bert were able to spend time in Suva with Wallace and his family and from there they caught a flying boat to Levuka, landing in the harbour and spending a full day exploring Bert's old stamping grounds. Struggling up the steep hillside with his walking stick, Bert was determined to spend time by his mother's grave, the sorrow of her death still a sharp pang in his heart when he remembered her loving and gentle nature that he knew for far too short a time. For Mary it was a strange sensation seeing her own name 'Mary Kienzle' on the gravestone. He then took his daughter to his old school and up the many steps to his home on the hill that now belonged to an elderly, wealthy plantation owner, Arthur Robinson. This home was still as solid as the day it was built, but Bert's grandfather's house, 'Qima', which had been high on the hillside overlooking the wharf, had been demolished and a new house built on its site by another prosperous local planter, R. A. Ricketts.

From Fiji they visited Hawaii, then on to San Francisco to visit more relatives from the Wilson branch of the family, then across to Chicago to spend time with Elsa, her husband Hans and their daughter HelenJoan.

Bert planned to call in on his US Army mate Colonel Arthur Bell, who had issued an invitation for them to visit him at his 'Creekside' Farm near Easton about 175 kilometres from Washington. After an illustrious career in the army, first in the 29th Division in World War I and then provost marshal of the Sixth Army in World War II, 'your ole cobber' Arthur, as he signed his letters to Bert, had done a short spell as a prison warden. Not long after the war, Bell had sent Bert some photos of his time in the army, addressed: 'To my good friend Capt H. T. Kienzle MBE, a real fine soldier, with admiration. Arthur S Bell Colonel Infantry US Army retired.' This was high praise from a highly decorated military man.

Bert then caught up with some of his other US Army pals when he attended a military parade at the marine base in Washington DC.

13

REMEMBRANCE AND RECOGNITION

Soon after their return from Bert's nostalgic overseas journey, Mary announced her engagement to John Hardy, whose father Nelson lived in Port Moresby and mother Gladys, in Sydney. John was a Trinity Grammar boy – handsome, charming and a talented sportsman. He would captain PNG's team for the 1963 first South Pacific Games in Suva, where he represented the Territory in swimming. John had won Mary's heart by courting her vigorously when she was working in administration in the junior school at Trinity Grammar and living at Homebush. Despite the persistent interference of her two younger brothers, at the tender age of 21, John asked Bert for Mary's hand in marriage. Bert gave his approval but made it clear he did not believe in long engagements – six months was his limit. Maybe the painful memories of the long wait for his Meryl prompted this policy, or maybe he was concerned for their moral fortitude. Whatever his reasons, he insisted on this time frame for both his daughters.

Mary and John were married at Mamba on Sunday 5 June 1960, and the Big House shone as a venue for the occasion. Guests were flown in by two Patair DC3s and accommodated at the various homes on Mamba or at Kokoda. The ceremony was held upstairs in the lounge room and the register signed in the library that had been blessed by Bishop Strong for just such purposes. The reception was a magnificent buffet spread downstairs in what the report in the *South Pacific Post* called the 'theatrette billiard room'. For the 'something old', Mary was honoured to carry a 100-year-old handkerchief lent to her by Rachel Cleland.

The process was to be repeated on another Sunday just short of five years later in May 1965 when Diane married Christopher Moloney. By now, Mary and John had two children, Greg, born on 14 May 1962 and newly arrived Jacquelyn, born 19 April 1965. This time, the marriage ceremony was held in Wallace and Ailsa's lounge room. The bridal party then hopped into two very new, very swish white VWs and 130 or so guests walked in perfect tropical sunshine across to the Big House where once again an impressive spread was laid out in the cool of the downstairs room.

Chris Moloney was a Sydney boy who had trained at ASOPA (Australian School of Pacific Administration) and had been teaching at various schools in the Northern District. He was indeed honoured to be given permission by Bert to marry his little Di, who had always had her father wrapped around her little finger and was the apple of his eye. This 'number two' daughter seemed to get away with a lot more than her older sister. After the time she had spent back at Mamba with a governess, Di had returned to Meriden to complete her Leaving Certificate and after a short stint trying nursing, opted for a business course then returned home to help her father in the office. During her years in Sydney, her charge account at David Jones was always stretched to the limit and the family would wait in trepidation to see what fashion statement she would be making each time she arrived home. When beehive hairdos were in, they joked that they needed to open both doors of the DC3 for her to be able to get out of the plane.

Life at Mamba in the 1960s was almost idyllic. The rubber and cattle were thriving and the company employed up to six European assistants at any one time. Everyone, especially family members, was expected to work hard but the social life and other benefits were attractive. Bert was generous to good workers. Salaries, paid on a calendar month basis of 12 times a year, were probably not anything to write home about but housing and house staff were provided and bread and meat were free. Boarding school education was paid for for the children of long-term employees, and school friends of his own children coming up for school holidays usually had their airfares paid by Bert. In medical emergencies his embedded memories of the loss of Carl meant he was always quick to act and generous in his assistance.

Life was a little lonely for the unmarried assistants. Bert had strict rules about fraternisation with the native women that if broken by anyone, be they family or employees, would mean a one-way ticket on the first plane out of Kokoda. The occasional female family friend, Volunteer Abroad or even missionary who paid a visit to the valley always looked good to the young men at Mamba and they were invariably greeted enthusiastically. Bert wasn't always so successful in controlling the fraternisations among his European staff, and between them and government expatriates in the district, so Meryl would sometimes have to step in and give some motherly advice to wayward husbands and wives. Bert believed strongly that the Europeans on his staff held a position of trust and responsibility and that they must earn and then keep the respect of the native employees. He frowned on undignified behaviour and it upset him noticeably if he witnessed any members of the European families on the estates behaving badly.

Evening meals continued to be a ritual, with everyone dressing formally for dinner and drinks being served sharply at six. Bert sat at the head of the table discussing the affairs of the world that had been listened to on ABC radio before the meal commenced. Three-course meals were prepared and served by the house staff – Beleni, Javoko, Gitavi and Boni – who had been trained by Meryl in all the necessities and niceties of a silver-service table. Weekends were filled with Saturday-night movies at the Big House and picnics by the Mambare near the school where a barbecue was built and a 'tinny' was provided for skiing and 'ironing boarding'. Sunday tennis with afternoon tea and home-made cakes was traditionally alternated between the gravel court at Mamba and the basically bare dirt one at Kokoda station. Bert would play a mean game, walking stick in one hand and racquet in the other, but the devil on the court was Wallace. One local school teacher always said that he made sure he was absent when Wallace was looking for either partner or opponent.

Boxing Day at Mamba in these semi-utopian years was a particularly big annual event, with steer riding, swimming races, high jumping, tug-o-wars, running races and a 'mu-mu' – several beef carcasses cooked native-style in hot rocks and covered in banana leaves. Mamba's native workers were involved in all these activities, and this they much appreciated. For their part, the many different tribes employed on Mamba would put on sing-sings and take pleasure in their natural penchant for pantomime, each year dressing in European garb and imitating their bosses. They particularly liked imitating 'Unk', the name given to Wallace by young Ted Johnston, friend and unrequited admirer of Mary for many years. Not sure what to call this imposing, rather scary man, Ted volunteered the name 'Unk', which he felt was appropriate to the mumbles that were Wallace's usual form of conversation. Unk had a reputation for being tough, taciturn and temperamental, although usually, but not always, fair. Despite his gruff manner, many a bloke would say of this tall, well-built 'man's man', with his Dean Martin-style ruggedly handsome looks, that they would follow him to the ends of the earth if required. Everyone who worked with him soon learnt that if you greeted him and got two grunts in response it was a good day; a one-grunt reply, and it was a good idea to keep your head down. The clowns would prepare re-enactments of things that Unk had done during the year, bringing a smile to everyone's face, even his. If a suitable movie could be found, the projector would be set up in the 'Women's Club', an open-sided cement-floored gathering place Bert had built for the local ladies, where they would be given lessons in mothercraft and family health. A sheet would be drawn tight between two trees outside and the workers and their families would gather en masse to watch this amazing invention of white man, the talking picture. They just loved westerns and always gave out a big cheer when the Indians had a win. Even a heavy downpour of rain would not deter them from sitting through until the very end of the credits and the last 5–4–3–2–1 countdown.

The pleasures of these prosperous times did not mean Bert lost sight of his loyal Papuan workers and as some of them were reaching the age where they could no longer handle the physical work they were used to doing for him he decided to set up his own superannuation scheme for those who had been with him before, during and after the war. The first beneficiaries were his two ever-faithful men, Morso Lellewa and Hitolo Jinga. He surveyed each of them a 40-acre block out of his Amada Plantation lease. He called this plan the Amada Superannuation Scheme, and the idea was he would help the men plant cocoa trees on these blocks that would then provide them and their families with an income once they retired. The Department of Labour thought this was a wonderful idea and wanted Bert to report to them regularly on the scheme and its progress. He later extended the scheme to several other workers but was quite disappointed when some of the old mens' families did not help them to maintain the blocks well enough to ensure successful 'plantations' were established.

The only real blot on the landscape in those halcyon days was the introduction of income tax in the Territory for the first time. Bert and Wallace had had their fingers burnt by bad advice from their solicitor with regard to Hally's income and in 1954 had to pay £16,000 to the Australian Government in back taxes. Any mention of taxation made Bert's blood boil. He felt that he had contributed significantly to the development of the Territory as a pioneer opening up the interior of Papua.

He had never been properly compensated after the war, but had still reinvested most of what he had made since back into his plantations, so he believed that he and others like him should remain exempt from such imposts. After all, they had to build and maintain all their own roads, bridges, electricity and water supplies, plus housing for all their employees. They mowed the Kokoda airstrip much of the time, keeping it like a golf course – for which it was occasionally used if planes were not due in! They even took on the contract in 1956 to virtually rebuild and extend the strip so it could take larger aircraft and heavier loads, like the RAAF Caribous, which would use the strip for 'circuits and bumps' training for their pilots.

In the middle of 1961, the family was thrilled to have a six-week visit from Elsa's daughter HelenJoan, who had arrived in Papua after an odyssey through the South Pacific where she visited Tahiti, Hawaii, Samoa, New Zealand and, of course, Fiji. Her visit was even mentioned in the *Post Courier* newspaper, alongside the story of the mysterious disappearance of Nelson Rockefeller's son, Michael. The super-wealthy New York Governor's 23-year-old son had gone to West Irian to buy art from the primitive Asmat tribe on the south coast of Dutch New Guinea. He supposedly disappeared when his overloaded 40-foot dugout canoe was swamped in the Arafura Sea near the mouth of the Eilanden River. Although this river was infested with sharks and crocodiles, rumours abounded that he had survived the ordeal. One story said that he had made it to shore, only to be eaten by cannibals. Another version was that he was still alive and hiding in the jungle somewhere and that an Australian adventurer of dubious reputation claimed to have spotted him some years after his disappearance. Whatever the truth, it made good media fodder and overshadowed the little paragraph about Mamba's US visitor.

§

The early 1960s saw problems and changes for Patair and Bert's involvement with the airline. In 1960, they were once again the subject of a takeover offer by Melanesian Airlines at a handsome figure, which the directors refused. The same year they were granted a permit for a second DC3. The following year, disaster struck when the company lost three aircraft in various accidents – a Piaggio, a DC3 and an Aztec. The Piaggio and the Aztec were lost in combinations of weather, mechanical problems and pilot error, but the DC3 was a different case altogether. VH-PAT, loaded with fragile medical equipment from the Public Health Department, was en route from Port Moresby to Minj when smoke was seen pouring from the cargo area. The pilot, Captain Miles Lewis, managed to make a near-perfect landing at Bereina airstrip only 110 kilometres from Moresby, despite being half blinded and asphyxiated by the choking fumes, which had by then saturated the cockpit. The captain and air-hostess Pat Gollum escaped unharmed but co-pilot Bill Vink received a bad burn on his wrist while trying to remove the smoking box. Soon after they disembarked, the aircraft became engulfed in flames and was completely destroyed. It would appear the Public Health Department had loaded what was dangerous cargo without advising the airline, and subsequent investigations cleared Patair of any blame and commended the pilot on his handling of the emergency.

Despite this outcome, the company barely managed to avert the withdrawal of their charter licence by the director-general. The directors stepped in and negotiated to keep their licence on the proviso that a thorough internal investigation of the company was carried out. Bert and other members of the board soon established that the operations would not stand a close check by DCA. There was no order, no discipline, inexperienced personnel were running the company, staff unity was non-existent and public relations poor.

Significantly, Meryl had been warning Bert that she could see the overpaid and underworked management of the company was living it up in Port Moresby while he and other directors remained ignorant of what was happening, stuck as he was out on the plantation. It was time to step in. Hans van Santen was recalled from leave and Frank Campbell was appointed to take over the accounts, which were in a chaotic state. It was realised that the only way to regain status with the DCA was to employ a team of experienced men as executives. The company appointed its own secretary, Kevin Tibbey, traffic manager, Phil Chandler, who had had 17 years with Qantas, and operations manager/chief pilot, Bill Forgan-Smith of 20 years' experience also with Qantas.

Bert was elected chairman and by 1962, despite showing an operational loss in that year, they had restored the faith of the director-general in Patair. Their charter licence was renewed and they were granted a full airline licence in the new company name of Papuan Airlines Pty Ltd. The company then went from strength to strength, and by late 1965 was looking to expand its range of aircraft and replace some of the ageing DC3s. Bert and managing director Cliff Jackson set off on a hectic five-week investigatory journey to Italy, France, Switzerland and Norway, as well as the UK, the USA and Canada. In Belfast, they visited Short Brothers & Harland to check out the Short Skyvan, two of which had already been ordered but would not be delivered until January 1967. In France, they looked at the four-engine Potez and the Nord 262 and in Switzerland, the Pilatus Porters. Two of these were ordered and flown out by Swiss pilots Guido Good and Emil Wick, who arrived on 15 May 1966 in aircraft with registration numbers HBFBZ and HBFCH, the first Pilatus Porters to arrive in Australasia. These aircraft would soon impress the military with their STOL capabilities combined with their ability to reverse on land by altering the pitch on the propeller, and many would later be used in the Vietnam War.

While in Europe, Bert and Cliff also took the opportunity to investigate the latest developments in quality hotels and to make contacts in the wine and liqueur export industries, particularly in Italy. On their return, they used the knowledge and contacts they acquired to design and build an international standard hotel in Port Moresby overlooking the airport, to be owned and operated by Papuan Airlines' subsidiary company Tourist Developments Pty Ltd. This hotel was erected in 1967 at a cost of around £250,000 and the name chosen for it by Meryl was 'The Gateway'. She played a big part in its design and interior décor and named the best room in the house 'the Yodda Suite'. She and Bert always stayed here on their visits to Moresby. The hotel included a very popular 'grog' shop they called 'The Wine Kellar', guaranteed to be well stocked with Bert's favourite wines – Mateus Rosé from Portugal and Liebfraumilch Riesling from Germany.

It was around this time that Bert also invested in a jewellery business in Port Moresby called Winston's Jewellery, indulging his passion for precious metals and gemstones, and resulting in both Meryl and Ailsa being spoilt with beautiful gifts for every special occasion.

§

For the family, apart from the spate of weddings culminating in John's marriage to Helen Mutton at Trinity Grammar School on 11 June 1966, there was to be a new addition to the household. With his remarriage and imminent departure to Killara in Sydney in 1962, Dr Harry White asked Meryl to adopt his Papuan son Sammy. Despite unsolicited advice from members of the family that he would be better off being sent back to his own people, for Laura's sake Meryl could not say no. Sammy was given all the benefits of the rest of the Kienzles, including education at Trinity Grammar School and living in the Big House with all the attendant luxuries. Being the closest in age to Soc, it fell to him to look after Sam, protecting him both at school and at home from the taunts he received because of his unusual position. Theirs was an awkward friendship that would ultimately collapse when the difference in cultures and loyalties would result in a violent clash of values.

Soc was busy doing his own thing most of the time and always knew how to make the most of his holidays at home from boarding school. After spending Christmas 1963 and New Year at home, he flew to Moresby to spend some time with a Trinity Grammar School mate. The plan was that they would then walk back to Kokoda together across the Trail. On 6 January, making a much later start than intended, they were taken up by his mate's mother to set off from P. J. McDonald's plantation, at what had become known as McDonald's Corner. Here they spent some time and had a few sandwiches while they waited for their guide, Yabi, a policeman who knew the track well, having worked with Bert during the Kokoda Campaign. At around 9.30 a.m., they set off together and PJ radioed Bert to tell him that the two boys were on their way and what time they left. The next day was Meryl's birthday and a small dinner party was being held at Mamba as a celebration. It was not expected that Soc would be there but David Ross, who owned Kokoda Plantation, which was situated at the very start of the Kokoda Trail, was invited and Soc knew this. As he made good progress along the track, he decided he was going to try to get back in time for Mum's birthday and so he kept going and going, stopping for less than six hours' sleep at Kagi. Soon after this when they paused at a 'rest house', Yabi came across a cache of smoked pork stored in the rafters. He proceeded to gnaw away at it but would not let the boys have any as he said their 'whitey tummies' could not handle it. Within an hour he was violently ill and had to let them proceed on their own. By the time they reached Isurava, Soc's mate had had enough and wanted to stop, but Soc was now more determined than ever to get home so he piggy-backed his exhausted friend on and off for the last few kilometres. He knew he would have to be at Kokoda by around 5.30 p.m. to catch a lift with David over to Mamba – drinks were served at 6 p.m. sharp. Much to David's surprise, there by the side of the road as he headed over to the birthday party was Soc and his exhausted mate. Bert and Meryl could not believe their eyes when their youngest son arrived home with David. He had covered the trail in less than 33 hours – the fastest ever done by a white man! Bert was indeed proud of both his tough young sons. John, also accompanied by Yabi, had covered the Trail in less than three days a few years earlier, without the incentive of a birthday party to drive him on.

This impressive feat by such a young white man would plant the seed for the Annual Kokoda Trail Race that Bert instigated and sponsored for several years thereafter, with Soc's time as a benchmark. Bert ran the event each year sometime between April and June, preferably around Anzac Day, giving a prize of $200 for the winner. The record was broken in the very first official event by a Papuan who ran the distance in 27 hours. These records for a white man and black man would hold for many years; in fact, they probably still have not been broken, as the track over which people race today is not the original wartime Trail and starts at Owers' Corner, not McDonald's Corner – a three-hour walk time difference.

For Bert's youngest son, the most important outcome of his achievement was an increased fascination with the war and everything that had happened around his home. Up until this experience, his only real interest in the history was when as a young boy he and his mates, instead of tennising with the 'oldies' at Kokoda, spent their time playing in the many Japanese air raid shelters that had been dug into the side of the plateau during the occupation of the area from August to November 1942. These cleverly constructed trenches were wide enough for three men's torsos, angled at 45 degrees along the side of the plateau edge, with a 10-foot-long, 45-degree fall into an underground chamber that could hold five or six men. Their layout meant it was very difficult for aircraft to fire into them, but the enemy could safely fire out of them at the circling Allied fighter planes. Many of these trenches remain intact to this day, but even in the 1960s there was a risk of them collapsing, not to mention the possibility of snakes and other unfriendly creatures having taken up residence there.

Soc now became a sponge for any information his father could give him about the campaign and began spending much of his holiday time heading off into the bush to find battle sites and collect war relics. His father would direct him and, when he was a little older, allow him to take a tractor and trailer and some of his men from the war on his quests. Soc found helmets and boots, water bottles, bayonets, bullets, belts and buckles. He found horseshoes and pack saddles, rifles, revolvers and pistols and many skulls, bones and teeth. For every load, he was under strict instructions to return them to the Big House where he would lay them on the lawn for his father's inspection. Bones he had found in mass graves were assumed to be Japanese. Those from individual sites Bert knew would be Australians, and he would carefully bundle them up and send them to Bomana Cemetery, where they were usually buried as 'Known unto God'. Bert and Soc always felt that missing men like Captain Sam Templeton were probably somewhere among these unidentified soldiers. Bert would cause his brother Wallace great consternation as he poked at the old ammunition, pushing anything he felt could be dangerous aside and instructing the houseboys to dump it into the nearby rubbish hole, where it would fall on previously added ammunition – a recipe for an explosion. Unk would say to Soc, 'What's the silly old bugger doing now? He's going to blow us all up if he keeps this up!'

Soc's best find in the mid-60s was the mountain gun that had been left behind by the Japanese at Gorari when the speed of their retreat did not allow them to carry it to the coast. This he took home with great pride and it was to later be mounted impressively on the front lawn of either the Big House or of his bachelor pad by the Mambare River, depending where Soc was living, where it always served as a great talking point. Much of this gear was later put into the original war museum at Kokoda, but a lot of it disappeared in the immediate post-independence year, including some of the bones of General Horii's horse that Bert had saved since he found them on the track in 1942.

§

Many changes occurred in PNG in the early 1960s. By now more than 15,000 Europeans lived in the Territories. Alcohol was legalised for the natives and the University of PNG was established. In 1963, C. E. Barnes replaced Paul Hasluck as minister for territories, inheriting an administration with well-established polices on education, health, economic growth and political development. Nineteen sixty-four was a very significant year in the political history of PNG, with the first parliament in the form of a House of Assembly being opened on 8 June. Just before this, on 30 May, the Kienzles were honoured to receive a visit from Australia's Governor-General De L'isle, who had arrived in Moresby on the *ANZAC II* as part of a trip that included an official visit to PNG and a cruise along the coast. De Lisle had an interest in cattle production and asked to inspect Mamba's herds on the way back to the airstrip after morning tea at the Big House.

Soon after this, Bert and Meryl celebrated their many good fortunes by taking their own cruise, a first-class trip around the Pacific on the *Monterey*. Bert carried with him a document headed with the Australian Coat of Arms and 'Commonwealth of Australia'. It read: 'The bearer of this document, Captain Herbert Kienzle of Kokoda Papua New Guinea, is proceeding on a visit overseas. Any facilities or courtesies which may be accorded the bearer while absent from the Commonwealth will be greatly appreciated.' The document was signed by J. McEwen, Acting Prime Minister.

Early in their voyage, they called in to Suva, where their visit was reported in the local newspaper and it was noted that they met up with Bert's cousin Wallace Caldwell, now deputy superintendent of police, and also with author Raymond Paull. They were then taken to lunch at the stylish Grand Pacific Hotel by R. W. Robson, now the publisher of Fiji's only daily newspaper, the *Fiji Times*. Robson was also known as a conservative commentator on local and regional issues through his *Pacific Islands Monthly*.

Their trip also took them to Germany, where they visited the house in Kanonenweg, now called Haussman Strasse in Stuttgart, where Bert had lived in the 1920s. The beautiful old home had been declared a Municipal Monument and so was well maintained and easily recognisable to Bert. To their relief, they were welcomed quite warmly by some of their Kienzle relatives.

Bert's contact with Australia's federal leaders continued when he received a personal letter from Prime Minister R. G. Menzies on 3 February 1965 asking him to support the Winston Churchill Memorial Trust, which was raising funds for its Churchill Fellowships. These fellowships were designed to benefit scholars in all Commonwealth countries and their territories, including PNG. Bert organised Operation Doorknock in the Kokoda District and raised about £300, for which he received a letter of thanks from W. J. Kilpatrick, National General Chair of the Trust.

At the age of exactly 50, on his birthday in October 1965, Meryl's only brother Stan died of a heart attack. He left behind his wife Helen and their only child Helen Evelyn, known as Lyn, at the time just 15 years old. Meryl and Ailsa had now lost both their parents and siblings, and Meryl particularly seemed to start worrying about all her family after the many early deaths they had experienced.

§

In 1966, Lady Rachel Cleland set out to complete one more significant project before her husband retired as administrator of the Territory. She decided she wanted to beautify the main highway and alternate routes from the airport to the town centre and to Konedobu in Port Moresby. She formed a committee with members from both government and private enterprise to fix the roads, plant trees and shrubs, position rubbish receptacles and build seating in suitable places along the routes. Initially, she had hoped that each tree planted would have a plaque beside it with the names of every native carrier, policeman and PIB soldier who served during World War II. She allocated Max Dryer of the Electricity Commission the job of collating this list of names, and he soon contacted Bert for assistance. Bert had to disappoint him with the information that 'Due to the urgent and continuous movement and action of men in and out of the Kokoda Trail and Owen Stanley Campaign, no complete records were kept. I never saw an accurate and comprehensible roll of all native carriers.' This idea was eventually shelved.

Rachel herself contacted Bert and asked if he would help sponsor a similar monument in Port Moresby to the one he had done to the carriers at Kokoda. Of course he agreed. Rachel and the brigadier visited Mamba in October 1966 to have another look at the carriers' monument and to discuss the plans with Bert. It was decided to locate the memorial, which would incorporate a seat, on the seaward side of the road at Three-Mile Hill overlooking Koki markets and out towards Fisherman's Island. A plain wall of stones brought down especially from the Kokoda Trail was constructed with replicas of Ray Ewers' circular plaques, paid for by Bert, inserted at either end. Two further rectangular sculptures, one honouring the police and one the PIB, were commissioned from Ray Ewers by Lady Rachel and sponsored by the RSL. These centred between the two circular plaques. Below all this was a plaque that read: 'This monument honours those Papuan and New Guinean servicemen, police and carriers who served their country during the campaign in Papua New Guinea 1942–1945.' All this took some planning and was not actually completed until mid-1967, by which time Donald Cleland had retired as administrator and been replaced at Government House by David Hay, with his wife Alison. The opening of the memorial was incorporated into the huge 'Return to Kokoda' celebrations that were held over four hectic days from 3 to 6 November. This pilgrimage to mark the 25th anniversary of the retaking of Kokoda involved diggers from all over Australia and a regathering of some of the top brass from the campaign. Lieutenant General the Hon. Sir Edmund Herring gave the address at the 'Unveiling and dedication of the memorial to Papuan & New Guinean Ex-Servicemen, Royal Papua Constabulary & Carriers at Three-Mile Hill' on 3 November 1967. Despite his large part in this project, Bert kept a low profile during the ceremony, only laying a wreath. On 4 November another service was held at Bomana Cemetery. The next day, the pilgrims flew out to Kokoda, where a memorial service was held on the plateau. Two plaques were taken out by the men of the 39th Battalion and unveiled on this occasion, one to commemorate the return of the 39th and one to commemorate the 25th anniversary of the re-entry to Kokoda of the 16th and 25th Brigades.

That day, the Kienzles were honoured to have as guests at the Big House Lieutenant General Herring along with Major General P. A. Cullen and Brigadier Ivan Dougherty accompanied by Bishop David Hand, who signed the visitors book in the traditional manner: '+David, New Guinea'.

This gathering was not the first held in what was a very nostalgic year for Bert. Earlier, on the anniversary of the first battle at Kokoda, a large contingent of 39th Battalion veterans also made the journey to Kokoda for a memorial service as part of a week-long commemoration similar to the one in November. On 18 August more than 40 guests, diggers and their wives flew to Kokoda and dined at Mamba after the activities at the station, which included the laying and dedication of a plaque to the 39th Battalion, this honour being performed by Bert and Alf Salmon. Bert and Meryl received many letters of thanks from the grateful veterans in the ensuing months. The importance of the year had been marked by the issue of stamps celebrating the 25th anniversary of the Pacific War, and Bert, with his interest in philately, arranged for the purchase of first-day covers for any interested guests. The whole occasion was reported in the *Australian Women's Weekly* in September 1967:

That evening there was a big dinner party at the Kienzle homestead at Kokoda, and a screening there of wartime newsreels made by Damien Parer. Some of the men recognized themselves or their friends in the young faces of the troops preparing to walk the Kokoda Trail . . . Officers of the 39th Btn thanked Captain Kienzle by presenting him with the battalion colours – 'mud over blood' – to be flown at Kokoda for ceremonial occasions . . . There were cheers of 'Good on you, Bert' and rousing hurrahs. It was a moment of tremendous emotion for everyone. Captain Kienzle was very moved but he managed to say 'If you ever want to come back, don't forget to let us know – you are always welcome.'

Bert was really chuffed by this attention, as he held the men of the 39th in high esteem, saying of them in an interview some years later, 'Great blokes, great battalion.' This mutual admiration was further demonstrated when a discussion broke out about the location of a particular battle. Bert was consulted for clarification and word came back, 'It's not marked on the map and Bert doesn't know where it is. If he doesn't know it, it's not there!'

Other visitors of note that year included Major Michael Jeffery, later to become governor-general, at that time stationed in Port Moresby with 1PIR. Major Jeffery presented Bert with a copy of Colonel Keogh's *South Pacific War 1941–1945*. A few years later, another future governor-general, this time of Fiji, George K. Cakobau, great grandson of the famous King who had lived in Levuka 100 years earlier, took time out from an official visit to PNG to fly to Mamba to catch up with fellow 'Levukans' Bert and Wallace. Ratu George, at the time minister of Fijian affairs and local government, was a bit younger than Bert, but they had a lot in common, having both attended Levuka Public School, and George also achieving the rank of captain when he served in the Fiji Military Forces in World War II. George was partly in the country to watch a rugby game between his Fiji team and PNG, and Soc was to play for the home side. They flew to Moresby together and discussed rugby all the way. George sang the praises of Fijian rugby and insisted that Fijians were better than the pure Polynesians at the game because the latter were too soft and fat, whereas the Fiji boys were pure muscle. As they descended the aircraft stairs in Moresby he wished Soc good luck, adding 'I feel sorry for you.' He could see what was coming – PNG was defeated by about 100 to nil.

In 1965, Bert had been appointed as an inaugural director of the newly formed PNG Development Bank, which was to later change its name to the PNG Agricultural Bank. This involved regular trips to Moresby for board meetings and tours of the whole Territory to investigate development projects, and it also meant some interesting visitors to Mamba. On 21 August 1967, Stephen D. Eccles of the World Bank paid a visit to PNG and spent a night at the Big House. Eccles had joined the bank in 1966, and eventually became its vice-president and controller. Having worked in a bank for a short time in Germany, the finance industry always interested Bert. He loved anything to do with numbers and money. He had actually set up the first agency of the Bank of New South Wales in the plantation office at Mamba and this provided a much needed service and education for the plantation employees. The Bank of NSW was the first to set up shop in PNG in 1910. Before that, Burns Philp were the bankers and they had their own notes that were redeemable in gold in both Australia and London. Bert encouraged his workers to try to save a little of their pay each week, but it was a losing battle. The minimum balance to keep an account open was two dollars and there were probably 40 savings passbooks in Bert's office with just that amount in them. Periodically, the account holder would put some more in one week then come and take it out again a week later just to be sure that it was still there! The concept of cash that you could not actually see or touch – just a number in a book – meant little to a Papuan.

Diane's husband Chris took up employment as an assistant at Mamba straight after they married, and threw himself into the many new skills he had to learn. One of his first big projects was to supervise the construction of improvements to Trinity Church, then called St Elizabeth's Anglican Church, at Saga Village – the large Orokaiva village situated beside the Mambare on Mamba's boundary. Bishop Hand had appealed to Bert's apparently unlimited generosity to help fund the upgrading of this place of worship that Bert had originally constructed in 1959, receiving a letter from Bishop George Ambo at the time saying thanks for 'putting up a nice church for the Saga Christians'. At its original opening, its first priest, Rev. Simon Peter Awoda, had lined up over 150 people and baptised them in the nearby Fala Creek. Two days after this first batch took the plunge, another 200 were dunked and blessed in Kebara Creek.

The current structure of the church was fairly basic but practical and strong. Chris commenced by building a gabled entry portico on the front of the church complete with gentle concrete steps. This got good reviews. He then seconded Carl Hansen, co-owner of Kokoda Rubber Plantation and an experienced builder, to construct a complete brick backdrop on a raised section where they planned an altar and pulpit. Although Chris noted that 'Michelangelo was not contacted for advice', they came up with the idea of inlaying four bricks in the shape of a cross every four feet along the backdrop. This looked stunning, especially with Carl's great workmanship. The carpenters had never made small house bricks with the brick machine before, so it was all an adventure. Chris and the carpenters built a besser block communion rail topped with a sturdy local cedar rail.

Next came the altar. Again, with help from Carl they built two precision forms with reinforced oiled masonite. One was for the cross and one was for the altar.

The altar was suspended atop two columns of white painted bessers. The cross was erected and they commenced work on the sides of the church. The sides were made of cedar in vertical louvre formation. This was a mammoth undertaking amidst much flak from Unk, who was keeping them supplied from the sawmill. However, the results were great, with the louvres providing both light and shelter. Meryl had had four eight-seater pews built in Moresby and Chris's brother-in-law Phil Booker, who had come to Mamba for a visit and while there French polished the family dining table, donated his time to polish the rails and the pews. So the edifice was complete and Meryl and Bert were delighted.

The day came for the opening of this great new asset to the village and Chris proudly led the bishop into the church, pointing out the construction and looking forward to his reaction to the altar. Instead of praise, however, the Bishop stopped in his tracks and commented: 'Oh dear, that altar will have to go – in Anglican churches the altar must always take up exactly one-third of the width of the room – that is not big enough.'

Of course, Chris was livid and at a loss as to what to do and Bert was speechless, no doubt pondering the cost to Mamba of the whole exercise already and the apparent lack of gratitude for his generosity. The next day Chris quickly made a substitute altar and added the extra 17 centimetres with no enthusiasm at all. The day after, they towed the offending unwanted piece down to the river where it made a wonderful, if unconsecrated, barbecue table.

David Hand remained in Papua until he died and was devoted to the country and its people, but he often seemed to 'open his mouth to change feet'. A few years later, Soc was in hospital in Port Moresby with a bad dose of malaria, so bad that the nivaquine had sent him temporarily blind, so that he saw nothing but black spots and squares. As he lay half asleep in the darkened room, he recognised the voice of the bishop talking to someone in the bed beside him. The subject came up of the need for funds for another Anglican Church project in the Northern District, an ambitious plan to go into the shipping industry. 'Plus David', as Chris had now unaffectionately christened him since the opening of the Saga Church and seeing how he signed his name, was heard to say, 'Try Bert Kienzle, he's got plenty of money and is always good for a touch-up.' Of course, Soc reported this event to his parents. Bert took it in his usual philosophical manner but Meryl was not quite so understanding. Having a grandfather and grand-uncle who were Anglican ministers, she felt both instances were behaviour unbecoming to the position and had little time for the bishop after that. He did, however, visit Mamba on several later occasions.

Up until this time, Bert had been developing his dreams of a dynasty at Mamba. He had designed the different leases so that there was a distribution of rubber plantings and cattle pastures on each one. He hoped that each of his children and their spouses would ultimately take over these leases and supply the central rubber factory, and the abattoir, which was constructed in the early 1960s. Mamba had now reached a level where they could supply beef to Port Moresby. Up to 15 beasts a week were killed, quartered, wrapped in stockingette and refrigerated, awaiting delivery by charter aircraft from Kokoda to Moresby. A butcher shop was established at Mamba and national staff were trained in the art of butchery. From the initial Aberdeen Angus and Red Poll Shorthorn, Mamba expanded into Brahmans, showing their stud animals at the agricultural shows in Lae and Port Moresby. Retail outlets were set up at both Popondetta and Moresby. Mamba Quality Meats were soon in demand throughout Papua, but it was a real challenge to ensure enough beasts were fattened up and ready each week to maintain supply. The cattle were a great interest of John Kienzle (known as JK), and with both he and Unk having completed their studies at Hawkesbury Agricultural College, while both of them were at Mamba it was a very efficiently run operation. They worked hard to create a top-grade line of cattle with first-class handling facilities.

Bert's dream began to unravel when, in 1966, John Hardy decided there was no real future for him at Mamba at a management level when both JK and Chris were also working on the estates. He and Mary with their two young children left and bought a farm they named 'Lautanu' (Motu for 'my land') at Tarana, outside Bathurst in New South Wales. Two years later, Soc finished his schooling and also made up his mind that there were already enough family at Kokoda and he would look elsewhere for employment. He started work in the mailroom of Winchcombe Carson in Sydney and saved what he could from his meagre wages to start his pilot's licence. Fate changed his course when Unk fell very ill with a twisted bowel and had to be shipped south for urgent treatment and a long recovery. Soc was summoned home by his father to fill the void, and there he stayed.

In 1968, the government built a third monument at Kokoda to hold the plaques that had been unveiled the year before.

They added a plaque in honour of Bruce Kingsbury VC and one to honour Bert's contribution to the campaign. A trust was then set up to maintain the precinct of the three monuments, now to be called Kokoda Memorial Park.

On 16 December 1968, Bert was thrilled to receive a letter from Government House in Canberra informing him that 'Her Majesty The Queen would be graciously pleased to promote you to a Commander of the Civil Division of the Most Excellent order of the British Empire', and on 1 January 1968 he received his official citation as CBE. His award noted that he was: 'Founder of Yodda Estate and associated cattle and rubber properties and chairman of directors of Patair. For service to the development of Papua and New Guinea.' Bert was listed in *Who's Who* and in *Debrett's Peerage, Baronetage, Knightage and Companionage*, which noted he was now a member of Tattersall's Club, The Papua Club and of course, Kosciusko Alpine Club.

At last, this fine, unassuming and rather shy gentleman of the old school, whose many generous deeds over the years had gone unnoticed and who never wanted trumpets or fanfare, was being recognised, and for more than just his war efforts.

14

DEATH OF A DYNASTY

The first half of the 1970s was an era of many changes in PNG, most not for the better. By the start of the decade, the push for independence of Papua New Guinea had reached unstoppable momentum and the future for expatriate land-owners was uncertain to say the least. Rubber prices were fluctuating from marginal to unviable and employment for Europeans could only be considered a short-term prospect.

Despite the caution urged by experienced and concerned businessmen like Tom Leahy, a well-respected member of the famous New Guinea pioneering family and a member of parliament, Gough Whitlam under pressure from both the United Nations and his Russian cohorts was keen to fast-track self-government and independence. According to Tom in his autobiography, *Markham Tom*, Whitlam said to him, 'You know, Tommy, it's better for us all to get out and let them run their own race. We've built the universities, the entire infrastructure is in place, and I think it's about time we let them go.' Tom replied to the effect that we would be throwing them in the deep end; that we still needed to build a middle class in both the public and private sector. His concerns fell on deaf ears. Gough had his own agenda.

In September 1964, the members of the first House of Assembly had voted in favour of a motion that rebuked the UN for interfering in their affairs, making it clear they were quite happy with the Australian administration. The motion read:

> We the elected representatives of the people of PNG desire to convey to the Parliament of the Commonwealth of Australia, the Trusteeship Council and the General Assembly of the UNO, the expressed wish of the people that they and they alone be allowed to decide when the time is ripe for self-government in PNG and the form such government will take.

Repeated warnings from other expatriates, and wiser Papuans, that the country was not ready, that there were not nearly enough educated and skilled nationals available to administer an independent nation, were ignored. Tei Abal (later Sir Tei Abal), leader of the opposition at the time, publicly stated that he believed his country was not prepared for independence, that they needed another 50 years. Whitlam, influenced by the educated elite and too arrogant to investigate the details of the issue, blindly continued on his idealistic path. After his flying visit in 1969, he had made the following statement, which demonstrated his naivety.

> PNG is not unique in its economy, in the difference of economic standards between sections of the country, its educational and social standards, its need for economic aid from abroad, its need for advisors, the diversity of local customs, or even the multiplicity of languages – none of these problems require colonial rule for their solution or easing. In fact, it well may worsen if foreign techniques, methods, laws and customs continue to exclude local custom, knowledge and experience. An outside administration cannot lead or impose unity. It can by its errors unite people against it. This is the very situation which Australians at home will not permit.

Unlike Tom Leahy and others, he can't have studied what was happening in African countries that had traded colonialism for self-government.

The sad reality is that despite his intentions to the contrary, the legacy he left through his overzealous, uninformed action in fast-tracking independence once he became prime minister, is one of which he surely cannot be proud.

The successful operation of a true Westminster system of democracy in PNG was doomed before it began. What Whitlam and his associates did not understand, and what even the expatriates did not want to say at the time, was that the PNG people do not have the same concept of nationhood that most Western countries have. They are a country made up of over 700 different language groups and tribes. Theirs is a tribal system, where they have survived for thousands of years by looking after their 'own' – their wantoks. As with most tribal cultures, anything you do – lie, cheat, steal, even kill – is justifiable if it is done to protect or help your family. It is only the cause of shame if you are caught; in the past that meant caught by someone from another tribe; now it included the legal system. The appalling culture of nepotism, graft and corruption that has thrived in the country since independence all comes back to the wantok system. Bert knew and understood his people well enough to know this would happen, and tried in vain to warn anyone who would listen, even though in his heart he knew there was little he could do to change the course of events.

Bert's relatives in American Samoa were to go though the same pains, and the similarity of their dilemma is seen in a statement made by Peter Talai Coleman in his report in *Samoa News*:

> We are all trying to cope with a Western system of government implanted by now departed administrating authorities, systems which were built on western experiences and assumptions of human behaviour and instincts which do not necessarily always translate well or fully into island societies.

Another respected political scientist, James Q. Wilson, wrote:

Enlightenment defined the west and set it apart from all the great cultures in the world, but in culture as in economics, there is no such thing as a free lunch. If you liberate a person from ancient tyrannies, you may also liberate him from family controls. If you enhance his freedom to create, you will enhance his freedom to destroy. If you cast out the dead hand of useless custom, you may also cast out the living hand of essential tradition. If you give him freedom of expression he may write 'The Marriage of Figaro' or he may sing gangster rap. If you enlarge the number of rights he has, you may shrink the number of responsibilities he feels.

The realities of the above statements was seen in the urban drift that began to occur as the young men and women shunned village values and family traditions to seek what they thought would be greener pastures and a more gratifying life in the towns, particularly Port Moresby. Unemployment was high and crime rates soared – there was little discrimination in choice of victims. Black or white, they were easy game for theft and rape. As more and more Australian police left and the responsibility of maintaining law and order fell to the nationals, the situation degenerated. The wantok system and the attitude of the people of 'an eye for and eye, a tooth for a tooth' – indeed a 'life for life' – the 'payback' system – meant police had little control over those not in their own tribes, and let their wantoks literally get away with murder.

As the influence of the 'left-wing libertarians' began to infiltrate the corridors of power in the Territory's capital, it also spread to outer areas and generated unrest and confusion among the village people and plantation workers. For the first time the Kienzles found themselves in a heated land dispute with the Orokaiva people from the nearby village of Saga. All the land that Bert and his family had leased over the years was crown land – they paid rent to the government of the day for those leases. Much of the Yodda Valley had initially been classed as 'waste-and-vacant' – a virtual no-man's land surrounded by many different tribes in all directions – but there was one lease near the airstrip and adjacent to Saga Village that the Saga people felt should be theirs, especially as it was now developed with rich pastures and a magnificent set of rosewood timber yards, and stocked with fat cattle. Encouraged by a few young, hot-headed members of the tribe, and egged on by the active left in the educated elite in government, they arrived en-masse one day brandishing axes and knives and gathering outside the office at the Big House. Bert, Wallace, Soc and Ian Blackwood, a plantation assistant, calmly went out among them, listening to their rantings, dodging axes being swung in circular motions around their heads.

Meryl – 'Juju' as she was now called by the family, a name given her by her first grandchild, Greg Hardy – attempted to make light of the matter by bringing her chair out and sitting down to watch the 'show', but things turned nastier when word spread to Mamba's many workers who lived on the place, the majority of whom were not Orokaivas. They also arrived wielding axes, knives and stones. Running screaming down the driveway, they hustled against the Saga people, many of whom panicked and ran as the workers slowly but surely pushed the angry mob towards the cliff.

The Kienzle men made the decision that the only way to prevent bloodshed was to remove the Saga people from the plantation, and so Soc was instructed to go and get the truck, pile them all in the back and take them to Popondetta for their own protection. This he did, passing the riot police just outside the town, on their way up to handle the problem. They were amazed when Soc told them that he had the culprits on board to stop them being killed. It was some days before the Saga people felt they could safely return to their village after which the whole thing died down. Although he would later look back on it with humour, Bert was very upset by this event. Those same people had held a huge ceremony making him and Wallace honorary chiefs of their village only two years before.

One other incident in those years that demonstrated the left-wing influence was the attempt at a strike by Mamba workers. The fortnightly, tax-free salary that employees received was set by the government. All labourers and rubber tappers at Mamba were paid this correct amount. Skilled workers and boss-boys were paid more. By now, Mamba also had some excellent national plantation assistants like David Jinga (son of Bert's old mate Hitolo) who had been educated at Charters Towers in Queensland and Peter Uari, who attended Vudal Agricultural College in PNG. Attempts to pay rubber tappers on productivity had not proved successful, as they abused the trees by rough tapping in order to increase their output. Some do-gooder had put the idea of unions and strikes into their heads, and so one day, instead of arriving for 'fall-in' on time, Mamba's worker sent a delegation saying they were going on strike for higher pay. Soc, who was in charge at the time, listened to their rantings and calmly explained to them how the system worked, but when they still weren't satisfied, he pointed out that if they did not work today they would not be paid – something their advisers had omitted to tell them. He then said, 'So, okay, you go on strike today, then I'll go on strike tomorrow – and as I give you your work, you won't be working or getting paid tomorrow either.' In fact, he said, 'I might go on strike for a week.'

Many of the plantation's workers were involved in what they called *kampanis*, where each fortnight when they got their pay they would take it in turns to all give a large portion of their cash to one member of the company. That meant that instead of their meagre pay-packet every two weeks, about every two months they would get a big dollop that they could spend on something worthwhile. This system mostly worked because really the Papuan was not dependent on his wage to eat – he could live out of his gardens, so the weeks it was not his 'turn' he would not starve. It fell down, however, when one of their members, for some reason like absenteeism or overspending on 'booking' (putting onto account) at the trade store, could not match what others had given. When Soc also reminded them that if it was their turn to collect on their *kampani* at their next pay, they would be left short, they soon dispersed and went back to their tasks.

Labour supply continued to be a challenge for Mamba as their requirements ebbed and flowed over time. JK, and later Soc, took over from Unk as the manpower gatherers, and were sent several times to Garaina and later the Chirima region up in the mountain ranges west of the Yodda. The airstrip for the Chirima was at Yongi, the site for a Catholic mission station manned by three somewhat eccentric French priests: Father Ceriso, Father Barte and Father Besson. These men had set themselves up to be fully self-contained, not only with food but with their own lethal banana wine, vodka made from sweet potato and all sorts of exotic alcoholic beverages that guests loved to sample on their visits. They had a water-power-driven sawmill and they made their own saddles for their horses that only understood French as Mamba staff had learnt the hard way. Some years before, Bert had purchased four packhorses from them – Paris, Maju, Brandy and Lise – who would only respond to '*allez*' and '*arrêtez*', not 'giddy-up' and 'whoa!' The Fathers ran a very tight ship at their mission. Any villager's pig found on the airstrip was instantly shot and all parishioners had to work hard to earn their rosaries. These men took leave only once every 10 years, at which time they were entitled to return to France for three months, but they rarely lasted the distance. Civilisation was more than they could handle and they would invariably cut their holiday short and return early to their jungle home. It took some persuasion, but they did eventually visit Mamba several times and seemed to thoroughly enjoy talking to Bert and the family and sharing their stories.

Attempts by the many patrol officers who ranged the country explaining to the people what independence meant and how it would impact their lives seemed to have limited effect. This was confirmed when a delegation of Mamba workers came to the office a couple of days before 16 September 1975, Independence Day, and asked if they would 'turn white' on that day. They certainly seemed to think that many of them would, overnight, become entitled to a 'Big House' lifestyle.

Most concerning was the introduction in 1974 of the Land Acquisition Act. First, the land rights of Papua New Guineans were to be protected in the Constitution of the Independent State of Papua New Guinea as an integral part of the human rights provisions; second, the Plantation Lands Redistribution Scheme was introduced to compulsorily acquire plantation lands owned by foreigners and redistribute them to the original customary owners of the plantation lands in the first instance, or to those citizens who are short of land; and third, the Unused State Lands Redistribution Scheme was introduced to return or redistribute unutilised state lands to original customary landowners or to land-short citizens generally, with a view to dealing with the perceived land shortage problems in the country. How could any plantation owners proceed to run their businesses with confidence with this threat over their heads? Why would they reinvest in their properties when there was no guarantee of ever getting their money back? Of course, at the same time, the government made it difficult to remove funds from the country, so as to discourage any 'scorched earth' activities once these Land Acts were passed.

Most saddening for people like Bert and his family, who had done so much for Papua and its development, was the attitude by some factions of the government to citizenship for resident foreigners. Initially it was proposed that they would be required to redistribute all their financial assets to indigenous parties before they would be eligible for citizenship. Then it was proposed that Europeans, Asians or mixed-race people should be completely excluded from obtaining citizenship and that the right to vote, to serve in parliament and be appointed to senior positions in the public service should be restricted to those with both parents and grandparents born in PNG. This proposal threatened to split the government, as one of the first casualties of such a law would have been the finance minister at the time, Julius Chan. Eventually, it was agreed 'aliens' could apply for citizenship provided they had been residing in the country for eight years, but only if they revoked citizenship of any other country. Other restrictions applied, and although some of the Kienzles initially considered the idea of taking out citizenship, they concluded that before too long they would just end up as second-class citizens of a third-world country, with no real rights.

Another disappointing trend in the lead-up to independence was the quality and attitude of the Europeans, mainly Australians, who came to work for the administration in the Territory. They were derogatorily called 'two-year tourists' by the expatriate plantation and business owners, and they came with supercilious attitudes and chips on their shoulders. They automatically assumed that all plantation owners were 'colonialist pigs' who had made heaps of money by exploiting the native people. These young 'blow-in' 'do-gooders' partook in wholesale lambasting of pioneers and long-time residents, hell-bent on tearing down this perceived colonialist society, which in fact had done a great job of developing this country, far better than they ever were capable of doing, as time would prove.

If they had bothered to investigate the facts they would have learnt they had it all wrong, but their ignorance meant that dealings with the government became more and more frustrating and the 'tall poppy syndrome' flourished. Bureaucracy and red tape were the bane of the existence of private enterprise, with more and more government departments interfering in people's day-to-day lives. And of course they all operated under acronyms – DASF, PWD, PHD – headed by other acronyms – DC, ADC. Whole songs lampooning the system were written entirely in acronyms, and the Kienzles and others would joke about who was the current DIC and the DDIC – the dickhead-in-charge and the deputy dickhead-in-charge.

Bert probably coped with all this better than Wallace, whose patience regularly ran very thin, but they were both bewildered by the attitudes of some after all they had done over the years to help the local people and the District Office at Kokoda. They never hesitated to help the government people out in an emergency. One amusing story of this assistance was when, back in the 1950s, long-serving assistant Jack Mason went across one day to help the station 'mechanic' get the generator working again. Pulling the necessary section of the machine apart, he spread the various components carefully on the lawn behind him. With his head down, backside up, hard at work, Jack did not notice a cassowary calmly walk past, pick up and swallow a large and vital bolt and walk off, observed only by Jack's stunned Papuan assistant, who proceeded to roll about laughing thus frightening off the hungry bird. Cassowaries eat stones and hard seeds to help with their digestion but this was a very expensive choice of roughage. They had to wait several days for the necessary replacement part to be delivered.

§

Back in 1961, in order to increase its competitiveness with Qantas and TAA, Ansett Airlines of Australia had taken over Mandated Airlines of New Guinea. Initially, they operated as Ansett-MAL, but in 1968 changed their name to Ansett Airlines of PNG. Around this time, Bert began to receive delegations of executives from other Australian airlines, particularly East-West, interested in acquiring Papuan Airlines because of its international status, held by virtue of the two flights a week it operated to Irianjaya. Nothing apparently came of East-West's approaches, but in May 1970 Ansett administrators visited Mamba and began negotiating with Bert and the other directors to buy Papuan Airlines, which by now had taken over STOL Airways, which owned about seven charter aircraft and had interests in several hotels throughout the Territory as well as a duty free shop and wine cellars. After a further visit to Mamba in August 1970 by a delegation of Ansett executives, including Sir Reginald himself, the deal was struck and the airline sold. Negotiations had stalled at one stage when Bert insisted that his airline staff not be affected by the takeover, until Sir Reginald publicly stated that employees' jobs would be safe and the airline's 'identity would not be lost'. All this became irrelevant only three years later when Ansett, Qantas and TAA's interests in PNG were forced to amalgamate under the banner of Air Niugini, which was 60 per cent owned by the government, 16 per cent Ansett and 12 per cent each to Qantas and TAA. Bert had seen this coming and knew that his decision to sell had been a wise one. In addition to the uncertain future of European-owned businesses, Mamba was now not so dependent on air transport for produce and supplies. The same year, with much fanfare and celebration, the road from Kokoda to the coast at Oro Bay via Popondetta was finally completed, with the construction of a proper vehicle bridge over the massive Kumusi River at Wairope and the upgrading of the road from there to Kokoda. The rubber and most supplies were now carried by road then sea, with only urgent supplies coming in and perishable beef going out on a once-a-week air charter.

Bert and Meryl's adopted son Sammy had by now left Trinity Grammar and was attending technical college in Port Moresby studying to be a mechanic. Although he would have liked to have returned to Mamba it was felt by both him and the family that his situation in the workplace would be too difficult. This fear would prove to be well founded on a disastrous visit he made around this time. Sam arrived to stay at the Big House after Soc had recently settled in to his bachelor pad, a native-style 'round house' he had built on another superb cliff top site above the Mambare. Most unwisely, Sam decided to take the daughter of one of the rubber tappers for some extra-curricular activities on Soc's bed. Unfortunately, her betrothed and father were not very happy about this and chose to carry out some 'payback' by slaughtering a poddy calf that Soc was raising in a yard near his home. Soc hated cruelty to animals even more than he was disgusted in Sam's behaviour, and a heated argument ensued that turned very physical. Soc told him he should leave the plantation for his own protection and this Sam did, never to return. Several attempts by Bert over the years to contact him and forward some money that was sitting in a bank account Bert had set up for him were unsuccessful. The family would later learn that Sam eventually married Vgara Rotona and had two daughters, Mary Ann and Pauline. His biological father later contacted him and welcomed him back into the family, giving him his rightful share of village land. Despite this, Sam struggled with his station in life, and when Soc and John ran into him many years later, in 1995, they were shocked at how badly he had aged.

§

In 1972, Diane and her husband Chris decided the time had come to move on from Mamba. They had two boys, Simon, aged four and David, aged two, who would be needing schooling and with two Kienzle sons now working on the plantation, Chris felt that he would probably soon become superfluous. They had found a business they liked the look of on the Gold Coast distributing refrigerated foods to retail outlets and so they left and Bert now really did have to accept that his dreams of a dynasty were unravelling and no longer realisable. This was confirmed when two years later JK and his family also opted to head south. John had been working at Mamba for 10 years and had three young children – Rachel, Julya and Nicholas – the older ones ready for school. He had commenced studying for his degree in accountancy with a view to helping his family and ensuring employment back in Australia and he now felt there was no longer a future for them all in this soon-to-be-independent nation, and was keen to head south to finish his degree and get established in his profession before his children got much older.

By this time, Soc and I had met when I'd come to stay at Kokoda with old schoolfriends of mine, patrol officer David Stent and his wife Mary Ann. Coincidentally, David's boss at the time, the local ADC (Assistant District Commissioner), was Frank Sabben, descendant of Hubert Sabben, who had been the great friend of Tom Wilson back in Fiji.

We became engaged in May 1975 and married in December the same year, just three months after independence and on the very date that Whitlam was ousted from power in Canberra – that infamous day, 13 December 1975. Just desserts, most Territorians felt, for rushing this fledgling nation into something for which it was ill prepared.

Probably the most enjoyable times for Bert during those difficult early years of his eighth decade were visits from family – his cousins Wallace Caldwell and Peter Schoeffel – and many veterans and researchers of the war. In 1969, Bruce Adams visited Kokoda when researching his book *Rust in Peace* and he went with Soc and some of Bert's boys to locate the remains of the Kittyhawk that had crashed after its victory roll over the airstrip in November 1942. Interestingly, it appears official reports of that incident recorded that the aircraft suffered engine failure and there is no mention of the unsanctioned aerobatics performed by the pilot. Adams made a return visit in 1972 when he wrote an article on Bert and this journey for the *Australasian Post*, which he titled 'King of the Angels'. All agreed this was a most apt name for Bert.

The year 1971 had seen another pilgrimage of diggers, this time 16 men of the 2/14th and their families, who timed their visit to attend Anzac Day at Bomana Cemetery, then called into Kokoda and on to Buna and Gona and other parts of PNG where their unit fought so gallantly. Names including Williams, Angus, Ferguson, Wilkinson, O'Halloran and Maher appear in Bert's visitors book. The next year saw the return of the 39th Battalion for the 30-year anniversary of the Kokoda campaign. More than 40 men and many of their wives made this journey, some of whom had been there only five years before, and once again a ceremony was held on the plateau, at which Bert gave the main address. In this speech, his final paragraph clarifies his determination that the path across the Owen Stanleys over which the Kokoda Campaign was fought should be called the Kokoda Trail.

Now, as we stand here on Kokoda plateau remembering those great men, Australian and Papua New Guineans, let us once and for all rectify the name which should carry on for all time now as well as into the future, the much disputed name 'Kokoda Trail' or 'Kokoda Track'. We, who fought and saved this emerging nation, Papua New Guinea, from defeat by a ruthless and determined enemy knew it as Kokoda Trail, not Track. A trail means a path through a wilderness and this is surely what it was for most of us. So I appeal to you and all those in Papua New Guinea who helped us defend this great country, to revere and keep naming it Kokoda Trail in memory of all those gallant men who fought over it . . . Lest we forget.

Another memorable occasion for both Bert and Meryl was the invitation they received to dine with Her Majesty the Queen and Prince Philip at the Papua Hotel in Port Moresby when the royal couple visited in 1974. Both of the Kienzles were honoured to spend some time talking to Her Majesty and were most impressed that she seemed to have done her homework about their interests in the country, discussing the problems of the world's rubber industry at some length with them. The Queen returned to Papua only three years later and on this visit she made a quick trip to Popondetta, where Prince Charles had spent some time when he attended Martyr's Memorial School with some other Timbertop boys in 1966. Her Majesty must have liked PNG, because she was back again in 1982.

§

At 5.15 p.m. on 15 September 1975 the Australian flag was lowered. At 10.25 a.m. on 16 September the Bird of Paradise flag of the new nation of Papua New Guinea was raised on Independence Hill at Waigani. The independence ceremony was presided over by Michael Somare, leader of the Pangu Party.

At Mamba, celebrations were arranged by the Kienzle family, but elsewhere they were fairly subdued. The Papuans really did not know what they were celebrating. They woke up on 16 September and nothing really had changed. There were still Europeans running most of the businesses and, they felt, occupying their land. They still had to go to work the next day to earn money.

However, things did start to change very quickly. There was a mass exodus of expatriates who were either told their positions were being nationalised or who could see the writing on the wall. This meant that suddenly untrained people were thrust into positions in both the public and private sector that were beyond their education or ability. This in itself added further to the reverse racism that was now surfacing, with anti-white sentiments resurging as the real meaning of independence, or what Papua New Guineans thought it should mean, sank in. Business efficiency plummeted, and particularly in rural areas problems with transport, communications, land disputes and theft all increased. Even ordering supplies over the radio became an exercise in frustration as the PNG operators flexed their power muscles and would continually ignore Europeans calling in, even when it was their designated 'schedule' time.

John Waiko, a highly educated member of the PNG elite, later wrote in his book *A Short History of Papua New Guinea*:

> PNG inherited from the colonial period a limited but stable and relatively efficient infrastructure with a relatively well-paid workforce, with some sectors such as health, education, transport and communications considerably in advance of other countries

How quickly this degenerated. In a newspaper article in the late 1970s, Kevin Egan, Public Prosecutor of Papua New Guinea commented:

> In the four short years since independence, there has been a definite and perceptible break down not only in law and order but in many areas of administration within this country. Without exaggerating, I estimate that in four years since

independence, 40 years of administrative achievement has been lost ... PNG is rapidly turning into an oligarchy.

This is the scene that I, as Soc's new wife, arrived at after our wedding in December 1975. There were now no plantation assistants left on the place. It was now just Soc, Unk and Bert. Bert was 70 years old and tired, in continual pain with his hip and angry at the way his beloved country was going. Unk just wanted out. Both Meryl and Ailsa were spending more and more time down south. From a plantation that had had between six and seven European assistants at any one time, there was now Soc and two elderly gentlemen to run the show. A series of assistants followed, including my brother Ian for a short time, but by 1978, with the future so uncertain and profits way down, for quite some time it was just Soc and me at Mamba with the closest other Europeans being at Popondetta. Soc was now trying to do what the six assistants plus Unk had done in the past – an impossible task. If he was away from the field, rubber production dropped; if he was not in the factory, output dropped; if he didn't regularly check on the cowboys, cattle died and disappeared; requirements for weekly slaughter were not met; and the jungle began to encroach on the pastures. Bert despaired for the future and rued his decision to refuse an offer he had received to sell the place for close to two million dollars in the late 60s.

Currency revaluations by a PNG government with no real understanding of what this did to exports in 1978 saw the Kina reach a value of AUD1.38, making rubber, and to a lesser extent copra and cocoa, uneconomical to produce. Dire warnings from expatriate plantation owners that this would see the collapse of agricultural export industries, and so increase the urban drift of unemployed workers, fell on deaf ears. At the same time as this was happening, the Minister for Finance Julius Chan was crowing in the press that rubber had a bright future and he foresaw its growth in the form of nucleus estates that provided processing facilities and support and advice for surrounding smallholders. This was a scheme that Mamba had been involved in for many years, with workers and their families being encouraged to raise cattle or grow rubber and cocoa on their blocks that adjoined the plantation, or on the areas Bert had allocated them on the actual estates. Trouble is, these projects don't work when there is no longer any real profit margin in there, even for the 'nucleus' of the estate.

After this stressful year, Soc and I planned a short trip overseas in February 1979, leaving only Unk and Bert to manage the place. Unk was delayed getting back, so for a while Bert had been alone – it was a difficult time for them both. The day before our return, Bert had got himself so stirred up over what he would normally consider a fairly minor issue that he had suffered a mild stroke. He had to be got back to Australia as soon as possible and it became more urgent to dispose of the properties. Fortunately, about this time the PNG Development Bank began to show some interest in acquiring the estates and this Bert felt was ideal, as it meant the land was virtually going to belong to the people.

§

In October 1969, a contingent of Japanese veterans, apparently part of a Ministry of Health delegation, had visited Kokoda and Mamba. Several of the men were from Kochi city, where many of the members of the Nankai Shitai, or South Seas Detachment, which first landed on the north coast of Papua in 1942, originated. They were greeted by Bert with the respect he felt they should be shown. He knew enough of the vagaries of war to accept that yesterday's enemies are best made into today's friends. He had seen first-hand in Germany how the Allies' treatment of their enemy after the World War I played a big part in creating the environment for another world war. Bert instructed Soc to take the group and show them some of the burial sites he had come across in his explorations as a teenager. This was a great help to them in their search for the remains of their comrades.

One particular high-ranking Japanese ex-soldier shook his hand and through his interpreter told Bert he remembered him from the war. When Bert responded 'How could that be?', he said he had seen him through binoculars on the Trail. This made the hair on the back of Bert's neck stand up and sent shivers down his spine, as he realised that if he could be seen though field glasses he had probably been within sniper range.

Among this group of eight Japanese visitors was Hirokichi Nakahashi, who was most excited when he saw the mountain gun that Soc had found at Gorari, now sitting on the front lawn of Mamba House. Once told where it had been found, he knew it was the one manned by his friend First Lieutenant Yohijo Takaki. Takaki had been ordered to bury the weapon as the Japanese retreated fast to the coast after the battle at Oivi/Gorari. Aged 24, Takaki believed strongly in the Japanese soldiers' tradition of never abandoning their weapon and once he had carried out the orders to bury the gun, he drew his pistol and committed 'hari-kiri'. Nakahashi later commented to Charles Happell, author of *The Bone Man of Kokoda*:

> When I saw the barrel of the gun which had been abandoned under such distressing circumstances, I was filled with deep emotion. Remembrance of those times brought a flood of tears. I, who had a lifetime of friendship with the officers and men of that unit, had been strangely destined to discover the gun barrel. I must have been guided by the spirit of First Lieutenant Takaki.

Also in the group was Sadashige Imanishi, one-time mayor of Motoyama City, and later senior member of the Kochi–New Guinea Association. Imanishi had amazingly survived a decade of war, from China to Papua New Guinea and all the way back to China. Along with the other men on this trip – Yoshimura, Ishida, Nabi, Shirakaya, Matsuya and Nakahashi – they managed to recover 300 bones of Japanese war dead that were taken home to Japan, cremated and interred at Chidorigafuchi, a cemetery for unknown soldiers in Tokyo.

As a follow-up to this visit, in 1972, not long after the 39th's 30-year reunion, another small delegation of Japanese visited, and in 1973 yet more bone collectors arrived, one of whom, Tafao Koitake, would return again in 1974. As a result of Bert's willingness to welcome and assist these old enemies, he corresponded with several of them when questions arose over the years that they wanted answered for their research. In return, they provided Bert with a definitive list of all Japanese deaths and casualties during the Owen Stanley Campaign.

In early 1979, another large group of veterans arrived, including Yoshitsugu Tsujimoto, and a Dr Hiroshi Yanagisawa who claimed that he had met Captain Sam Templeton in 1942. Bert later replied to a thank-you letter from Tsujimoto and asked him to get Dr Yanagisawa to put his memories of his contact with Templeton in writing. This the doctor did, and Bert soon received a very interesting letter dated 14 April 1979. Hiroshi's English was not good but what he had to say was extremely interesting in light of what Templeton's men always believed had happened to him. He wrote:

> . . . with great honour I would like to describe the fact as much as I remember, because you eagerly want to know about Captain Sam Terupleton [sic], a friend of yours, the situation I was facing at the time and the details of the medical treatment I gave for him.

He goes on to describe the progress of what he calls his 'advance party' from the coast to Kokoda where they first met resistance, which indicates they must have gone through after Templeton's men had met the first wave of Japanese at Oivi on 26 July, at which time it was believed Sam had been killed. However, Yanagisawa goes on to say that on 8 August at 3.15 they marched into Deniki and:

> . . . a soldier shouted 'there is a wounded man under the building'. I could see the person who was an officer to all appearances, his right femoral region were injured badly by

the broken pieces of shells, exposed broken bones, scattered skin and muscle. On carrying him from under the floor, I set the broken bone and stitched up the scattered skin and muscle and moreover I wrapped it in gauze and bandaged and splinted it. His physical and mental powers became so weak that I injected morphine in order to relieve his pain . . . he seemed to me to be relieved by knowing I was an army surgeon. 'I am Captain Templeton, come from Sydney Australia. I have parents, and elder brother and two younger sisters . . . What is the reason why Japan makes a war against Australia? In the First World War the navy of both nations invaded together into the Mediterranean . . . we should be real good friends.'

The doctor writes that he agreed with him, then continues that he had to move on with the advance party towards Isurava so he left Templeton with another surgeon: 'When I saw him last we stared each other tightly. I will never forget this moment forever . . . from the bottom of my heart I pray for the repose of his soul.'

Bert quickly sent a copy of this letter to the 39th Battalion Association but they agreed with him that because of the large discrepancy in dates, it was really almost an impossibility. Bert would later receive a copy of a letter from a digger, Les Arnel, who was a runner for Templeton at the time of his disappearance. Les recalls that they took up positions on the edge of the small plateau on which the village of Oivi was located, but when they saw the Japanese swarming up the ridge they pulled back to the actual village and spread around its perimeter. Sam told Les to stay put while he reconnoitred back towards Kokoda to see if there were any enemy along that route. Les said Sam disappeared fast into the jungle and not long afterwards a shot rang out. Les would never see Sam again and he writes that he understands all that was found was his holster and haversack. Les and his mates were the ones then led to safety by the heroic Sainopa. There were also some rumours that Templeton may have been killed by natives who sympathised with the Japanese, which Les says is possible, as quite a few of their Orokaiva carriers did desert them around this time. He concludes that Sam was killed by a person or persons unknown and his body removed some distance away.

The Japanese doctor must surely have misunderstood the name of the soldier he treated. Then again, it is not beyond the realms of imagination that Sam, wounded near Oivi but determined and resourceful and knowing his way back, managed to stumble back through the jungle, avoiding the Japanese who would have been swarming all around him, to find himself unable to continue at Deniki, where he collapsed under the hut where he was found. Eleven days, wounded, hiding in the jungle, trying to rejoin his company?

In 1972, Sam's son Reg had written to Bert saying that he had been disappointed not to attend the August reunion at Kokoda that year, but that it was his dream to one day return to Kokoda and stand on the site where his father was killed. Bert never advised Reg of this controversial letter, probably not wanting to get his hopes up and feeling it would upset him unnecessarily unless it could be proved correct. Had there been any truth in this theory, it was surmised that Sam's identification was removed by the Japanese, his body then hurriedly buried with others on the Australian advance more than three months later, and ultimately ending up in among the many graves of unknown soldiers at Bomana. All this was later complicated by the family of Yanagisawa telling the authors of *The Path to Infinite Sorrow*, Craig Collie and Hajime Muritani, that is was at Oivi that he met and treated Sam. Memories, but not imaginations, appear to have dimmed with time for these old soldiers.

Soon after this visit, Bert was approached by a representative of the Japanese Embassy, a Mr Yasho Hori, to assist in the construction of a cairn at Kokoda that members of the Japan–Papua New Guinea Goodwill Society wished to fund in memory of the Japanese dead. Bert would later admit that initially he was against the idea but then his philosophical nature took over and he decided to work with the RSL and members of the Provincial and Central Government to assist in the project. It was agreed that the plaques should acknowledge all war dead – Japanese, Australian and Papua New Guinean. A site was eventually agreed upon on that placed this memorial in a continuation of the arc created by the three other cairns on the plateau, and Bert nominated Soc, being the only one left at Mamba, to make all the arrangements for the construction in a similar form to the others. After countless letters back and forth, concerns from the RSL and delays in permission from the government, the memorial was eventually opened with much Japanese style pomp and ceremony in February 1980. Bert was not able to attend but Unk was there, on his last visit before the properties were sold. Yoshitsugu Tsuijimto, on his second visit to Kokoda, gave the closing address and Mikio Abe, chairman of the Goodwill Society, presented Soc and me with a certificate of acknowledgment and numerous other gifts for our work in completion of the project.

The Kienzle family agreed to do the right thing and give over the mountain gun to be mounted in front of the memorial. As had been done at its previous locations, the barrel was pointed at a 45-degree angle above the ground. Soon after its place-ment, the Kienzles received a hot letter from the government saying that it was pointing at the District Office in a most threatening manner, so they pointed it away towards the old tennis court. They were then advised by the RSL that it should not be pointing skyward, but to the ground as a symbol of surrender. The resultant positioning really just makes it look like a piece of septic plumbing, but at least it is now where all Japanese pilgrims can see and appreciate it.

§

The year 1979 was a sad but significant one. Negotiations were finalised for the PNG Development Bank to buy the Mamba Estates at a price about one-tenth of their real worth. Takeover would be in March 1980. Soc and I would stay on to manage and facilitate as smooth a transition as possible to a Mamba without Kienzles.

Around this time, Bert received a copy of a map surveyed by the Department of Works in 1978. For reasons known only to them, they did not take the time to visit Bert, the man who knew more about the Trail than any other. They set out to map the track as it was being walked at the time – no longer the Kokoda War Trail. The errors they made would lead to many misunderstandings and misrepresentations, and unfortunately, this was the track that the many trekkers would take as gospel when they started to visit the area in the following decades. Some of the worst mistakes were in identifying the locations of the various dumps and stations that Bert had established during the campaign. One of the most glaring errors was 'Camp 1900' – supposedly a staging point during the war at an altitude of 1,900 metres – because during the war they didn't talk in metres and there was no 'camp' at this point. The war track did not even go along this route.

Then there was the track from Deniki to Isurava. The one being used in 1978 was not what was traversed in 1942. It was in fact a cattle pad that Soc has been forced to cut in the early 1970s when his father instructed him to deliver 11 heifers and a bull to the people of Isurava. The cattle headed up the war trail, but when it got too steep they just dug their heels in and sat back on their haunches like mules, refusing to budge. Soc got his boys to find a route that was not quite so steep and they set out to blaze this track. Even then, halfway up the cattle packed it in, so Soc called down all the villagers from Isurava and they proceeded to make stretchers for the cattle. They carried them to their village like wounded soldiers – only it took 16, not eight, carriers per beast. This track is now heavily overgrown with the choko vine naively introduced to the area by Meryl and Ailsa without realising how it would thrive and become almost a pest to the whole valley. Fortunately, the local people have learned to use this voracious vine to advantage – not that they like the actual choko fruit, but they value the tips of the vines as a form of green salad vegetable, sometimes cooking it like cabbage.

Another area where these surveyors didn't bother to research the war trail was from Kagi to Templeton's Crossing via Mt Bellamy. This part of the real trail was a problem because there were no watering points. Wisely the locals had redirected it over the years to pass by water sources but this does not therefore give a picture of how hard it was for the troops in this section. For some other inexplicable reason, perhaps because their native guides had no idea where Templeton's Crossing was and couldn't agree on which crossing was which, they named two different crossings of the Eora Creek Templeton's 1 and Templeton's 2. There was only ever one Templeton's Crossing, and it was the junction of two tracks. Also, the old track around Iorabaiwa meandered through quite a lot of kunai grass – a hot and exposed area that the locals had since by-passed. The Golden Stairs, the alternative route around Nauro – all are incorrectly marked. The list goes on. If only they had taken advantage of the knowledge of the one man who knew!

Bert made one final trip back to Mamba in late October 1979 and took the opportunity to hire a helicopter to fly to his old stamping ground at Myola, landing there for the first time in 37 years. There had been quite a lot of activity at Myola in the previous 12 months. In 1978, the Koiari people who now claimed ownership of the area, its *tabu* status having slightly faded, had approached Soc to help them promote some development of the lake region. The obvious first step for this would be to reopen the airstrip. After a couple of reconnaissance trips with helpful pilot mates, Soc managed to get a landing strip cleared by the locals well enough for a plane to land. On board were he, the pilot, a lawnmower, some markers and a 44-gallon drum of petrol. Soc singlehandedly mowed the strip sufficiently for the aircraft to take off. In appreciation of his work and in acknowledgement of his father's long association with Myola, the people said they wanted to 'hand over' the land to Soc and me as a gesture of good will. An official ceremony was held on site, attended by us, and Greg and Rosemary Jacobsen who had just commenced working at Mamba and 100 or so Koiaris and Biagis. Soon after this, in

October 1979, staff at the Big House were surprised one day by the arrival of an unscheduled helicopter that landed on the tennis court. On board were Bruce Hoy of the PNG War Museum and some RAAF personnel plus Charlie Lynn who were planning to collect Tommy O'Dea's crashed Trimotor Ford, the remains of which still rested by the airstrip at Myola. The local people had told them they were not allowed to touch it without Soc's permission. In fact, on landing on the lake they had been greeted with a party carrying shotguns and bush knives. With them they had a tape recorder into which Soc had to say, in Motu of course, that he approved the removal of the relic. The Koiari people had been assured that it would be repaired in the aviation section of the Port Moresby National Museum. Soc gave his permission, and a Chinook helicopter lifted the old plane, initially in two trips: one with the fuselage and a second trip for the engine. A third trip was needed the next year to collect the remnants of the wings and there was a bit of excitement when the wings began to 'fly' independently of the helicopter. The whole event was covered in several newspapers, and Bruce Hoy corresponded with Bert about the arrangements. In his final letter on the matter, Bert wrote: 'If only we had helicopters in those dreadful, tortuous days in 1942, it would have been very different.'

The Trimotor Ford has a fascinating history. This strange looking aircraft was constructed of a tubular aluminium framework, covered with corrugated aluminium. Two hundred of them were made between 1926 and 1933, ending up in unusual places like China, for use by Chinese warlords; and one, which ultimately ended up in PNG, was used by the British Earl of Lovelace for elephant hunting in India. Four of them were acquired in 1935 by Guinea Airways: one crashed at Wau in 1941, one was destroyed by enemy action in early 1942 and the last two were impressed into the RAAF. Of these two, one was strafed and burned by the Japanese while on the tarmac and the last one was the one at Myola, which, as previously mentioned, hit some mud on landing and flipped.

The day before, the same pilot, Tommy O'Dea had flown out seven wounded in the plane from the lake.

So when Bert landed there in late October, the Trimotor was gone and the airstrip was looking pretty good, although it had rarely been used. It was a great moment for Bert to tread again on what was hallowed ground for him. He vacillated between joy and sorrow as the memories flooded back of his role, and the important part of Myola in the Kokoda Campaign; of his mates Doc Vernon and Sydney Elliot-Smith; of his loyal 'boys', nearly all of whom were now dead; and of the huge task he had carried out with them in 1942. As he flew home, getting the pilot to take him all over his properties for one last nostalgic look, he knew this would be the last time he really saw his beloved Yodda Valley.

The following month, he boarded a small aircraft at Kokoda to make his final flight out of the valley. He did not tell the people of Mamba that he would not be returning. The emotional upheaval for all concerned would have been too much and too disruptive for those left behind but the heaviness in his heart stayed with him until his last breath eight years later.

His feelings were poignantly expressed in the final words he wrote in answer to a list of questions about the usage of Police Motu during his time in Papua, sent to him by Dr Tom Dutton of the ANU.

Bert wrote:

Papua taudia be namu herea – lau diba; tor lau noho Kokoda negani momo, lau bogasisi momo idia dekena, lau Taubada Kienzle. Bahmahuta namuherea.

The men of Papua are wonderful – I know. I lived at Kokoda a long time. I miss them a lot, I Taubada Kienzle. A heartfelt goodbye.

EPILOGUE

When Bert left PNG in 1979, he eventually settled at the unit that he and Meryl had bought in Bay Street, Tweed Heads. Situated next door to the shopping centre and close to both Twin-Towns RSL and Tweed Bowls Club, people often asked how they could live there after years in a large home with unforgettable views. Meryl's comment was that she had looked at great scenery for over 40 years; what she needed now was a bit of civilisation and fun – she had a lot of living to do yet! She loved to visit the pokies and would drag Bert along at least twice a week for a good meal and three or so hours feeding the machines. Bert would keep tally but was only allowed to tell people of the wins, not the losses.

Bert set himself up in the garage of the unit as an office and spent much of his time managing his investments, monitoring his children and grandchildren and their activities, and answering the many letters that started to come in with the sudden surge in interest in the history of Kokoda. People like Peter Brune, Peter Ryan and Peter Dornan communicated with and visited Bert for research for their books, and different battalions writing their histories asked his advice. Every letter he wrote was meticulously typed by him, with a carbon copy on green A4 paper.

By this time he had developed low-grade diabetes and angina, and had been told to take it more quietly. In a letter to his cousin Wallace Caldwell at the time, he wrote: 'Damned if I know how much quieter as I do bugger-all now!'

He was bored, and when Soc and I left Mamba in 1983 and bought a farm near Allora on the Darling Downs, he soon bought the property next door. Meryl got some pleasure renovating the old home on the hill – those damned views again! They shared their time between the Tweed and Allora, Bert enjoying it most when he could sit on the verandah and watch Soc working the farm, occasionally testing Soc's patience by waving frantically from his viewpoint until he got out of the tractor and rushed to the house, only to have Bert say, 'What are you doing now?' Meryl enjoyed spending time with her grandchildren Carly and Suzanne and pottering in the garden, but she would soon have itchy feet to get back to the club life on the coast where Di and Chris and Mary also now lived. JK and his family were not far away in Brisbane.

Back in Papua, Bert had not been forgotten. In fact, his family's absence was being felt quite markedly. In April 1986, the premier of the Northern – now called Oro – Province, Dennis Kageni said at the celebrations for the 10th anniversary of independence:

> My government and its people pay tribute to the Kienzle family who had been trying to educate Papua New Guineans to work hard if successes are to be achieved. My government commends the Kienzle family for setting an example of how the private sector was working alongside the government to bring about development in the isolated rural areas of Papua New Guinea. I call upon foreign businesses operating in the Oro Province to follow the example of the Kienzle family and give support to the Oro people to develop the Oro Province.

On this occasion, both Bert and Wallace were awarded Papua New Guinea Independence Medals – Bert Number 5965 and Wallace Number 5966 – for 'rendering outstanding service to PNG'. MacLaren Hiari, a well-known politician and active promoter of the Oro Province, said of Bert:

> Herbert Thomson Kienzle was a monument to private enterprise and devoted to his chosen country. He spent 53 years of peace and war between Port Moresby and the Yodda … As an example of individual enterprise, Mamba and its associates in this, his country, are a monument to what men can accomplish providing they accept the rigid conditions of existence which this land demands. There have been no short cuts for the Kienzle brothers, no outside capital to boost things along, no concessions and no interest to follow narrow personal paths. The running of the properties has not been an easy task for the Kienzle family. If Papua New Guinea wishes to become an independent people, then this is an extremely good example of personal effort for them to study.

§

Life continued happily for some years, although Bert was on regular medication for his heart. On 6 January 1988, John and Helen offered to drive Bert and Meryl to Sydney to their house at 18 Delecta Avenue, Clareville Beach – a beautiful place right on the Pittwater that Helen's mother Eve Mutton was living in at the time. Because of concerns about the effect of the warfarin he was on necessitating frequent toilet visits, Bert decided to stop taking the medication for the day of the big drive. Meryl's birthday, 7 January, was celebrated with lunch out at their favourite club nearby. The next morning, when Bert seemed to be taking a long time in the bathroom, Meryl went to check on him. She found him sitting on the bathroom stool slumped back against the wall. He was gone. There was no sign of pain, just a look of peace on his face. His heart must have just stopped and all could imagine him taking one last sigh as he left this world of continual hip pain and frustration at his failing stamina. A dignified departure for a dignified man.

Bert was flown back to the Gold Coast where a funeral service was held at Holy Spirit Anglican Church, Isle of Capri at 12 noon on Wednesday 13 January 1988, and his ashes interred at Allambe Gardens. Meryl stayed on in the unit, with Mary who lived at Southport to keep an eye on her, but the joy had gone out of life for her. All her children rallied around and helped, with John as the accountant taking over the finances. But the pokies were not the same without Herbert. Nothing was the same without Herbert. She even visited the farm for a few months but his absence was even more palpable there. In November of the same year, Mary received a mumbled phone call from her mother and rushed down to find her on the floor beside her bed having suffered a stroke. In Tweed Hospital for about a week, a final massive stroke mercifully took her on 11 November – 10 months without her Herbert was more than enough for Meryl. Her ashes lie beside his at Allambe.

BIBLIOGRAPHY

Adams, Bruce, *Rust in Peace: South Pacific Battlegrounds*, Antipodean Publishers, Sydney, 1975.

Archbold, Richard, *New Guinea: Expedition Fly River Area, 1936–1937*, Robert M. McBride and Co., New York, 1939.

Austin, Victor, *To Kokoda and Beyond: The Story of the 39th Battalion*, MUP, Melbourne, 1988.

Braga, Stuart, *Kokoda Commander: A Life of Major General 'Tubby' Allen*, OUP, Melbourne, 2004.

Brune, Peter, *A Bastard of a Place: The Australians in Papua*, Allen & Unwin, Sydney, 2003.

Brune, Peter, *Those Ragged Bloody Heroes: From the Kokoda Trail to Gona Beach 1942*, Allen & Unwin, Sydney, 2005.

Cleland, Dame Rachel, *Papua New Guinea: Pathways to Independence*, Artlook Books, Perth, 1983.

Collie, Craig and Muritani, Hajime, *The Path to Infinite Sorrow*, Allen & Unwin, Sydney, 2009.

Cyclopedia of Fiji, Cyclopedia Company of Fiji, 1907.

Derrick, R. A., *A History of Fiji*, Government Press, Suva, 1968.

Fischer, Gerhard, *Enemy Aliens: Internment and the Homefront Experience in Australia 1914–1920*, UQP, St Lucia, 1989.

Fitzsimons, Peter, *Kokoda*, Hodder Headline, Sydney, 2005.

Foskett, Alan, *The Molonglo Mystery*, Alan Foskett, Canberra, 2008.

Gibney, Jim, *Canberra 1913–1953*, AGPS Press, Canberra, 1988.

Gordon, H. J., *The Reichswehr and the German Republic 1919–1926*, Princeton University Press, Princeton NJ, 1957.

Grahamslaw, Tom, Recollections of Angau <www.pngaa.net/Library/RecollAngau.html>

Ham, Paul, *Kokoda*, HarperCollins, Sydney, 2005.

Happell, Charles, *The Bone Man of Kokoda*, Pan Macmillan, Sydney, 2008.

Hawthorne, Stuart, *The Kokoda Trail: A History*, CQU Press, Rockhampton, 2003.

Hetherington, John, *Melba: A Biography*, MUP, Melbourne, 1967.

Hiari, Maclaren, Manuscript.

Inder, Stuart (Ed.), *Tales of Papua New Guinea: Insights, Experiences, Reminiscences*, Retired Officers Association, Sydney, 2001.

Johnston, George H., *New Guinea Diary*, Angus & Robertson, Sydney, 1942.

Kavanamur, D., Yala, C. and Clements, Q. (Eds), *Building a Nation in Papua New Guinea*, Pandanus Books, Sydney, 2003.

Kienzle, Herbert T., Personal papers, diaries and reports of Captain Herbert T. Kienzle.

Kienzle, Wallace & Campbell, Stuart, 'Notes on the natives of the Fly and Sepik River headwaters, New Guinea', *Oceania* 8, pp. 463–81.

Lal, Brij V., *Broken Waves: A History of the Fiji Islands in the Twentieth Century*, University of Hawaii Press, Honolulu, 1992.

Leahey, Tom, *Memoirs of an Australian Pioneer in Papua New Guinea*, Crawford House, Belair, SA, 2004.

Lett, Lewis, *Papuan Gold: The Story of the Early Gold Seekers*, Angus & Robertson, Sydney, 1943.

Lett, Lewis, *The Papuan Achievement*, MUP, Melbourne, 1944.

Levuka Public School, *Levuka Public School Diamond Jubilee 1879–1939*.

Lewis, D. C., *The Plantation Dream: Developing British New Guinea and Papua 1884–1942*, Journal of Pacific History, London, UK, 1996.

Lodge Polynesia, History Notes.

Luvaas, J. (Ed.), *Dear Miss Em: General Eichelberger's War in the Pacific 1942–1945*, Greenwood Press, Westport, Conn., 1972.

Macaulay, Lex, *Blood and Iron: The Battle for Kokoda 1942*, Hutchinson, Sydney, 1991.

McCarthy, Dudley, *Australia in the War of 1939–1945: South-West Pacific Area, First Year, Kokoda to Wau*, Australian War Memorial, Canberra, 1959.

McDonald, Neil, *Damien Parer's War*, Lothian Books, Melbourne, 2004; *Chester Wilmot Reports*, ABC Books, Sydney, 2004.

Neil, Marie H., *Trial Bay Gaol: Public Works Prison and Wartime Detention Camp*, Macleay River Historical Society, 1975.

Nelson, Hank, *Black, White and Gold: Goldmining in Papua New Guinea 1878–1930*, ANU, Canberra, 1976.

Nelson, Hank, *Taim Bilong Masta: The Australian Involvement with Papua New Guinea*, ABC Enterprises, 1990.

Nk Mar (Translation), *Last Hours of the Imperial Army*.

Norris, F. Kingsley, *No Memory for Pain: An Autobiography*, Heinemann, Melbourne, 1970.

Oakes, Bill, *Muzzle Blast: Six Years of War with the 2/2 Machine Gun Battalion, A.I.F.*, 2/2 Machine Gun Battalion History Committee, 1980.

Paull, Raymond, *Retreat from Kokoda*, Heinemann, Melbourne, 1958.

Robertson, John, *Australia at War 1939–1945*, Heinemann, Melbourne, 1981.

Rybarz, Beverley, *The Bridge Builder*, Wakefield Press, Adelaide, 2005.

Scott, Geoffrey, *The Knights of Kokoda*, Horwitz, Sydney, 1963.

Sinclair, James, *Last Frontiers: The Explorations of Ivan Champion of Papua*, Pacific Press, Queensland, 1940.

Sinclair, James, *Wings of Gold: How the Aeroplane Developed New Guinea*, Pacific Publications, Sydney, 1978.

Stuart, Ian, *Port Moresby: Yesterday and Today*, Pacific Publications, Sydney, 1970.

Vernon, G. H., Diary of field services on the Owen Stanley–Buna campaign, 1942.

Waiko, John, *A Short History of Papua New Guinea*, OUP, Melbourne, 1993

Ward, G. R. T., *Diamond Jubilee of the Kosciusko Alpine Club*, Kosciusko Alpine Club, 1970.

Watson, R. M., *History of Samoa*, Whitcombe & Tombs.

Webb, William, 'A Report on Japanese Atrocities and Breaches of the Rules of Warfare', 1944.

Whonsbon-Aston, C. W., The Romantic Story of Lodge Polynesia No 562 On the Roll of the Grand Lodge of Scotland, 1975.

Wilkinson, Jack, Personal diary.

ACKNOWLEDGEMENTS

The first person I should acknowledge is my father-in-law, Bert Kienzle. The fact that he recorded and kept everything that he felt was important was of immense help – and I hope that he is smiling down at my efforts from somewhere.

I also acknowledge the work of Peter Brune in two of his books, *A Bastard of a Place*, and *Those Ragged Bloody Heroes*; and Paul Ham's book, *Kokoda*. Classics such as Dudley McCarthy's *Australia in the War of 1939–45: South West Pacific Area, Kokoda to Wau*, and Raymond Paull's *Retreat from Kokoda*, were also invaluable. Bill James' *A Field Guide to Kokoda* was very useful when it came to issues of mapping and casualty figures. My sincere appreciation too, of Peter FitzSimons, both for his comment on Bert, and also for his book *Kokoda* – probably the most readable book on the campaign.

For the earlier years, particularly the internment in World War I, I am thankful for the publications of Gerhard Fischer, and for the generosity and enthusiasm of Ann McLachlan from the Bourke Library; and also Alan Foskett, author of *Molonglo Mystery*, who took the time to show us around the site of the old camp near Canberra. Peter Southwell-Keely and his helpers at the KAC were also of great assistance.

On the immediate family side, my thanks to Diane for her generosity with photos, books and documents, giving comments on the draft that helped me see my work from the perspective of another of Bert's children. Thanks to Mary for her many insights, and John for his comments. The American 'wantoks', Helen-Joan and Tom were also the source of much interesting family information.

Big thanks to my husband Soc, who I believe to be one of the foremost experts on Kokoda, and the Trail and all its facets. I depended very much on him to check for inaccuracies, and help contribute many of the anecdotal tidbits that give the story extra character.

Finally my thanks to my mother, Joan McLellan, who critiqued the book from the perspective of a non-Kienzle and, as always, encouraged me and gave me confidence I could complete this project; and my darling daughters, Carly and Suzanne, and their partners, for their pride and patience, despite the obsession in our household with all things Kokoda for the last five years!

INDEX